CONTENTS

ACKNOWLEDGEMENTS

Rowan wishes to thank Tracy Boakes very warmly. She word processed this book quickly, accurately and resiliently, and her calm approach to his handwriting, and especially to his tangled, tortuous rewriting, was a vital contribution.

Pattie would like to thank Bernhardt, her wonderful life-companion. His ongoing support has empowered her work in this book. Thank you so much!

Gordon would like to thank Debra for her support and encouragement and Graham Dexter for his long-term and continuing positive influence.

INTRODUCTION

This book is for counsellors, psychotherapists and people who use counselling skills. Our main aim is to offer ideas, evidence, arguments, information and occasionally advice on central aspects of adult, individual, integrative counselling and psychotherapy. We have included some apparently peripheral aspects too, but essentially it is a concise discussion of central, non-partisan elements of counselling with, where appropriate, practical guidelines.

For this new edition, we have revised most of the entries, deleted a few and added many new ones. The new entries are mainly on client groups (e.g. Ageing, Alexithymia, Autistic spectrum disorder), and concepts, strategies and techniques which are integrative (e.g. Action planning, Bibliotherapy, Body scan).

We selected the client groups on the basis of our expertise or a particular interest and recognise that many other groups could have been included. We discuss a directly relevant issue in the entry on Specialisms in counselling. Similarly, we have included more exercises and techniques in this edition but still only a small proportion of those available. Our criteria were supporting evidence; our experience of them as useful; and their compatibility with integrative counselling. For a wider range of techniques, see Milner and Palmer (1998), Leahy (2003) and Jinks (2006). We discuss the impact and role of techniques in the entries on Common factors and Relationship between counsellor and client, principles for using them in Exercises, and we touch on individual differences in responding to techniques (an area which is not yet well understood) in Psychological type.

We have deleted or not included entries on theorists, contexts for counselling, children, counsellor education and training (apart from in passing, for example in the entry on Continuing professional development) and approaches to counselling (other than a general entry on Theories of counselling).

Two other factors in revising for this new edition were the increasing power of the internet and the growing emphasis on evidence-based practice. The internet is a spectacular development but it can be overwhelming, with too much information, some of which is excellent, some dubious, some dangerous. We have mentioned websites which we have found helpful and judge to be trustworthy (the URLs for these websites are available on the publisher's website – www.nelsonthornes.com). Evidence-based practice similarly has marked strengths and limitations. We discuss these in the entry on Evidence-based practice, but our general policy is to include both research findings and clinical wisdom.

Using this book

The book is organised alphabetically, with the entries as their own index, and it is cross-referenced so that everything we have written that is relevant to a particular topic can easily be found and read. We want counsellors with a pressing query or a vague disquiet to be able to find entries that stimulate, crystallise, challenge or support their own thoughts, values and feelings. Further reading (e.g. longer discussions and research papers) is suggested for follow-up if desired, and we hope that the book will be enjoyed in more leisurely, less-pressured times too.

The Authors

Of the five authors of the previous edition, only Rowan Bayne was centrally involved in this new edition. Tony Merry died, much too young. Liz Noyes retired from her academic post at UEL and is counselling and supervising. Gladeana McMahon also left UEL and is very active in the media, in coaching and counselling and in writing several books. Ian Horton has retired from his academic post at UEL and continues to be part of the counselling world in a variety of roles. He contributed to the planning of this new edition.

The two new authors, Gordon Jinks and Patrizia Collard, bring a wide range of experience and knowledge. Gordon worked in mental health (NHS) for many years and as a student counsellor. He is a BACP Accredited Counsellor. Pattie works in private practice as a psychotherapist, coach, stress management consultant, trainer and supervisor. She is an accredited CBT psychotherapist with the BABCP and is registered with the UKCP.

Counselling and Psychotherapy

None of the many attempts to distinguish between counselling and psychotherapy has been generally accepted (Feltham, 1995a; McLeod, 2003a; Thorne, 1992). What Thorne called the 'dismal quest' in 1992 is no nearer to being fulfilled 15 years later.

One strong argument is that if we take what counsellors and psychotherapists (and practitioners whom Feltham called their 'cousins') actually do with their clients there seems to be no difference. Rather, there is considerable overlap (at least) between them in several central respects: the theories, methods and techniques used, and the goals sought. Moreover, the differences that do exist, like length of training and fees, have little impact on therapy itself; differences in orientation (whether espoused or actual) seem much more significant. We do not therefore distinguish between counselling and psychotherapy in this book and, but for considerations of continuity and crispness, would have called it 'The Counsellor's and Psychotherapist's Handbook'.

Feedback to us

Finally, if there are aspects of integrative counselling which you think should have been included but are not, please let one of us know. Our address is School of Psychology, University of East London, London E15 4LZ. E-mail addresses are rowan@uel.ac.uk; g.h.jinks@uel.ac.uk; p.c.collard@uel.ac.uk.

ABUSE

See also: Anger, Bibliotherapy, Boundaries, Catharsis, Challenging, Collusion, Counselling, Empathy, Post-traumatic stress disorder, Power, Referral, Specialisms in counselling, Stress, Touch, Trust

Counselling the survivors of emotional, physical or sexual abuse requires great sensitivity. Both establishment of trust and exploration need to proceed at the client's own pace. Collusion of silence is a hazard in this type of counselling; it can be tempting to let clients avoid the painful expression of their past experience. Shillito-Clarke (1993, p219) recommended the accounts in Walker (1992a) as a way of exploring reactions: 'I found it difficult to read without pausing between accounts or resorting to defensive strategies. In this respect, the book may prove an interesting testing ground for anyone interested in, but unsure of their ability to work with, survivors.' Sanderson (2006) and Draucker and Martsolf (2006) integrate ideas, practice and research on sexual abuse, and much of what they write is relevant to emotional and physical abuse and to counselling in general. Two key themes are that the impact of child sexual abuse varies enormously and that counsellors need to be particularly aware of the effects on themselves of working with clients who have been abused.

Clients often benefit from exploring their experience at the time the abuse was happening, and sometimes a large amount of previously unexpressed material pours out. This is likely to include having felt alone, frightened and confused by the experience, with no clear picture of 'normality'. They may have been afraid of telling anyone about the abuse because of threats from the abuser to themselves, their siblings, or their family, or fear that they would not be believed. They may have experience of not being believed. They may have felt guilty: through having been told by the abuser that it is their fault; as a result of a child's tendency to take responsibility; on the assumption that adults must be right; or as a result of having experienced some gratification. They may have developed some coping strategies, for example dissociation, which can be problematic later in life.

The impact of the abuse in later life can include disturbing recollections in the form of flashbacks or nightmares; low self-esteem and distorted self-concept as a result of shame and guilt, which can lead to self-harm, suicidal ideas, depression, eating disorders, substance abuse, and sexual and relationship problems; anger towards the abuser or others; fear of being permanently tainted by the abuse, of being unable to form 'normal' relationships, or indeed of becoming an abuser themselves; and isolation and stigma – fear of telling, or fear of others knowing.

Therapeutic goals should be negotiated carefully with the client and avoid conveying any expectations on the part of the counsellor that particular goals are 'essential'. Clients who have experienced abuse often have therapy at different stages in their lives when particular issues come to the fore, and they should be supported in working in ways which best address their present concerns. These are some guidelines:

- The client should feel safe and contained in the relationship. The counsellor should respond calmly but genuinely to disclosures about past experiences, memories, or current behaviour and feelings.
- Trust is often an issue. Abusers are often trusted members of society, as are counsellors. Therefore, 'trust has to be worked at and earned and may be constantly tried and tested and retried by the client' (Walker, 2006, p466).
- Disclosure of abusive experiences needs to be managed effectively:
  - It should be under the client's control. For example, if the client says 'bad things happened to me' the counsellor should respond at that level, not reframe the comment as 'abuse'. 'Many abuse survivors disclose hesitantly and gradually, otherwise it can be too much to bear' (Walker, 1996, p135).
  - Some cathartic work may be indicated, but it is vital that the counselling does not in any way recreate the invasion of the abuse, of body or mind, and that boundaries are therefore very secure and clear.
  - Challenge distortions (for example about responsibility) sensitively.
  - Tolerate, and work with, uncertainty – clients may be unsure about their recollections.
- Clients may need help in dealing with blame and challenging guilt. It may be helpful to explore what can reasonably be expected of an individual at the age when abuse took place. (For example, a photograph of the client as a child may help to reinforce this. It can be an emotional but potentially healing experience for clients to see themselves at the developmental stage when the abuse took place.)
- Work to develop self-esteem and positive self-concept. The notion of 'survivor' rather than 'victim' can be a helpful starting point. Recognise strengths, resources, and resilience. Help the client to develop self-care: both physical and psychological.
- Work on instillation of hope:
  - Develop a vision of a better future and long-term goals.
  - Identify realistic short-term goals, enabling the client to experience success.
- Identify helpful and unhelpful coping strategies. Some strategies may have been useful at an earlier life stage, but be problematic now.
- Work to identify and use appropriate outlets for feelings. Help the client to think through any possible consequences of taking legal action (expert legal advice is crucial) or confronting the abuser.
- Help the client to explore any needs for support from others and consider how to balance these with needs for privacy.

Bibliotherapy is sometimes a helpful strategy in working with survivors of abuse (e.g. Ainscough and Toon, 2000; Bass and Davis, 2002). Haines (1999) addresses the particular issue of developing a healthy sex-life.

The idea of 'repressed memories' is a potential problem in treating abuse. In the USA, people with recently unearthed memories of sexual abuse have sued the alleged abusers for events that happened 20 or even 40 years earlier (Loftus, 1993). Major problems with this are the power of suggestion and that remembering things is a creative process – we simplify, shape and distort our memories. For example, there are cases in which people were led to believe – by a therapist or therapy group – that they were abused and later reinterpreted these 'memories' as false.

Studies of counsellors whose clients report previously repressed memories conclude that the memories are seen as authentic because of accompanying symptoms ('body memories' such as a rash), emotional pain and occasionally corroborating evidence from others (Loftus, 1993; Wright et al., 2006). On the other hand, cognitive psychologists generally regard 'repression', and therefore the idea of 'recovered memories', with some scepticism. One line of argument is that extremely painful events are often remembered vividly by those who experienced them, for example children who have seen their parents murdered, survivors of concentration camps, and victims and observers of catastrophes. However, severe abuse or trauma, perhaps especially in early childhood, may lead to repressed memories in some people.

We recommend avoiding the use of hypnosis or fantasy exercises in recovering 'buried memories'. In our experience, clients who recover memories tend to do so at times when they are in some way ready or able to deal with them and it is unwise to try to force the process. Nevertheless, memories can surface at unexpected times and leave the survivor feeling extremely distressed, frightened and vulnerable. It is helpful to discuss and clarify the support available between sessions for such clients, whether this comes from friends, significant others, support groups, telephone helplines, or internal resources.

ACCEPTANCE

See also: Core conditions, Empathy, Respect, Warmth

Most counsellors try to adopt a nonjudgemental attitude towards their clients. The distinction between a client's actual behaviour and that client's impulses or fantasies is central. Most of us have experienced impulses or fantasies involving violent and/or destructive behaviour without acting on them. It can be very important for clients to know that they can give voice to these things without being judged or rejected for having them. The progress of counselling may get stuck if your clients feel unable to express the dark side of their nature (if they have one), because they fear rejection or disapproval from you. *Positive* feelings or self-evaluations by clients also need to be accepted without evaluation. The acceptance of all feelings and impulses offers clients the opportunity (perhaps for the first time) to understand themselves as they now are (Mearns and Thorne, 2007; Merry, 1995).

ACTION PLANNING

See also: Behaviour, Brainstorming, Contingency plans, Counselling, Force-field analysis, Goals, Homework, Imagery, Scaling, Values

Helping clients to make changes in their lives outside of therapy sessions is often a key part of the counselling process, and a systematic approach to action planning is likely to be helpful. Egan (2007) pays particular attention to this stage of counselling and recommends that counsellors help clients to make a clear distinction between identifying goals (*what* they hope to achieve) and strategies (*how* they hope to achieve it). In a simple analogy, this is the distinction between choosing a destination (goal) and then planning the means of travel to get there (strategy). Egan's approach to action planning is highly structured, and some counsellors have reservations about the level of directiveness which might be involved. However, it is important to note that the direction given to the client is about the *process* of developing an effective plan, not the *content* of the plan, which will be determined by the client.

Once the client has established a clear goal, action planning begins by brainstorming a list of possible strategies and strategy elements (things/people/places/organisations/programmes, etc.) that might help. It is important to encourage creative and divergent thinking at this point in order to generate a wide range of possibilities for action. The client can then be encouraged to review the brainstormed list and select 'best-fit' strategies (Egan, 2007), i.e. those which are most in tune with the client's personal preferences, available resources, specific circumstances and environment; most within his or her control; and most likely to be successful in achieving the client's goal. The chosen strategies are then broken down into a detailed sequence of actions needed to implement them. The client now has a clear action plan in the form of a list of intended actions and a timetable for implementation. Some contingency planning is likely to be helpful, with the client identifying factors which might get in the way of, interrupt or divert his or her plans, and developing strategies to deal with these should they occur.

ACTIVE LISTENING

See also: Empathy, Nonverbal communication, Paraphrasing, Questions, Silence, Summaries and 'moving interviews forward', Thoughts, Values

'Active listening' is a term used to describe a set of skills involved in listening carefully to the client, reflecting on the client's communication (both verbal and nonverbal) in order to develop a clear understanding and communicating the level of attention and understanding back to the client. The skills involved are nonverbal attending skills (open, attentive posture; eye contact; appropriate facial expressions and responses; encouragers such as nods; allowing clients appropriate space); hearing the client's words and the nonverbal content of his or her speech (intonations, inflexions, pace, hesitations, etc.); observing the client's nonverbal communication; internal processing of the client's whole communication; and the verbal skills involved in communicating understanding and checking accuracy of understanding (paraphrasing meaning and emotion, summarising, and clarification questions).

ADMINISTRATION

See also: Client information handout, Contract, negotiating a, Evaluation, Fees, Record keeping, Website (personal)

It is almost impossible for a counsellor to avoid administration. Administrative tasks may be limited to booking rooms, arranging appointments, keeping case notes, and writing letters to other professionals, although a counsellor may need a higher degree of general and financial administrative skills (McMahon *et al.*, 2005).

Administration can be seen as falling broadly within four categories, which are:

- **general administration:**
  - keeping an appointments diary for recording clients' appointments
  - devising advertisements and placing them in appropriate places such as local papers and referral directories
  - running a filing system to cater for documentation relating to items such as insurance, utilities and rent and information from professional associations such as the British Association for Counselling and Psychotherapy (BACP) and the British Psychological Society (BPS)
  - using a telephone message service (e.g. an answering machine or call minder service), which must be monitored on a regular basis
- **administration relating to client work:**
  - producing a client information handout outlining the service(s) offered and any relevant terms and conditions such as fees, cancellation policy and confidentiality
  - keeping client details forms containing basic client details such as name, address, telephone numbers, doctor's details and a paragraph clearly outlining the client's consent to the terms and conditions of the counselling offered
  - producing client consent form(s), which may include forms outlining the client's permission for taping of counselling sessions, for her or his details to be used for the purposes of case studies or for therapeutic purposes such as permission for therapeutic touch to take place if appropriate

- note taking and recording supporting documentation (this requires the counsellor to have a reliable formula for recording case notes and for storing relevant documentation such as referral details, letters written to other professionals about the client, relevant therapeutic questionnaires and assessment material)
- preparation of evaluation forms to provide feedback to the counsellor concerning therapeutic outcome and client satisfaction
- keeping secure storage facilities to ensure that the ethical requirements for the protection of client confidentiality are met, including registration under the Data Protection Act for all computer-based client records (Bond, 2000)

- **financial administration:**
  - entering income and expenditure, compiling profit and loss accounts, organising receipts, working out how much to put aside for income tax and reconciling bank statements (book-keeping skills will be required by counsellors in private practice for such tasks)
  - invoicing systems (these may be needed in addition to the provision of simple receipts)

- **professional administration:**
  - keeping reasonably accurate records of (amongst other things) the number of hours of training received (skills and theory), professional development activities, personal therapy, supervision received (and over what time) and number of hours of counselling undertaken each year. Accreditation schemes, such as those now offered by the BACP, require the counsellor to complete a comprehensive application form, and to be able to provide the relevant information for the initial application; and for reaccreditation such records are required.

ADVERTISING

See also: Client information handout, Ethical Framework, Marketing, Website (personal)

In some professions, medicine for example, advertising of services is illegal. In counselling, it is both legal and professionally acceptable to advertise as long as you do not state or imply that you can cure people of any sickness, ill health or disturbance. You can say that you can help with these problems and others like them, but you should not claim to be in possession of special knowledge or skills that guarantee any form of success.

It is, therefore, advisable to restrict advertising to straightforward statements of any areas you specialise in (such as stress or depression), the approach you use, and how potential clients can contact you. The costs of advertising can be claimed against tax, provided that they are 'wholly and exclusively' incurred for the purpose of business.

For advice, contact the Advertising Standards Agency (ASA) by phone (020 7492 2100, 9–6 weekdays) or send an email to copyadvice@cap.org.uk. The ASA's website includes a search facility.

ADVICE

See also: Challenging, Counselling, Empathy, Frame of reference, Giving information

A basic aim of counselling is to support clients in taking responsibility for their decisions and in being more independent. Generally, advice can be seen to be inconsistent with this aim, and many counsellors therefore do not give advice. *Not* giving advice can be therapeutic in itself: it says, in effect, 'When you've explored what's troubling you, you'll see it more clearly and know what to do.'

However, the place of advice in counselling varies to some extent across the spectrum of approaches. A useful distinction is between advice relating to the client's content (e.g. 'This is what I think you should do') and advice relating to the therapeutic process (e.g. 'This is a way I think you might work out what to do'). The latter can be seen to be more consistent with the aim of counselling described above. An exception is that if you suspect that clients are physically or mentally ill you should advise them to see their general practitioner, and there may be other issues involving the safety of the client or others where you would be wise to give clear advice.

Lazarus offered a radically different view: 'I would often be fairly free with my advice', although he added that he always phrased it as 'This is the way I see it' (Dryden, 1991, p60). And Yalom sometimes offers advice '*not as a way of usurping my patient's decision, but in order to shake up an entrenched thought or behavior pattern*' (2001, p150, italics in original).

Advice is not the same as information. Advice is suggesting particular actions. Information is facts or ideas which clients may find helpful in deciding what to do or how to make sense of something.

AFFECT

See: Emotions, Feeling

AGEING

See also: Assertiveness, Dementia, Hot flushes, Loss, Multiculturalism, Transitions

> Age comes down like a cosh. One minute you're a lively young stud and the next you're wearing underpants the size of a sheet. (Nancy Banks-Smith, *Guardian* TV critic)

Ageing can be a problem and a shock – like a cosh – but it can also mean greater freedom and zest for life. Nancy Banks-Smith was writing about older people (hard to define, although in the UK the arbitrary figure still given most significance is 65), but the effects of ageing, and the effects of worrying about them, occur much younger. For example, many 30-year-olds are less able to socialise until 3am and work well the next morning than when they were 20.

In 30-year-olds, extra responsibilities and the cumulative effects of lifestyle are likely to be important factors in how quickly they age. In older people, beliefs about ageing seem more central. Stereotypes like slow, infirm, rigid, etc. are toxic, and therapeutic interventions with older people may need to focus on challenging such beliefs. Facts can be useful here (e.g. that in the USA the mandatory retirement age was generally abolished in 1986).

At the same time, there are, with age, real decreases in some respects: for example, skin loses elasticity and some illnesses become more common (although *not* inevitable). Other problems related to being older are:

- multiple bereavements and loss generally (e.g. of aspects of identity, strength and agility)
- alcoholism, alcohol dependency
- chronic pain
- depression (this is more likely to be masked by physical symptoms and overlooked because it is 'part of being older' – when it is not).

Topics to be worked on in counselling may therefore include:

- greater freedom from former responsibilities and restraints – a capacity to rise above worries and put them aside
- active coping skills for bereavement
- skills that maintain and improve cognitive functioning (e.g. memory, although 'senior moments' can be caused by various factors, including stress and tiredness)
- spirituality
- mobility and exercise
- relationships
- helping people to grow old in ways that suit them, from having a long rest to trying new activities and skills or returning to earlier ones
- anxiety about death (counsellors probably also need to accept, to a great extent, the reality of their own death in order to work well with older people)
- deafness, which can be frustrating and irritating for the deaf person and others. It can also be isolating and affect confidence yet is a neglected problem in older people (see the Hearing Clearer website).

For health advice, and details of the evidence on which it is based, see the RealAge website, which also allows you to assess your 'real age' (as opposed to your chronological age). A useful recent finding is that older people are more willing to discuss falls and preventing them as part of *balance* training (Nyman,

2007; see also the Balance Training website). The research also found benefits in tailoring advice about balance to each person.

Markides (2007) has 250 entries, again with an evidence-based, practical, positive emphasis, on topics like cataracts, optimal ageing, public policy, sleep disturbances and wisdom. Sugarman (2004) relates some of the research and ideas on ageing to counselling.

A group counselling technique that may be 'particularly suited' to older people is Gestalt reminiscence therapy (O'Leary and Barry, 2006). It involves 'story-telling, unfinished business, the present, the expression and location of emotion, the acknowledgement of contextual dimensions, the enhancement of contact, the sharing of spiritual values and attention to both interpersonal and group procedures' (p544).

Overall, age in years does not tell us much about an adult's abilities. It defines what we can do less than many people believe, and counselling is as effective with older people as it is with other age groups (Hill and Brettle, 2005).

AGGRESSIVE AND VIOLENT CLIENTS

See: Violence and its prevention

ALEXITHYMIA

See also: Autistic spectrum disorder, Dyslexia, Emotions, Psychological type

'Alexithymia' means 'lacking words for emotions'. If asked about their emotions or feelings, people with alexithymia say 'I don't know', 'I feel bad', or report bodily states or behaviour. They are not being reserved or defensive: rather they are not able to identify emotions or communicate about them; they are not psychologically minded (Lumley, 2004).

The notion of alexithymia can be helpful to counsellors in three ways. First, you may be less likely to view a client with this limitation as resistant. Secondly, self-awareness skills can be taught, for example learning emotion labels and recognising emotions in others. (Alternatively, some cognitive-behavioural therapy (CBT) interventions may be the most effective because they do not rely as much on self-awareness.) Thirdly, alexithymia is 'fairly prevalent in such problems as addictions, chronic pain, eating disorders, hypertension and panic attacks' (Lumley, 2004, p290), which may provide a useful new perspective and suggest some therapeutic strategies.

ANGER, IN CLIENTS

See also: Assertiveness, Body scan, Catharsis, Contract, negotiating a, Emotions, Empathy, Nonverbal communication, Relaxation, Thoughts, Touch, Violence and its prevention

Some clients are so angry that you may feel, or actually be, threatened. Empathy or – when your client is calm – an 'anger management' approach may be helpful.

This generally applies the same principles and techniques as CBT, including relaxation training, responding constructively to relapse, and assertiveness training. It is an approach to anger (sarcasm, explosive temper, etc.) rather than to premeditated or instrumental violence. However, the most effective strategies or treatments vary, for example relaxation with one client who is very tense, listening to other clients' stories about being angry to help them identify core values and develop assertive ways of expressing them, changing or stopping negative thoughts with another. See also Nay (2004), Williams and Scott (2006) and, for current information on anger management, the website of the British Association of Anger Management.

A contract establishing the difference between 'feeling angry' and 'aggressive behaviour' (and agreeing not to behave aggressively during counselling) can clarify the situation and increase confidence. However, the inclusion of details on what will happen if the client becomes violent may either be useful or may reduce trust, depending on the situation. All angry clients require recognition of their anger and a chance to talk about it, although for some the thought of talking about it is too threatening. It needs to be made explicit that clients can decide what is right for them: they are then more in control and less likely to feel threatened or to resort to violence.

How you respond to potentially violent clients if they become upset also needs to be established early on. Touch is risky, and in some areas and cultures maintaining eye contact may be interpreted as 'eyeballing' and responded to aggressively; in others, *not* looking can be seen as furtive and might cause unease and aggression. Comfortable 'personal space' also varies from person to person and culture to culture. You should be clear about these factors and agree that the client will take deep breaths and (literally) 'count to 10' or, more distractingly, backwards from say 100 in threes or focus her or his attention 'out', for example by looking for all the things of a particular colour in the room. These strategies aid self-control, although a balance between self-control and clarifying emotions needs to be kept in mind.

Expression of anger is often encouraged in counselling, on the grounds that:

- suppressed emotions cause problems which are helped by the releasing of anger and/or
- experiences are more likely to be understood and assimilated if spoken about, and that experiencing emotions facilitates this process.

Some approaches see expression as vitally important; others see anger as a manifestation of depression or as an expression of fear, with fear as the emotion really needing to be expressed. In contrast, research on anger suggests that expressing it is usually unhelpful, and that the question of whether or not a person should express or suppress anger is better put as 'When does a person benefit from expressing anger? What kind of person? And, more subtly:

> When should an individual neither express nor suppress anger,
> but stop generating the emotion in the first place? Why does the
> same action (say, talking about one's anger) produce a feeling of

communication in one circumstance and the opposite feeling in another? (Tavris, 1984, p172)

Tavris's general conclusion about expressing anger was that just 'releasing it' tends to consolidate the anger, excludes other emotions and makes other people angrier too (Tavris, 1984, 1989). Anger can be expressed constructively, but the view that not expressing it is stressful and that releasing it is healthy in a 'cathartic' way is too simple.

There are many ways of helping clients become more aware of their anger: empathy; holding a conversation with it ('How long have you been there? What do you want?'); drawing it; writing to it. Sometimes more physical techniques, such as punching cushions, lead to clearer understanding.

ANGER, IN COUNSELLORS

See also: Anger in clients, Immediacy, Self-disclosure, Stress, Supervision

Faced, in the session itself, with his or her own anger, the counsellor is sometimes in a dilemma about whether to talk about it then or later. In other words, do you use the skills of self-disclosure or immediacy in the session, or wait until supervision? There is no easy answer; it depends on the circumstances. The first consideration is whether or not disclosing your anger will help your client. This is not as straightforward as it seems: what you might see as being helpful to your clients (in that you are letting them know their effect on people) they may not, and the counselling could be disrupted. If in any doubt, it is better to discuss your angry response in supervision. There you can clarify whether you are picking up on your client's anger, or if it is your own anger that is being stimulated. It will then be possible to examine how you could enable your clients to get in touch with and manage their own anger while you talk about your feelings with your own counsellor.

ANXIETY

See also: Bibliotherapy, Depression, Emotions, Evidence-based practice, Exercise (physical), Exercises, Giving information, Mindfulness, NICE, Panic attacks, Post-traumatic stress disorder, Stress, Thoughts

Anxiety is common and causes considerable distress and disability. Although some anxiety is overt, it can also underlie depression, obsessions, hysteria, bodily symptoms, phobias and possibly addictions. Counselling aims to help clients face up to anxiety through, for example, empathy, restructuring of thoughts, facing 'existential givens', or physically facing whatever is anxiety provoking.

In studies comparing psychological treatments of anxiety, the most effective changes found so far have been through CBT interventions (Beck *et al.*, 2005; NICE, 2004a). These are structured and collaborative with shared decision making. Explicitly expressed goals are chosen and the person experiencing anxiety learns new ways of behaving and thinking. Thus dysfunctional habits can be abandoned in time and new neuropsychological pathways formed. CBT interventions for anxiety have been studied more than other approaches; they seem to have more enduring effects than drug treatments (Hollon *et al.*, 2006).

Components of CBT treatment of anxiety include:

- telling your client about the physiology of anxiety and assessing misinterpretations of physiological symptoms
- identifying and replacing negative thoughts
- relaxation/mindfulness training to reduce arousal (Brantley, 2003)
- defusing anxiety by experimentation and rationalisation
- increasing physical activity
- increasing exposure to feared situations
- bibliotherapy
- support groups
- exposure to feared situations.

Some counsellors use questionnaires such as the Beck Anxiety Inventory completed before, during and after therapy to help to evaluate client progress. It may be helpful to give clients a choice as part of the process of encouraging them to take responsibility (do they want to look at thoughts, feelings, or actions, or any combination of the three?). Yalom (2001, p200) commented that he generally finds it useful to say to a client who is very anxious and pleading for relief, 'Tell me, what would be the perfect thing for me to say. What exactly could I say that would lead to you feeling better?' The quality of the relationship and the tone would obviously be important in such an intervention.

APPROPRIATENESS OF COUNSELLING

See: Assessment, Contraindications for brief counselling, Referral, Specialisms in counselling

ASSERTIVENESS

See also: Boundaries, Contract, negotiating a, Immediacy, Multiculturalism, Self-awareness, Sexual attraction, Stress, Thoughts, Values

Assertiveness is most relevant to counsellors themselves in three ways: as part of such skills as negotiating a contract, immediacy, and negotiating problems with boundaries; as a strategy for self-care; and as a strategy for most interpersonal problems.

Assertiveness can be defined as 'being able to express and act on your rights as a person while respecting the same rights in others' (Nicolson *et al.*, 2006, p78). Lists of assertive rights vary, but the left-hand column of Table 1 is representative. The table's format, taken from Bond (1986), is unusual and

Table 1 Assertive rights

1.	I have the right to be treated with respect	**and**	Others have the right to be treated with respect
2.	I have the right to express my thoughts, opinions and values	**and**	Others have the right to express their thoughts, opinions and values
3.	I have the right to express my feelings	**and**	Others have the right to express their feelings
4.	I have the right to say 'No' without feeling guilty	**and**	Others have the right to say 'No' without feeling guilty
5.	I have the right to be successful	**and**	Others have the right to be successful
6.	I have the right to make mistakes	**and**	Others have the right to make mistakes
7.	I have the right to change my mind	**and**	Others have the right to change their minds
8.	I have the right to say that I don't understand	**and**	Others have the right to say that they don't understand
9.	I have the right to ask for what I want	**and**	Others have the right to ask for what they want
10.	I have the right to decide for myself whether or not I am responsible for another person's problem	**and**	Others have the right to decide for themselves whether or not they are responsible for another person's problem
11.	I have the right to choose not to assert myself	**and**	Others have the right to choose not to assert themselves

makes explicit the 'respect for others' element in assertiveness. Rakos (1991) drew a distinction between assertiveness therapy (a more remedial approach, in clinical settings) and assertiveness training (for professional groups and the general public). Assertiveness training is for people who are already relatively assertive but who wish to develop particular skills and qualities further.

Approaches to assertiveness training differ radically. In those which focus on skills, 'saying no' and 'making requests' are fundamental. Saying no includes the key skill, strongly supported by research (Rakos, 1991), of 'empathic assertion'. Other assertive skills are giving and receiving compliments and giving and receiving criticism. The terms used by Dickson (1987) for styles of behaviour which are *not* assertive are fairly standard: aggressive, passive and manipulative (indirectly aggressive). Her very practical book is for both sexes despite its title.

The elements of each skill are outlined in Nicolson *et al.* (2006). Here, as an example, is the skill of saying no:

- Basic skill:
  - Be brief.
  - Speak clearly and confidently (e.g. watch for unwanted, potentially sabotaging, smiles and apologies).
- Refinements:
  - Notice your first reaction (to take into account, not necessarily to act on).
  - Calm repetition may be useful.
  - Offer an alternative.
  - Empathy first (more appropriate if it is someone you know well).

Assertive values are clearly for autonomy and against subservience. Cultural bias is therefore a problem. One solution is 'bicultural competence' (Rakos, 1991), when the person or group practise assertive skills for the 'mainstream' culture and for their own subculture and those of clients, colleagues, etc. Another solution is to emphasise individual style and self-awareness. Assertiveness training is then seen more as consciousness raising, to allow greater choice, including whether or not to use skills to challenge a particular social context, than as prescribing how or when to use the skills.

Cooper (2007) discussed the structure and some of the practicalities of a four-session assertiveness training group (plus homework, plus a follow-up a few months later) which she runs at Cambridge University. It could be an alternative to the skills approach emphasised in this entry or could complement it. The four sessions are 'Looking at assertiveness'; 'Rights and responsibilities'; 'Speaking our minds and listening without getting hooked in'; and 'Protecting ourselves'.

ASSESSMENT

See also: Beginnings, Challenging, Contract, negotiating a, Contraindications for brief counselling, DSM-IV, Expectations (clients'), Giving information, Intake interviews, Multiculturalism, Nonverbal communication, Psychodiagnosis, Referral, Therapeutic planning

Assessment is the attempt to describe 'what's going on for your client', with varying degrees of formality.

Counsellors vary radically in their attitudes towards assessment. Some counsellors use a range of procedures which may involve lengthy intake interviews or case histories and diagnostic classification systems (e.g. DSM-IV). For others, the whole idea of assessment is anathema. They regard it as something 'done to the client', synonymous with the medical model of diagnosis, prescription and treatment in which the balance of power, responsibility and role of expert is held by the counsellor. Some person-centred counsellors attempt to address the concerns highlighted above by carrying out a 'person-centred assessment', which avoids the use of preordained checklists or pro formas but places clients at the centre of, and in control of, the process of developing a comprehensive picture of themselves, their work, their hopes, and areas to be explored. This will be shared with the client as an explicit aim for the first session and set the tone for further sessions. However, while many counsellors prefer not to use any type of formal procedures and may avoid using the term 'assessment', few would argue with the need to obtain some information when starting work with each client.

Assessment is typically concerned with one or more of the following objectives:

- to help you and your client understand the nature of the client's presenting issues
- to identify the factors that may be associated with the issues and the client's experience or behaviour
- to determine the client's expectations and desired outcomes
- to assess the client's strengths, abilities, resources and successes
- to collect baseline data that can be compared with subsequent data to evaluate progress
- to facilitate the client's learning and motivation by sharing the counsellor's view of the problem (this may in itself contribute to therapeutic change through increasing self-awareness)
- to produce an initial assessment (formulation) which provides the counsellor with a basis for, first, making a decision about whether to offer a counselling contract, to initiate referral or to suggest that counselling would not be appropriate, and, secondly, to provide the basis for developing a therapeutic or counselling plan with the client, including the length and pattern of contract.

For detailed discussions of assessment in counselling, see Milner and O'Byrne (2003).

Assessment categories

Various kinds of information can be gathered or areas explored during assessment:

- presenting issues – including affective (emotions, feelings, mood), somatic (body-related sensations), behavioural (what the client does or does not do) and cognitive (thoughts, beliefs, attitudes, values, images, fantasies, internal dialogue) elements
- antecedents – factors that may have influenced or caused the presenting problem
- consequences – factors that may be maintaining it, at least in part
- previous attempts to solve or cope with the problem
- client resources and strengths

- the frequency, duration and severity of the problem (i.e. how long or how often the problem occurs, when it first started and its effects).

An assessment formulation is an attempt to construct a picture of what is going on for the client and to describe and offer some explanations of the presenting issue(s), possible targets for change, and ideas about how you and your client might work together. It may include some tentative ideas about emerging themes or possible connections between the client's past and present behaviour and experience. Depending on your theoretical orientation, the formulation may hypothesise about the possible origin and development of the problem and why it persists, or it may focus more on goals for the future.

The formulation integrates information from a variety of sources:

- the client's account and understanding of his or her experience
- the client's developmental history and social context
- your experience of the client, including his or her nonverbal communication
- your own theoretical framework(s).

These sources may be supplemented by such techniques and resources as:

- client diaries which may address specific issues or may be more general
- genograms, life-space diagrams, autobiographical narratives, self-descriptions
- psychological tests
- DSM-IV classifications.

AUTISTIC SPECTRUM DISORDER (ASD)

See also: Alexithymia, Multiculturalism, Specialisms in counselling

Autistic spectrum disorder (ASD) is a developmental disability and affects social, communication and imagination skills. It presents in varying degrees of severity and affects the lives of around 1 per cent of the population in the UK and worldwide. People with autism seem disinterested in the social world, whereas people diagnosed with Asperger's (or high-functioning autism) want to be more sociable but struggle with nonverbal communication, such as interpreting facial expressions. This makes social interaction (including job interviews) more difficult.

ASD appears to affect more males than females, has no ethnic or social regard and is a lifelong condition for which there is no cure. Some widely held and damaging myths about ASD are countered in the following statements:

- Not all individuals with ASD 'live in their own world'.
- Parents do not cause their children to have ASD.
- People with ASD have a developmental delay but they can, to some extent, be taught what they are lacking. Ideally, one should not expect them to multitask or interrupt them unnecessarily.

- Many people with ASD are very intelligent and excellent workers. Their strong tendencies to collect things, to be meticulous and loyal and to like things to be the same and in order are a great asset in many occupations.

Specialist training is usually needed to be helpful and effective in working with this client group. Alston (2003) discussed working with couples, one of whom has Asperger's syndrome, and recommended either referral or 'a completely different way of counselling'.

Both Action for ASD and Mental Health Care and the National Autistic Society have websites.

AVOIDANCE, BY CLIENTS

See also: Boredom, Challenging, Contract, negotiating a, Denial, Empathy, Immediacy, Referral, Reluctant clients

Sometimes, clients avoid topics that they consciously do not want to talk about. When they do not say that they are doing this and just avoid the topic, it can make counselling difficult and frustrating. This problem may be overcome by agreeing (in the contract) that, if there is an area that clients wish not to talk about, they must make this clear and the counsellor will respect their wish. Once clients realise that their wishes are respected and that they can trust the counsellor, they are able to relax and usually quite quickly are able to talk about the area they were originally avoiding. However, we do *not* recommend expecting this outcome or using the agreement as a manipulative technique.

When clients are unaware that they are avoiding a topic, it might be for some general reason, such as finding it difficult to talk about emotions and feelings, or they might be suppressing a specific event. Usually, counselling will gradually (at the client's pace) encourage more openness, but for very deeply suppressed fears it may take many months. One form of avoidance is for clients to talk about everybody and everything but themselves. Often the best strategy is a good empathic statement: for example, 'You seem upset by your parents' behaviour' could bring clients back to themselves after complaining about their parents.

AVOIDANCE, BY COUNSELLORS

See also: Collusion, Contract, negotiating a, Emotions, Empathy, Feeling, Immediacy, Paraphrasing, Questions, Self-awareness, Thoughts

It is easy to avoid a subject, either by colluding with the client's wish to avoid it or by (consciously or unconsciously) failing to pick up clues from the client indicating that he or she wishes to address, or is now ready to address, particular aspects of his or her experience. This is especially likely if it is also a difficult subject for the counsellor. Each time the client approaches the subject the counsellor might focus on a safer topic or ask an unnecessary question, encouraging the client to continue avoiding the issue, or diverting the client into an area where the counsellor feels more comfortable. Counsellors need to work to be aware of (and keep track of) their own blocks, resistances and areas of vulnerability. It is important that clients do not feel that their counsellor wishes to avoid talking about particular issues. Clients should feel that they have permission and indeed the counsellor's full cooperation to explore the issues which are important to them. It is useful for client and counsellor to be able to discuss areas which may be difficult and may be being avoided, either at review/evaluation sessions, or at the time when a particular resistance or reluctance arises. The skill of immediacy is important at such times and enables counsellors to raise the possibility that an issue is being avoided, to own their part in the process, and to model such congruence for their clients. If avoidance can be discussed openly, ways to move forward can be negotiated. Counsellors often find supervision a useful forum in which to explore their own contributions to avoidance, and personal therapy may be useful in dealing with any issues which are identified as limiting.

BABCP (THE BRITISH ASSOCIATION FOR BEHAVIOURAL AND COGNITIVE PSYCHOTHERAPIES)

The BABCP was established in 1972 and is the main multidisciplinary body for people involved in the practice and theory of CBT in the UK. It offers workshops, conferences, training programmes, local branches, a journal and newsletter, a code of ethics, complaints procedures, accreditation and access to United Kingdom Council for Psychotherapy (UKCP) registration.

The BABCP's address and telephone number are given below; it has a website:

23 Partridge Drive
Baxenden
Accrington
Lancashire BB5 2RL, UK
01254 875277

BACP (THE BRITISH ASSOCIATION FOR COUNSELLING AND PSYCHOTHERAPY)

The BACP was established as a voluntary association and charity in 1977 (it was then known as the BAC). Today it is registered as a company limited by guarantee. Its rapid growth in membership reflects the increasing general interest in counselling in the UK. In 2006, it had over 26,000 members, of whom 26 per cent were accredited. The members represent diverse views and degrees of involvement in counselling: the title of the Association embodies the idea of an association *for* counselling rather than an association *of* counsellors. The BACP has a strong emphasis on diversity, for example through its recognition of a wide variety of approaches to counselling and psychotherapy, its development of an Equality and Diversity Forum and its broad interpretation of diversity, including age, culture, class, physical disability, socioeconomic factors, gender and sexual orientation. There is an inevitable but often creative tension among different interest groups within the Association.

The BACP's address and telephone number are given below; it has a website:

BACP House
15 St John's Business Park
Lutterworth
Leicestershire LE17 4HB, UK
0870 443 5252

BAP (THE BRITISH ASSOCIATION OF PSYCHOTHERAPISTS)

The BAP runs training programmes in individual psychoanalytic (Freudian) and analytical (Jungian) psychotherapy for members of the helping professions and for those working in child psychotherapy.

The BAP's address and telephone number are given below; it has a website:

37 Mapesbury Road
London NW2 4HJ, UK
0181 452 9823

BEGINNINGS

See also: Assessment, Confidentiality, Contract, negotiating a, Difficulties in being a client, Ethical framework, Expectations (clients'), Fees, Frequency of sessions, Giving information, Questions, Rapport, Referral, Working alliance

The beginning of counselling can be crucial. Some clients are optimistic and ready to work hard; others are very anxious about counselling (Manthei, 2007; Pipes *et al.*, 1985). This is not surprising: they are putting themselves in the hands of a stranger at a point in their life when they feel vulnerable, and when they may have limited or inaccurate knowledge about counselling.

From the counsellor's point of view, beginning work with clients involves both content and process: helping your clients explore what is troubling them and establishing a relationship. Different counsellors and approaches to counselling place more or less emphasis on each of the following:

- **Role induction:** this includes helping clients explore any fears, fantasies and expectations, in particular how long counselling might last and what will happen in the sessions. You may find it helpful to prepare a brief account of your own view of counselling. It is most important that you and your clients work towards and negotiate a common understanding of what is involved. Other questions that are quite likely to matter to clients generally include 'How long do you think I'll need to see you for?' and 'Will counselling help me?'

- **Establishing rapport:** this is sometimes called 'the therapeutic alliance' or the 'working alliance'.
- **Information-gathering:** this refers to encouraging your clients to talk openly about themselves and their problems. Other possible topics are the 'trigger' (why they came to counselling at this point), previous experience of counselling, their own assessment, and their attempts so far to help themselves.
- **Assessment:** see separate entry.
- **Practical arrangements:** this includes times and days to meet, how to cancel or change an appointment, and fees.

BEHAVIOUR

See also: Action planning, Counselling, Theories of counselling

In counselling and psychotherapy, behaviour is often seen as one dimension of human response or experience and complementary to other dimensions such as thinking and feeling. Behaviour refers to what people do – generally what is observable. Different approaches place different emphasis on behaviour as a target for change in therapy. What might be termed 'insight-oriented' approaches, such as the person-centred and psychodynamic approaches, tend to see behaviour change as secondary to changes in the client's understanding of self, and so the primary focus is on developing greater self-awareness and insight; whereas behaviour therapy sees behaviour as the primary target for change, on the assumption that, if clients are able to change their behaviour in order to be more effective, other benefits are likely to follow. Cognitive-behavioural therapy sees the three dimensions of thinking, feeling, and behaviour as mutually and causally connected, usually formulated in terms of the central importance of how the client *thinks* about any given issue determining how she or he then *feels* and *behaves*. The success or otherwise of a given behaviour will then further influence the client's thinking and feeling and therapeutic interventions can be targeted at various points along this chain.

Behaviour therapy encompasses a variety of therapeutic methods that aim to change self-defeating behaviour through direct action. The behaviour may be labelled a behavioural deficit (e.g. phobic avoidance) or excess (e.g. compulsive behaviour). The main aim is to alter behaviour that detrimentally affects the quality of the client's life. Behaviour therapy is successful in its pure form for the treatment of a variety of problems, such as using graded exposure programmes to desensitise individuals to feared situations (Lovell, 2006). However, in more recent years behaviour and cognitive therapy are more likely to be integrated to form cognitive-behavioural therapy. Broadly speaking, there are four steps in the process of client change in the behavioural approach:

1. Problem assessment and rating – determining the specific nature of the behaviour to be addressed

2. Explaining the principle of the behavioural change technique to be applied (e.g. exposure, desensitisation, response prevention etc.)
3. Behavioural tasks, designed to implement and reinforce change
4. Maintenance – strategies to consolidate change and avoid relapse.

For example, a client might be frightened of travelling in lifts and on a scale of 0–8 (0 = no discomfort, 8 = panic) may produce a hierarchy of different types of lifts and associated fear responses:

1. Large enclosed lifts I cannot see out of: 4
2. Small enclosed lifts I cannot see out of: 6
3. Enclosed glass lifts on the outside of buildings: 8

The principles of an exposure programme are explained to the client. It is important that the client understands the nature of fear and the principle that avoidance of feared situations maintains and may even increase fear, whereas regular exposure to the feared situation usually eradicates it. Clients may fail to complete the behavioural task because they do not fully understand the principles behind an exposure programme or have not been properly prepared with coping strategies for the feelings that they might experience. Failure is likely to reinforce the fear and any negative views clients may have of themselves. In severe cases the therapist may accompany the client on an exposure task, for example accompanying someone with agoraphobia to a shopping centre.

Behavioural tasks are set, with the client, as homework. For example, the client might decide that she or he will spend 20 consecutive minutes a day for one week travelling in a large enclosed lift at the local shopping centre. (The duration needs to be of sufficient length to allow anxious feelings generated by the experience to subside.) When deciding on behavioural tasks, it is usually helpful for clients to choose an activity in the middle of the range on their rating scale of feared activity. Attempting to tackle the most feared situation first may lead to failure, reinforcing negative evaluations of self and risking refusal to continue with the work.

Once the client's fears have become extinct it is important that the client continues to integrate the once-feared situation into her or his life. Failure to do so may lead to recurrence of the problem. Clients also need to be prepared for the possibility that, in times of stress, old feelings may resurface. However, they should be assured that, if old fears do start to surface, exposing themselves to the feared situation is likely to ensure that the problem does not escalate (Lovell, 2006).

BELIEFS (IRRATIONAL)

See also: Thoughts

It can be useful to make a distinction between beliefs, which are relatively stable ideas that one holds about particular issues, aspects of experience, people, the world, etc., and thoughts, which can be seen as more immediate responses to the situations one experiences. Frequently, underlying beliefs will be a strong influence on thoughts. For example, if one holds a belief such as 'people must always like me' then it is quite likely that, upon encountering criticism from another, thoughts such as 'this is very bad' and 'I must somehow ingratiate myself with this person' will occur, accompanied by feelings of discomfort and/ or anxiety. Rational emotive behaviour therapy (REBT) places great emphasis on the identification of self-defeating or irrational beliefs so that they can be challenged: the evidence for and against the belief weighed up and hopefully a more rational, balanced and adaptive belief developed (Ellis and Dryden, 1998). In the example given, a more rational and less self-defeating belief might be 'it's nice when people like me but it's not always possible (or even desirable)'. The thoughts, feelings and behaviours following on from this new belief would then be explored with the client.

Some irrational beliefs, for example judgements about oneself and beliefs about 'other people' in general, may have their origins in early life experience. Parental influences can be powerful in fostering beliefs such as 'I always mess things up' or 'I always have to be tough or other people will take advantage'. It can be useful to explore the origins of such beliefs in order to challenge them, and interventions such as 'What is the earliest time you can remember thinking that?' may be helpful. The client can then be enabled to explore the appropriateness of the belief (which may have had some coping or survival value in childhood) in relation to his or her current developmental stage, environment and relationships.

BENEFITS OF COUNSELLING

See: Effectiveness of counselling, Evidence-based practice, NICE

BEREAVEMENT

See also: Crisis counselling, Loss

The loss of a loved one is a common presenting problem in counselling, and the type and intensity of grief experienced depend on a number of factors. It is particularly important that counsellors should be open-minded about what is a 'normal' or appropriate way to react to death: for example, people who are not distressed may be resilient rather than insensitive (Bonanno, 2004; Wortman and Silver, 1989, 2001).

Individual responses to bereavement are affected by personality factors, attachment patterns, social, cultural or ethnic context, previous experience of loss or bereavement, the level of support available, responses of significant others such as family members, and the role of the individual in the family or other groups. The nature of the bereavement is also important, including whether the death was expected or unexpected, the nature of the death (such as whether violent, an accident, suicide, illness, suspicious, etc.), the life stage of the deceased and the role of the deceased in the life of the bereaved. It may be necessary to explore any or all of these factors during the course of bereavement counselling. (It is also worth noting that for some people the death of pets can lead to intense grief reactions.)

A number of models have been developed to describe grieving. Worden (2004) suggests a useful distinction between 'uncomplicated' grief, which may still take months or years to integrate, and 'complicated' grief, which is characterised by more extreme reactions and an inability to negotiate some or all of the tasks of mourning. He identified four *tasks* of mourning, which the bereaved can take on if they wish to integrate the death into their experience and move on with life:

1. Accept the reality of the loss.

2. Experience the feelings associated with the loss.

3. Adjust to an environment in which the deceased is no longer present.

4. Psychologically 'relocate' the deceased and reinvest energy in life.

Worden's model has the great advantage for counsellors of seeing the bereaved as an active agent in the process of grieving, not someone passively experiencing 'stages'. Therapeutic work can be aimed at enabling the client to achieve each of the tasks. It is of course important to be aware that the tasks are in themselves quite complex and are likely to overlap, and that clients are likely to move back and forth between tasks as they negotiate the grieving process, sometimes needing to revisit tasks at successively deeper levels and sometimes choosing to reject or adapt one or more of them.

BETWEEN-SESSION TASKS

See: Homework

BIBLIOTHERAPY

See also: Evidence-based practice, Exercises, Homework

Bibliotherapy is recommending books, handouts, tapes, etc. to clients. You can suggest that your client takes notes or underlines important points, which you later discuss during counselling (Collard, 2006). There is a large selection of self-help books on the University of Cambridge's Counselling Service's website (go to 'Help with Common Difficulties', then 'Self-help booklets').

There is now strong evidence that bibliotherapy can be very effective, and it is included in the NICE (2004a, b) guidelines for anxiety, depression and eating disorders. Bibliotherapy can be used in its own right, as preparation for counselling (the NICE emphasis), or as a supplement to it (Frude, 2005), and it has obvious advantages compared with medication: no side effects or delayed action, low cost, and more appealing and acceptable to most people. There are limitations too, of course, especially the high level of motivation needed. Frude also discussed the details of a 'book prescription' scheme involving libraries and heath professionals, begun in Cardiff in 2005, and concluded that bibliotherapy 'deserves greater recognition, wider implementation, increased systematic research, and energetic development' (Frude, 2005, p31).

Although bibliotherapy sometimes works well, there are also some problems (Rosen, 1987; Rosen *et al.*, 2003). These are some questions to consider asking:

- Does the book or tape etc. claim or promise too much?
- Is the advice specific or vague?
- Is there a warning about placebo effects?
- Is sound evidence of effectiveness (i.e. more than opinions, anecdotes and testimonials) included or cited?

BIG I

See also: Exercises, Self-awareness

This intervention is based on the concept of the 'egoless self' (Lazarus, 1977). Adapted by Ellis *et al.* (1997), the technique is a way to describe and teach clients self-acceptance. The counsellor draws a big, hollow 'I' on a whiteboard or large sheet of paper to represent the client in his or her totality. Then the client chooses two colours: the 'good' colour is for the things the client likes about him- or herself, or positive actions that he or she does or did; and the other colour (the 'critical' colour) is for things and actions that he or she does not like. The counsellor starts off the process by drawing, in the 'good' colour, a little 'i' inside the big 'I' to represent something positive the counsellor has noticed about the client. The client is then encouraged to remember more examples of positive actions and abilities. The small 'i's representing these are drawn anywhere inside the big 'I', not in any particular order. Then, in the critical colour, the counsellor draws a little 'i' for the particular problem the client has come to therapy for (e.g. a phobia, a loss, a negative emotion) and asks the client to add further to-be-improved 'i's.

Thus, the client hopefully realises that the problem has been blown out of proportion and can actually be reassessed in the larger picture of things. So even if clients feel like a failure owing to having lost a job or a relationship, they may realise that this is only one aspect of themselves. Usually clients are encouraged to continue this exploration at home and to ask a couple of close friends to add their insights to the list of little 'i's.

The idea is that they will eventually be encouraged to accept themselves, 'warts and all', but still polish the areas (little 'i's in the critical colour) that they want to improve in their life.

BLIND SPOTS

See also: Challenging, Games, Immediacy

'Blind spots' refer to ways in which we may not be seeing the whole picture in our appraisal of a particular issue or situation. Clients may benefit from the counsellor's input (often in the form of challenging) in order to uncover their blind spots and thus develop a clearer and more empowered perspective on issues or aspects of their experience. Egan (2007) has examined the issue of blind spots and challenging skills in some detail. He identified some useful categories of potential blind spots including:

- ownership (this is about who *owns* a particular problem, or how a client's problem might be reframed in order to be something that she or he does own; for example, note the difference between 'my problem is that my boss is really demanding', and 'my problem is that I'm afraid to be assertive when my boss is demanding')
- self-defeating beliefs (about oneself or the nature of people/relationships/the world)
- faulty interpretations, evasions, and distortions, including a tendency to define problems in terms that seem unsolvable
- failure to understand the consequences of one's behaviour
- hesitancy or unwillingness to act.

Clients will benefit from a counsellor who is able to challenge them effectively to develop alternatives to these potentially limiting perspectives and enable them to look at situations in ways which imply a greater level of choice and autonomy for themselves and more potential for change.

Of course, counsellors are human too and also prone to blind spots. They may need to challenge themselves or be challenged in supervision in order to overcome limiting perspectives about particular clients or issues.

'BLOCKED' CLIENTS

See: Avoidance, Challenging, Referral, Reluctant clients

BODY SCAN

See also: Mindfulness, Self-awareness

The body scan is seen as one of the core skills taught in mindfulness-based therapies (Segal *et al.*, 2002).The key objective in doing the body scan is to enhance awareness of physiological sensations and to train one's mind to stay focused over a longer period of time, on a particular task in 'the now'. The client is first asked to lie down on a mat or bed or to sit upright on a chair, then focus for a while on the movement of his or her breath before directing attention to each region of the body and observing what happens when doing this. Each body scan is a new beginning, a new 'now'. Clients are invited to practise the body scan for around 40 minutes, six times a week and not to expect or judge a particular outcome. Here is a shortened version of the exercise, based on Kabat-Zinn (1990).

1. Lie down, making yourself comfortable, on your back on a mat or rug on the floor or on your bed, in a place where you will be warm and undisturbed. Allow your eyes to close gently.

2. Take a few moments to get in touch with the movement of your breath and the sensations in the body. When you are ready, bring your awareness to the physical sensations in your body, especially to the sensations of touch or pressure where your body makes contact with the floor or bed. On each out-breath, allow yourself to let go, sinking a little deeper into the mat or bed.

3. Remind yourself of the intention of this practice. Its aim is not to feel any different, relaxed or calm; this may happen or it may not. Instead, the intention of the practice is, as best you can, to bring awareness to any sensations you detect, as you focus your attention on each part of the body in turn.

4. Now bring the focus of your awareness down the left leg, into the left foot and out to the toes of the left foot. Focus on each of the toes of the left foot in turn, bringing a gentle curiosity to investigating the quality of sensations that you find, perhaps noticing the sense of contact between the toes, a sense of tingling, warmth or no particular sensation.

5. When you are ready, on an in-breath, feel or imagine the breath entering the lungs and then passing down into the abdomen, into the left leg, the left foot, and out to the toes of the left foot. Then, on the out-breath, feel or imagine the breath coming all the way back up, out of the foot, into the leg, up through the abdomen and chest and out through the nose.

6. Now when you are ready, on an out-breath, let go of awareness of the toes and bring your awareness to the sensations on the bottom of your left foot – bringing a gentle, investigative awareness to the sole of the foot, the instep, the heel, to the ankle, the top of the foot, and right into the bones and joints. Then take a slightly deeper breath, directing it down into the whole of the left foot and, as the breath lets go on the out-breath, let go of the left foot completely, allowing the focus of awareness to move into the lower left leg – the calf, shin, knee, and so on in turn.

7. Continue to bring awareness, and a gentle curiosity, to the physical sensations in each part of the rest of the body in turn – to the upper left leg, the right toes, right foot, right leg, pelvic area, back, abdomen, chest, fingers, hands, arms, shoulder, neck, head and face. In each area, as best as you can, bring the same detailed level of awareness and gentle curiosity to the bodily sensations present. As you leave each major area, 'breathe in' to it on the in-breath, and let go of that region on the out-breath.

8. When you become aware of tension, or other intense sensations in a particular part of the body, you can 'breathe in' to them, using the

in-breath gently to bring awareness right into sensations and, and as best as you can, have a sense of their letting go, or releasing on the out-breath.

9. The mind will inevitably wander away from the breath and the body from time to time. It is what minds do. When you notice it, gently acknowledge it and then gently return your attention to the part of the body you intended to focus on.

10. After you have 'scanned' the whole body in this way, spend a few minutes being aware of a sense of the body as a whole and of the breath flowing freely in and out of the body.

BORDERLINE PERSONALITY DISORDER

See: DSM-IV, Personality disorders

BOREDOM

See also: Challenging, Congruence, Immediacy, Intuition, Process, Self-awareness

When you feel bored in a counselling session, it is usually better not to be stoical about it. One strategy is to focus on the client's nonverbal behaviour; another is to 'change gear' into a free-flowing attention and see what comes to mind. A third possibility is to say in a positive and constructive way that you are bored and that you want to find out what is going on. This strategy is not itself boring.

A fourth possibility is to be more concrete. Yalom (1989, pp95–99) discussed in detail his decision to confront Betty about boredom as the outstanding characteristic of his experience of their relationship and how he proceeded. First, he clarified how much of the boredom was his problem and identified two characteristics of Betty that were boring: the fact that she did not reveal anything intimate about herself and her 'forced gaiety'. Then he chose to confront her, initially about how much she revealed and later with her being 'jolly' and 'entertaining'. A principle which Yalom (1989, p114) drew on is that 'if something big in a relationship is not being talked about ... then nothing else of importance will be discussed either'.

BOUNDARIES

See also: Abuse, Assertiveness, Burnout, Confidentiality, Contract, negotiating a, Drama triangle, Endings, Friendship with clients, Power, Privacy, Sexual attraction, Stress, Supervision, Time boundaries

Boundaries are a part of being clear with yourself and with clients and of being reliable and trustworthy. Boundaries create a framework for the development of the therapeutic relationship and enable clients to *know* (rather than have questions or anxieties about) what is expected of them and what they can expect of the counsellor. Relevant boundaries include those of time, space (privacy), confidentiality and the counselling contract. They offer stability and apply the idea (and existential fact) that there are limits to relationships, including the counselling relationship. However, counsellors do sometimes become too involved and want to give more and more to clients, or to a particular client. This is counterproductive for everyone. Clear boundaries are also a useful defence against the possibility of exploitation within the relationship, either of the client by the counsellor or vice versa.

Walker (1992b, pp126–129) discussed the boundary of availability, under the heading 'Ring me whenever you need to'. She acted 'with good intentions but poor judgment' with a particularly distressed client, by offering to be available between sessions. It is not that this was undesirable in itself, but it was ill considered at the time and reflected her own needs and anxieties. It also did not help the client.

BRAINSTORMING

See also: Counselling, Freewriting, Goals, Power, Values

Brainstorming is a useful technique for developing new ideas and introducing creativity into the client's thinking about how to move forward with an issue. Once a client is sufficiently clear about a problem, it may be useful to brainstorm possible goals or desirable outcomes that she or he would like to see in place. Once the client has made a clear commitment to a particular goal, it may be useful to brainstorm a list of possible strategies and *things that might help* to achieve that goal. It is likely to be most helpful if you can facilitate brainstorming in an atmosphere of freewheeling thinking, where, at least for a while, 'anything goes'.

The usual procedure is simply to encourage the client to think of as many ideas as possible and record them in some way, without judging or censoring them at all, and going for quantity, including what may seem absurd ideas. A large sheet of (flipchart) paper and coloured pens are often useful props in this process, helping to inject some activity and energy into the process and allowing both the counsellor and client to see what is being produced. The counsellor can help the client by offering encouragement and support and by using appropriate prompts to encourage divergent thinking. ('What else?' 'What people/places/things, etc. might be involved?' 'Any other ideas along those lines?' 'How else might you approach this?' 'What is the most way-out idea you can think of?') In some circumstances it may also be useful for the therapist to offer *some* ideas to a brainstorm, provided that these are put 'into the pot' along with the client's ideas and are not seen as the definitive answers.

It is important in brainstorming to separate the generation of ideas from evaluation of those ideas, and clients may need some encouragement to share freely any ideas which occur to them without prematurely editing their thoughts.

The output of a brainstorm begun in a session may be taken away by the client to add to when further ideas occur. The next step is usually to try combining and grouping the ideas and, finally, to select the most appealing options and evaluate the possible benefits and consequences of implementing them.

BRIEF COUNSELLING

See also: Contract, negotiating a, Contraindications for brief counselling, EAPS, Effectiveness of counselling, Evaluation

Brief or time-limited counselling is generally understood to be around six sessions. Many agencies, including general practitioner (GP) surgeries, see this as the limit, while others allow a review after six sessions, with an extension possible. In practice, most counselling relationships are for fewer than six weeks (Feltham, 1997), but there is an obvious issue: is the time in counselling of clients who need longer to be limited by economics? Thorne's view was that market forces are too influential and are barbaric in their effects:

> The creeping contamination of almost all areas of our corporate life by the forces of the market place means that more and more people experience themselves not as persons but as consumers or providers and as potential victims on the altars of cost-effectiveness and efficiency. (Thorne, 1995, p35)

On the other hand, it is unethical for clients to be encouraged to stay longer in counselling than they need – they may be exploited; another client could be seen – and many people can be helped in a few sessions. Thorne (1999, p7) described an investigation of his practice, stimulated by the thought that 'lives can be changed in the twinkling of an eye … The notion that meaningful change can only come about as the result of long and painstaking processes is clearly untrue.' He offered just three sessions of person-centred counselling to clients with concerns such as delayed grief, the aftermath of rape, performance phobia and physical abuse. To his surprise, he judged the sessions to be effective, and he was impressed by how much clients prepared for them. Similarly, Mann (1973) also tried using the element of time in a constructive and deliberate way to motivate clients to face up to the source of their problems. He offered, say, 12 weekly sessions of 45 minutes and from the start consulted his calendar so that the client could see its role in setting the exact date of their last meeting. Mann, like Thorne (1999), suggested that a client's rate of progress may be influenced by an understanding of how long the treatment will last.

However, Thorne (1999) also wondered if his investigation was really 'a charade, an abject capitulation to a mad world', if the counselling had worked only because it fits 'a world which is constantly on the hoof', a world of management values like short-term effectiveness performance indicators and accountability. His values are to put down roots, reflect, not be 'forever in a rush, consumed with busyness' and to know how to wait. These values led to a further twist in his argument: he believes that they and related personal qualities are necessary for brief counselling to be effective.

Brief counselling demands a high level of counsellor skill and is not an easier option than longer-term work. Generally, short-term counselling is suitable for clients who are not severely disturbed and who, apart from the presenting problem, are functioning adequately in other areas of their lives. Clients tend to be actively involved, work between sessions to try out new behaviours and practise what they have learned, and are well motivated to change. Although some approaches to brief counselling make claims to the contrary, it is doubtful whether it is suitable for all clients, for example people who have not resolved early issues concerning basic trust and who therefore find it difficult to establish a good working relationship with the counsellor. One risk is that such people will be harmed by the experience of further loss and that this overshadows any gain in more immediate problem management.

Brief counselling has developed largely out of economic necessity, with the pressures of increasing demands for counselling and often diminishing financial resources. However, valuable outcomes can be achieved over relatively short periods, so financial pressures and effectiveness are in harmony to some extent.

BURNOUT

See also: Difficult clients, Role conflict, Stress, Supervision, Support groups

'Burnout' is a vivid but unclear term, with deep exhaustion probably at the heart of the various definitions. Other characteristics are anger, frustration and cynicism, and a sense of futility and failure (Maslach and Goldberg, 1998). The positive, enthusiastic person is transformed by burnout. Moreover, like the stress which precedes it, burnout approaches insidiously, aided by such thoughts as 'It's only one more' and 'I've coped with extra work before'.

What is so poignant about burnout is that it mainly strikes people who are highly committed to their work: You can only 'burn out' if you have been 'alight' in the first place. While exhaustion can be overcome with rest, a core part of burnout is a deep sense of disillusionment, and this is not experienced by people who can take a more cynical view of their work.

Given what burnout is, the symptoms of burnout are much as you would expect them to be. Physical symptoms can include physical fatigue, frequent illness and sleep problems. Emotional symptoms include disillusionment with the job; the loss of a sense of meaning and cynicism towards our organisations or clients; feelings of helplessness; frustration of efforts and a lack of power to change events; strong feelings of anger against the people we hold responsible for the situation; feelings of depression and isolation. Behavioural symptoms can include increasing detachment from co-workers; increased absenteeism; increased harshness in dealing with colleagues; marked reduction in commitment to work; increased alcohol consumption.

Chronic overload and persistent conflicts with colleagues appear to be two of the main sources of burnout in the helping professions (Maslach and Goldberg, 1998). These, and other factors such as lack of a sense of control and unfair treatment, probably interact. For example, counsellors who work in an organisation which has values they respect may be able to cope with greater workloads. Generally, strategies for coping with burnout are the same as those for stress. However, Pines and Keinan (2005) suggested, from an existential perspective, that the focus in treating burnout (but not stress) should be on enhancing people's sense of the significance and value of their work.

BUSINESS

See: Advertising, Coaching, Fees, Marketing, Private practice, Stress

CATHARSIS

See also: Abuse, Anger, Assertiveness, Counselling, Crying, Emotions, Exercises, Literal description, Writing (expressive)

Catharsis is the idea that expressing emotions is healing in itself, as in the expressions 'getting it off your chest' and 'Don't keep it bottled up'. The co-counselling concept of 'discharge' (e.g. Evison and Horobin, 2006) has something of this flavour too although it is also associated with 'spontaneous insights'. An alternative view of catharsis is that expressing emotions can be a relief but only briefly: the emotion may then return and perhaps more intensely. On this view, the aim of counselling is to help your client clarify his or her emotions and make sense of them rather than to 'ventilate'; expressing emotion is most helpful when it leads to greater understanding (Kennedy-Moore and Watson, 1999).

Indeed, in Yalom's view, as a therapist, 'you encourage acts of emotional expression but you always follow with reflection upon the emotions expressed' (2001, p164). Earlier in the same book, he puts this idea more fully: 'effective therapy consists of an alternating sequence: *evocation and experiencing* of affect followed by *analysis and integration* of affect. How long one waits until one initiates an analysis of the affective event is a function of clinical experience' (p71, italics in original).

Moreover, for some clients, emotional avoidance may be the best way to cope. For others, cathartic work is appropriate (Jinks, 2006, pp 14–15).

CHALLENGING

See also: Assertiveness, Blind spots, Boredom, Challenging, some guidelines for, Collusion, Counselling, Empathy, Games, Giving information, Immediacy, Nonverbal communication, Patterns, Questions, Self-disclosure, Thoughts

Challenges are invitations to change or to look at things from a different angle. The idea is to help clients move where they need to go rather than push them to where you (the counsellor) think they ought to be. The intended result of a challenge is a broader horizon, deeper perception, or changed point of view, and hopefully one which allows the client increased choice, autonomy, or awareness of available resources. Challenging is more likely to be effective if you have earned the right by being empathic and developing a trusting relationship; if you are open to being challenged yourself by your client; and if you listen hard to the impact of your challenge (which may after all be wholly or partly wrong, or at the wrong time).

As the following list of skills shows, some effective challenges involve picking up what the client has (in your view) implied but is not very aware of, while others involve inviting clients to consider a different interpretation or appraisal of their situation:

- **Advanced empathy:** this means responding to the deeper messages which may be 'between the lines' in what is said, i.e. feelings or perspectives that are not fully experienced and acknowledged. For example, when clients talk a lot about their partner and very little about themselves, you might say, 'You've spoken with great feeling about X's behaviour. You seem to feel overwhelmed and powerless about X.' Thus the focus of attention is brought back to your client, who might move deeper into his or her feelings (whether your advanced empathy is accurate or not).

- **Linking ideas and identifying themes:** this involves bringing together things your client has said and suggesting probable patterns or connections in his or her behaviour, e.g. 'You say your boss ignores you and makes you feel unwanted. I think I heard you say the same thing last week about your mother.' Essentially, you are suggesting (very tentatively) a pattern or causal connection among various behaviours, emotions or ideas.

- **Contrasting ideas:** e.g. 'You say you feel disorganised and out of control at work, but when you talk about home you seem really on top of things. I wonder what the difference is for you.'

- **Immediacy:** e.g. 'When you stare at me like that, I sometimes feel a bit intimidated and wonder what you are thinking.' This is more direct and there would normally need to be a good deal of trust between you before you said it.

- **Questioning:** in our view questions should be used sparingly in counselling. The risk is of working with what *you* are thinking about rather than staying in your *client's* frame of reference. Usually, a good empathic statement is better. However, questions can sometimes help the client move further, e.g. 'How else could you look at that situation?' or 'What else was going on for you?' Skilled and sparing use of questions can also be useful in helping clients to challenge self-defeating beliefs or interpretations (e.g. 'I can't be happy unless I'm in a relationship') by exploring the evidence for and against.

- **Moving-on statements:** these are perhaps the simplest form of challenge but can be very effective in helping clients move deeper into a topic. It may be necessary to repeat only one important feeling or word for your client to explore it further, e.g. 'upset'.

- **Giving information:** see separate entry.
- **Self-disclosure (by counsellors):** hearing about someone else's experience is sometimes helpful, e.g. 'What I've sometimes felt (but you may not) is …' (see also separate entry).
- **Confrontation:** this is a more insistent way of challenging, when a counsellor describes apparent distortions or discrepancies in the client's emotions, thoughts or actions, for example:
  - blocking and avoiding: e.g. 'You talk about your family quite often, but I notice you never mention your daughter.'
  - self-defeating attitudes and beliefs: e.g. 'I hear you frequently calling yourself silly, which sounds as though you are being hard on yourself.' You could stop talking at this point or add 'What evidence do you have for thinking you are silly?' (See entry on Thoughts.)
  - discrepancies: e.g. 'You say you are quite happy, yet I see you here looking sad and sitting hunched up which gives a different picture.' (See entry on Nonverbal communication.)
- **Concreteness:** concreteness is the skill of inviting clients to be more specific. The purpose is to get below the surface communication that may not fully or accurately represent the client's experience or meaning. It also helps to ensure that you do not project your own meaning onto your client as it gives the client an opportunity to explain his or her, often idiosyncratic, definition of common feelings or experiences, e.g. anger, depression, anxiety. For example, your client says, 'Things are going badly.' You might respond in many ways, perhaps with a paraphrase or silence. If you chose concreteness, you would say something like 'Can you give me an example?' or 'Which things?' The potential benefit is much greater clarity and therefore opportunity to empathise; the risk is sounding intrusive or like an interrogator. Concreteness therefore more often has the 'flavour' of a challenge and should be used accordingly.

CHALLENGING, SOME GUIDELINES FOR

See also: Challenging, Counselling

Aspects to consider challenging

These include:

- what is implied; thoughts and feelings on the edge of the client's awareness; what seems vague or confused; underlying meanings
- verbal and nonverbal mixed messages; discrepancies; contradictions, distortions, evasions or 'game playing'

- failure to own problems, or to identify the aspects of problems which the client does own or can do something about
- resistance to change or to applying learning; self-defeating behaviour; underused strengths or resources; dysfunctional interpretations or irrational thinking
- the relationship between counsellor and client, particularly if relevant to other relationships or to the progress of the counselling
- themes, patterns, connecting 'islands' where the client seems unaware of the 'big picture'.

Principles

- Start by considering whether you have earned the right to challenge, i.e. by developing an empathic understanding of the client's experience and communicating that to the client.
- Where possible, encourage your clients to challenge themselves.
- Be tentative in the way you challenge.
- Be concrete: challenge specific examples of thoughts, feelings or behaviours rather than making vague inferences.
- Use 'successive approximations' rather than all-at-once challenges that make heavy demands on clients in a short time.
- Give time and space for your client to respond; avoid 'hit and run' or a string of challenges, especially towards the end of a session.
- Challenge on the basis of your client's values rather than your own.
- Challenge strengths and resources rather than weaknesses or deficits.
- Be sensitive to the impact of your challenge. Elicit and explore your client's reactions to any challenge and respond with empathy; help your client to share and work through any defensive emotions.

CHANGE

See: Common factors, Effectiveness of counselling, Metaphors in counselling, Personality, Psychological type, Readiness to change, Theories of counselling

CLIENT INFORMATION HANDOUT

See also: Advertising, Confidentiality, Contract, negotiating a, Fees, First session, Private practice, Record keeping

Client information handouts are provided by the therapist during the first contact hour with a new client. They provide the client with essential information about the counsellor and about counselling, as shown in Figure 1.

Name	....
Role, e.g. Psychotherapist, Coach	....
Address	....
Telephone number	....
Webpage (if applicable)	....
E-mail address (if applicable)	....

TRAINING
Doctor of ... , Diploma in ... I am a registered Life Coach and a Psychotherapist. I received further training in ...

EXPERIENCE
I have been working as a counsellor and trainer since ... My work includes treating private clients, running groups in medical settings and workshops as a trainer, etc.

MEMBERSHIPS
I am a registered psychotherapist with ...

CODE OF ETHICS
I adhere to the BACP Ethical Framework (available on request).

FEES
If you wish to cancel an appointment I require *a full 48 hours' notice*, otherwise you will be *liable for the full cost* of the session. *One session lasts for 50 minutes.* If you arrive late we still terminate at the previously arranged time, so as not to delay my next client. Cost: ... Concessions: ... Payable by cash or cheque at the end of each session.

SUPERVISION
Good therapeutic practice in the UK requires counsellors, regardless of how well qualified or experienced they are, to be in regular supervision. I receive one hour of supervision for every 10 hours of client work.

CONFIDENTIALITY
Trust between client and counsellor is crucial to the success of the therapeutic process and I treat all information disclosed as confidential. My records are kept securely and anonymously and destroyed seven years after our sessions end. Any (anonymous) details my Supervisor receives are also treated as confidential by her. However, if I feel a client is either a danger to him- or herself or to others I do reserve the right to inform appropriate agencies.

THERAPEUTIC PROCESS
I offer all prospective clients an Assessment Interview (rates apply as above). This gives us both the opportunity to consider whether we wish to work together. Thereafter, it very much depends on the individual needs of each client as to how long therapy will last. In general, I work in a brief, integrative approach unless otherwise indicated.

HOW CAN PSYCHOTHERAPY HELP YOU?
A trained therapist seeks to help you gain a perspective about issues troubling you. Together we explore the causes of your problems, why and how you maintain them, and consider what might be stopping you from reaching your full potential. Finally, we determine what you need to do to change things for yourself.

MY APPROACH
There are many different types of therapy to choose from. I work as a multimodal cognitive-behavioural therapist. The approach is essentially psychoeducational and contends that many problems arise from misinformation or missing information. Thus I see my work as being a 'coach', attempting to offer my clients a wide array of life skills that they may want to implement into their daily lives.

Figure 1 Example of a client information handout

CLIENTS WHO DON'T COME BACK

See also: Beginnings, Contract, negotiating a, Difficulties in being a client, Distress at the end of a counselling session (clients'), Endings, Expectations (clients'), Missed sessions, Multiculturalism, Readiness to change

It can be worrying when a client does not show up, especially if you know that he or she is having a number of serious problems or if the last session was unsatisfactory in some way. The most obvious form of positive feedback is when your clients come back, so a client's not turning up can cause you to question your effectiveness as a counsellor. However, dropping out can also be positive feedback, when your client has found what he or she needs from counselling but does not want a 'proper' ending.

Even the most experienced counsellors have clients who do not come back, or who break off the counselling relationship unexpectedly. It is important to explore your reactions in supervision, and to consider different ways in which you might contact these clients. Telephone calls, although encouraged by some agencies, can be intrusive or unwelcome. Perhaps the best way to respond is to send such clients a brief, friendly note enquiring after their welfare and inviting them to get in touch. If your client does not reply, we think you have been sufficiently caring and done enough: clients have the right not to reply and chasing after them does not respect that right.

If you are particularly concerned, more direct action may be needed – but again this is something to think through carefully in supervision. There may be times when a telephone call or, in the last resort, a visit is necessary. But visiting clients at home should be considered only in extreme circumstances and should be done only after you have explored the implications in supervision.

Clients may drop out of counselling for a variety of reasons, and it is useful to be aware of some common problems and to try to adopt strategies to minimise their impact.

Factors which may lead to dropout

- The client is not ready for counselling or is not ready for the nature of the work being undertaken.
- There may be impasse because the client does not feel understood or accepted or because of:
  - inadequate problem definition
  - poor therapeutic alliance
  - mismatch with the client's expectations
  - lack of negotiated goals/intentions
  - incompatible personalities
  - misunderstanding of cultural dynamics
  - inappropriate or poor intervention.

Some strategies to minimise dropout

- Take time to explore what the client wants from therapy: expectations, any anxieties, outside pressures, etc.
- Be sensitive to cultural factors and allow these to be discussed in sessions.
- Agree clearly defined appointments, time limits, etc. and stick to them.
- Conclude each session effectively, with a summary of major themes, progress and achievements, and goals agreed.
- Do not begin new topics near the end of a session.
- Build bridges between sessions:
  - Discuss future direction.
  - Negotiate between-session tasks.
- Hold a periodic review/evaluation with the client.
- Prepare for sessions effectively by reviewing previous notes.
- Avoid being or seeming rushed, preoccupied or distracted before and after sessions.

COACHING

See also: Action planning, Counselling, Specialisms in counselling

Coaching overlaps considerably with counselling as defined in this book (Neenan and Dryden, 2001; Rogers, 2004). As with psychotherapy, there are strongly held views about the differences, but none has been generally accepted. One possibility is a negative definition such as 'coaches do not treat disorders like obsessive-compulsive disorder or depression', but then nor do some counsellors. Some counsellors also work as coaches. Coaches vary as much as counsellors in the models they use, but most coaches probably emphasise action and the future.

The 'images' of coaching and counselling (and psychotherapy) are significantly different: for some people, there will be less of a stigma (but for others, less cachet) in seeing a coach. Coaches typically charge higher fees than counsellors.

A political criticism of coaching is that it is a means of helping people to 'fit in' with dominant and controlling ideas of what it means to be a 'successful' person, rather than enabling people to challenge existing ideas and helping them to make changes in their own lives that may not be approved of by others but are more personally satisfying to the individual concerned. However, many coaches are concerned with the personal development of their clients, and some of those clients do not feel that they have a 'problem' as such but would rather explore how they operate and who they are in a bid to improve the way they function in the world. As in counselling, the agenda is then based around the client's own wishes and goals. Moreover, in both coaching and counselling there are practitioners who think they know better than their clients and try to influence them accordingly (perhaps with very good intentions).

Two main kinds of coaching are business or executive coaching, which focuses on senior managers and their performance at work (the coach needs to feel comfortable with aspects of business), and life coaching, which is more general and includes helping clients become more assertive or lead a healthier lifestyle. However, what seems like a business problem may of course be related to factors outside work and vice versa. There are also speciality or niche coaches, who focus on a particular group (e.g. doctors or youths) or on a particular area (e.g. stress or career development). See the website of the Association for Coaching for further information. Rogers (2006) recommends finding a niche and discusses finding clients, fees and other aspects of setting up a coaching business.

CODES OF ETHICS

See also: Complaints, Ethical dilemmas, Ethical Framework, Mistakes

The main purposes of codes of ethics are to help maintain standards of practice, to inform and protect clients, to provide a framework for counsellors to consult when trying to clarify an ethical dilemma and within which to operate a complaints procedure, to demonstrate the maturity of an organisation and profession and to encourage recognition and discussion of ethical issues (Bond, 2000). When the BACP (2002) adopted the term 'Ethical Framework' rather than 'code of ethics', the intention was to signify a move away from a prescriptive approach of specifying 'do's and don'ts', which can lead to an increasingly long and complex code as new situations need to be addressed, to a framework which identifies guiding principles and values to be applied by practitioners and their supervisors in addressing ethical dilemmas. See the BACP's website for further information.

Other professional bodies and associations, for example the BABCP and the UKCP, also publish codes or guidelines of relevance to counsellors and psychotherapists.

COLLUSION

See also: Avoidance, Boundaries, Challenging, Drama triangle, Games

People come to counselling with many needs, some overt and others covert. Sometimes, the overt needs are in opposition to the covert ones. For example, clients might state that their friends are very important to them, so the overt need is to have friends, but underneath may be a fear of being left alone. In this case, the covert need (of which the client may or may not be aware) is motivated by fear, and the overt need is a desperate attempt to avoid the more painful covert one. It would be collusion if the counsellor concentrated solely on the client's issue with his or her friends. It is particularly easy to collude with avoidance if the subject is difficult for either the client or the counsellor.

COMMON FACTORS

See also: Change, Contraindications for brief counselling, Core conditions, Counselling, Effectiveness of counselling, Emotions, Evidence-based practice, Good counsellors, Integration and eclecticism, Readiness to change, Relationship between counsellor and client, Respect, Self-awareness, Specialisms in counselling, Trust, Values

The term 'common factors' is used to refer to those factors which different approaches to counselling and psychotherapy have in common (as opposed to what makes approaches different). Findings from outcome research have consistently failed to find any significant or consistent differences between approaches in terms of their general effectiveness. This has directed some researchers to the task of determining what it is that is effective, on the assumption that these factors must be present in all approaches. A variety of studies have attempted to identify these common factors and, while the lists arrived at vary, a consensus is emerging (Hubble *et al.*, 1999; Lambert, 2004). It seems that there are four categories:

- **Client variables and extra-therapeutic events:** the nature of the client's problems, their beliefs, motivation, capacity to relate, psychological resources and ability to identify a focal problem, as well as external support and events account for about 40 per cent of the change that occurs in therapy.

- **Relationship factors:** the quality of the therapeutic relationship, particularly as perceived by the client, accounts for about 30 per cent of client improvement.

- **Expectancy and placebo effects:** the hope engendered by taking part in counselling and being offered a convincing framework accounts for about 15 per cent of the variance in client improvement.

- **Technique and model factors:** while examples of specific techniques which are particularly effective with specific issues have been identified (e.g. CBT for panic disorder), there is generally little evidence for the effectiveness of any particular technique over others even with particular problems (in spite of recent enthusiasm for evidence-based practice). Specific techniques are estimated to account for about 15 per cent of the improvement experienced by clients.

The results of this synthesis are important in discouraging two assumptions: that any one approach has all the answers and is superior to others; and that any one factor (such as the relationship) is the key to successful therapy. Instead, the common factors approach suggests that what works in therapy is a combination of identifiable factors relating to the client, the relationship, the instillation of hope, and the selection of techniques which 'fit' either the particular problem or the client's characteristics and beliefs. It suggests that counsellors should listen well to their clients, respect and trust their strengths and values, and form genuinely *collaborative* relationships with them, rather than aim to be therapeutic heroes or wizards (tempting though this can be).

Research on the common factors approach provides strong support for particular *ways of working* which are consistent with an integrative model. The following are some guidelines:

- Relate to clients in ways which are genuine, accepting, and empathic.
- Treat clients as capable and as having the strengths and resources to deal with their problems. Encourage them to take this view of themselves.
- Focus on change: listen carefully and draw attention to any evidence for positive change, encouraging clients to see this as a result of things they have done.
- Help clients explore their readiness to change. Build motivation and commitment by helping them develop a vision of a better future.
- Help clients explore their expectations of counselling.
- Convey confidence in techniques or approaches used.
- Encourage clients to use resources outside counselling.

COMPLAINTS

See also: Assertiveness, Codes of ethics, Ethical Framework, Insurance, Legal system, Referral, Supervision

Complaints can be seen as 'an important source of learning for the profession' (Bond, 2006) and as opportunities to create trust and goodwill (Calnan, 1991). To use complaints in these ways, it is crucial to respond speedily and to remember that the client is probably upset and disoriented. Calnan's suggestions include treating every complaint, however trivial it may seem, with respect; staying calm; dealing with a complaint on the day it was made (or at least reporting progress); listening until the client and the person dealing with the complaint agree about 'the heart of the matter'; investigating; explaining in a straightforward way; apologising if appropriate.

If you have a complaint made against you, it is much less likely to be valid or upheld if you can show that you reflected on your relationship with your client and consulted your supervisor or supervision group. The personal, moral quality of humility is part of the BACP's Ethical Framework (BACP, 2007) and includes, in practice, using supervision to check relevant decisions, being open to challenge and knowing the limits of your professional competence.

Calnan also recommended three steps to take in response to being accused of professional negligence or incompetence. In a different order from Calnan's, these are as follows:

1. Inform your manager and ask a colleague to take over the client's care.
2. Inform your administration.
3. Contact your professional insurers quickly. Send a brief statement and photocopies of relevant documents.

Other types of complaints include those about relatively minor errors like missing an appointment; poor practice (e.g. counselling in a way that is inconsistent with the model you described to your client); and, of course, gross misconduct. All the major counselling and psychotherapy organisations *require* their members to report serious concerns about the conduct of others (Bond, 2000).

Preventing complaints

Like all professionals, counsellors are legally required to exercise 'reasonable care and skill' in their work. 'Reasonable' is defined by the profession itself in its statements about ethics, in major textbooks and in the views of leading practitioners or (in a profession, like counselling, in which there is much disagreement) those of a subgroup of responsible practitioners within the profession. Professions tend to be trusted by the courts to set and maintain reasonable standards and methods.

The following actions, apart perhaps from the fourth, are part of counsellors' normal professional practice and will prevent many complaints:

- Do not guarantee improvement (or nondeterioration) to a client.
- Do not give advice to clients.
- Be sure that any information given is accurate and that 'homework' assignments are both legal and ethical.
- Check your office for physical dangers (slippery floors, sharp edges, etc.) – 'reasonable care' again.
- Recommend that the client sees a doctor if you suspect that his or her emotional problems have a physical cause.

CONFIDENTIALITY

See also: Contract, negotiating a, Ethical Framework, Giving information, Legal system, Record keeping, Suicide, Supervision, Trust

Many people believe that counsellors offer absolute confidentiality. However, counsellors and counselling organisations do not usually consider confidentiality to be an absolute. Given that you respect a client's privacy as far as you can, but that there are limits, a key question is, 'In what circumstances might I break confidentiality?' Perhaps the most problematic circumstance here is breaking confidence to protect your client's welfare or to protect another person, maybe one who is threatened by a potentially dangerous client. Are *all* threats by your clients to be reported? What if you have a hunch that a client is suicidal or dangerous, but no evidence? Discussing such concerns with your supervisor is strongly recommended unless it would cause undue delay in taking needed action. The BACP's *Ethical Framework for Good Practice in Counselling and Psychotherapy* (BACP, 2007) states that in such cases:

> the aim should be to ensure for the client a good quality of care that is as respectful of the client's capacity for self-determination and

their trust as circumstances permit ... Any disclosures should be undertaken in ways that best protect the client's trust. Practitioners should be willing to be accountable to their clients and to their profession for their management of confidentiality in general and particularly for any disclosures made without their client's consent.

Such judgements are complicated but not uniquely so: the law rests on notions like 'reasonable care' and trusts professionals to make such judgements.

These are some guidelines for practice:

- Inform clients early (as part of your contract with them) about limitations on confidentiality: for example, that what they say may be discussed with your supervisor or supervision group, and that threats to the safety of the client or others may not be able to remain subject to confidentiality.

- Tell clients about any legal or organisational factors. Some agencies require their counsellors to inform them of incest and child abuse for example.

- Consult professional colleagues when you are unsure.

- Records should be brief and kept securely; however, see the next point.

- If you decide to break confidentiality, the following are important:

  - Whenever possible discuss your decision with your client first, perhaps encouraging him or her to inform the appropriate authority if possible.

  - If the client is unwilling to do so, inform him or her that you will make the disclosure, giving a clear account of your reasons.

  - Discuss the implications for your future work with the client and try to agree a plan which takes account of the client's wishes and needs as well as the need for disclosure.

  - In this instance, keep detailed records, including the rationale for your decisions. It may be necessary to account for your actions within the organisation you work for, or if there is a complaint against you.

Bond and Sandhu (2007) discuss in depth the legal and ethical implications of providing confidentiality.

CONGRUENCE

See also: Boredom, Common factors, Core conditions, Counselling, Immediacy, Self-awareness, Self-disclosure

'Congruence' is a term usually associated with client-centred counselling but which has become part of the everyday language of many counselling approaches (Mearns and Thorne, 2007; Merry, 1995, 1999). 'Genuineness', 'sincerity' and 'authenticity' are related concepts. Many counsellors, particularly those from the humanistic approaches, see congruence in the sense of sharing some of their feelings with their clients as part of the counselling process, although most psychodynamic counsellors would be more circumspect.

Rogers' definition of congruence includes these words: 'when self-experiences are accurately symbolised (in awareness), and are included in the self-concept in this accurately symbolized form, then the state is one of congruence of self and experience' (1959, p206). This definition is expressed in terms of the distinction between self and experience, not in terms of the behaviour of the counsellor, and is consistent with Rogers' earlier definition where, in discussing his ideas about the six necessary and sufficient conditions for therapeutic personality change, he wrote:

> the therapist should be, within the confines of this relationship, a congruent, genuine, integrated person. It means that within the relationship he is freely and deeply himself, with his actual experience accurately represented by his awareness of himself ... It should be clear that this includes being himself even in ways which are not regarded as ideal for psychotherapy. His experience may be, "I am afraid of this client", or, "My attention is so focussed on my own problems that I can scarcely listen to him". If the therapist is not denying these feelings to awareness, but is able freely to be them (as well as being other feelings), then the condition (congruence) we have stated is met. (Rogers, 1957, p97)

Ideally, the core conditions of empathy, respect and congruence (all subjective states or attitudes existing within the counsellor) would all be fully present together, but in practice it is rarely possible for a counsellor to be so consistent. The theory of client-centred counselling predicts that the extent to which the therapist experiences these attitudes determines the extent to which the relationship is likely to be effective in promoting change. Because the therapeutic attitudes are seen as existing together rather than separately, it is not usually helpful to ascribe more importance to one or other of them, but Rogers believed that therapist congruence sometimes takes priority (Rogers, 1959, p215). In other words, at those times when counsellors are unable to experience empathic under-standing, or are unable to be unconditionally accepting, they should be aware of those experiences, attend to them and allow them accurately into awareness.

The question often arises about the degree to which it is necessary for counsellors directly to communicate their feelings and thoughts to their clients in order to be 'congruent'. Congruence does not require that a counsellor *should* communicate thoughts and feelings that arise from within his or her own frame of reference.

> Being real involves being thoroughly acquainted with the flow of experiencing going on within, a complex and continuing flow. It means being *willing to express* the attitudes that come *persistently* to the fore, especially perhaps the negative attitudes, inasmuch as the positive ones can rather easily be inferred from behavior and tone. If the therapist is bored with the client, it is only real to express this feeling. (Rogers and Sanford, 1980, p1381, our italics)

Rogers and Sanford (1980, p1381) realised that this concept could create difficulties and was open to misinterpretation:

> It certainly does not mean that the therapist burdens the client with all her problems or feelings. It does not mean that the therapist blurts out impulsively any attitude that comes to mind. It does mean, however, that the therapist does not deny to herself the feelings being experienced and that the therapist is willing to express and to be any persistent feelings that exist in the relationship ... When the therapist is feeling neither empathic nor caring, she must discover what the flow of experiencing is and must be willing to express that flow, whether it seems embarrassing, too revealing, or whatever.

CONTINGENCY PLANS

See also: Action planning, Force-field analysis

Action plans developed in a counselling session are rarely simple to implement in the real world, and it can be useful to pay some attention to the things that might not go smoothly. This can be particularly important with clients whose lives might be chaotic, who are impulsive, or where there are problems with addictive/compulsive behaviours. Egan (2007) identified 'inertia' (the tendency for things to need a push to get started) and 'entropy' (the tendency for things to deteriorate if energy is not sustained) as useful targets for contingency planning. In practical terms, you can encourage clients to review the action plans that they develop and identify 'no start' and 'fall apart' factors which might interfere with their plans. They can then consider how to avoid or circumvent these influences.

CONTINUING PROFESSIONAL DEVELOPMENT (CPD)

See also: Psychological type, Research, Stress, Support groups

Continuing professional development (CPD) is now required by most professions and trades. The aim is partly to reassure the public that practitioners' knowledge and skills are up to date. In addition, person-centred counselling demands a lifelong commitment to a continuing process of increasing self-awareness because of its emphasis on congruence; in the psychodynamic tradition, personal growth and development are seen as equally crucial because of the need to minimise the effects of counter-transference.

Many activities can legitimately be considered as appropriate for personal growth. What you choose to do will depend on your approach to counselling and your individual circumstances. In our experience, people have found some combination of the following activities helpful, although this list is not exhaustive:

- keeping a journal
- being part of a network or support group that encourages personal exploration

- going on short courses and to conferences and workshops to keep up with developments in your field
- reading
- watching a TV programme or film
- researching and writing
- undertaking further formal study
- being in a personal growth group
- exploring particular aspects of counselling or counselling with specific client groups
- learning how to manage stress better.

On the more general issue of the relationship between reading the counselling literature and being an effective counsellor, McLeod (1997a) argued that reading can increase 'cognitive flexibility', a desirable characteristic in counsellors. However, it is also possible to read too much and become too theoretical or find it difficult to communicate directly. The literature can be 'a place of irrelevance, illusion, even of danger' (McLeod, 1997, p162).

You might also consider developing aspects of yourself that you have hitherto neglected, such as your spiritual development (if you have an interest in this) or your creative and artistic sides, by taking art classes, writing poetry, dancing, listening to or playing music, for example. Exploring the many forms of meditation can help you to deal with areas of confusion or anxiety. The more 'body-oriented' approaches to meditation, like some forms of yoga or t'ai chi ch'uan, suit some people. Similarly, some attention to physical fitness and/or the adoption of a healthier lifestyle (if you need and want it) might also be considered as a contribution to personal development if it enables you to give better attention to your clients.

Most people start counselling by offering a direct service to individual clients. Their work tends to be remedial. Counsellors may at some point want to shift the target of their efforts from individuals to couples, families, groups or organisations. They may also be interested in moving from remedial into more psychoeducational work. Social skills, relaxation and assertiveness training are all examples of interventions with a positive preventive and developmental purpose. Your approach to counselling may also develop, from working directly with clients to consultation, counsellor training, training of trainers, supervision, research, writing, broadcasting or the production of audiovisual curriculum materials.

Whatever you choose to do, it is important that you feel challenged and stimulated and that what you do helps you to question the assumptions about yourself that affect the way you relate to your clients and others. Holding the notion that you are fully trained and have no need for further personal work is likely to result in your practice becoming stale and lacking creativity. Rogers' idea of the person as someone continually in a process of becoming more fully functioning (Rogers, 1961) is helpful whatever your counselling approach.

In practice, CPD often occurs routinely during a normal working day: for example, reading an article can update your professional knowledge. There is therefore considerable autonomy in choosing what to do for CPD but, to qualify as CPD, the activity must be relevant to your development as a counsellor. However, the *process* itself is fairly formal and systematic, with some professional bodies requiring learning needs and objectives to be specified, with each activity analysed and evaluated in those terms, and it is therefore sometimes experienced as controlling. Moreover, keeping detailed records comes more easily to some personality types than to others, when the particular personality characteristics are not likely to be related, positively or negatively, to competence. The same general arguments apply to the related procedures of accreditation and registration. Some practitioners will probably continue to rebel, some to be pragmatic with varying degrees of resentment and irritation, and others to embrace the procedures with enthusiasm.

CONTRACT, NEGOTIATING A

See also: Boundaries, Brief counselling, Client information handout, Expectations (clients'), Fees, Frequency of sessions, Giving information, Goals, Multiculturalism, Psychological type, Time boundaries, Trust, Values

A contract is an agreement negotiated between you and your client at the beginning of your work together. Commonly, it has two elements: a therapeutic element concerned with the purpose of counselling and your approach, and a business element concerned with practical arrangements and conditions. Some counsellors prefer an informal approach to contracting, almost to the extent that it is not an explicit process. They feel that their client's understanding of what is going on, what can be achieved and how, needs to evolve gradually through their work together. Other counsellors are more formal, in some instances making use of written contracts (these may include such details as specific goals, strategies to be followed and duration) which they invite the client to sign, thereby giving informed consent to the process. These represent extreme positions on the degree of formality of negotiating a contract.

Closely related to the issue of formality is the degree of specificity: how concrete and detailed the contract is. Some counsellors and clients agree on working towards greater self-awareness. Other contracts may be much more concrete and specify clear objectives, such as 'to eliminate or significantly reduce the frequency of panic attacks'. Such a contract may also identify some of the steps and strategies towards achieving this goal. Greater specificity can help to communicate a sense of direction and purpose, stimulate clear thinking and motivate the client to change. It can also provide a rational basis for evaluation. On the other hand, clients and counsellors do not always know where they are going until they get there. This is not to imply a lack of purpose, but it does make specific goals written into a contract rather pointless.

The therapeutic contract is sometimes described as the counselling or treatment plan. It is a negotiated agreement about what you and your client want to achieve together and how you might work towards it. This element of the contract may follow from an initial assessment and, typically, is reviewed from time to time. Sometimes, a more explicit form of agreement about what needs to be achieved and the strategies involved will be relevant only at a later or action-planning stage of counselling.

The business contract is intended to protect both counsellor and client by specifying the arrangements for counselling and the boundaries within which it will take place. Part of this element will be information giving and may be non-negotiable or negotiable only within limits, for example time and fees. Typically, the conditions include the length of each session, frequency and pattern of attendance, duration of the contract, fees and timekeeping. The contract on timekeeping may involve an explicit commitment to punctuality on the part of both counsellor and client, with an additional commitment to cancel an appointment in advance rather than simply not turn up to a session. It should be made clear whether, if a client arrives late, any additional time will be allocated. Making these conditions explicit from the very beginning should save misunderstanding and resentment.

Sills (2006) offers a wide-ranging review of contracts in counselling and psychotherapy, including such factors as goals, orientation, modes, personality, and ethical and legal issues.

CONTRAINDICATIONS FOR BRIEF COUNSELLING

See also: Assessment, Avoidance, Brief counselling, Common factors, Emotions, First impressions, Mental health and mental illness, Referral, Relationship between counsellor and client, Trust

Some clients may not be suitable for counselling, and counselling is not the answer to all psychological problems. The difficulty is in judging accurately whether or not someone is likely to benefit from counselling. However, it is possible to identify various characteristics in a potential client that may serve as contraindications for brief counselling. In making such clinical judgements, it is appropriate to be cautious, for the following reasons:

- It is not always possible to identify contraindications in the first session.
- Patterns of behaviour provide a more reliable basis than single items of evidence.
- It is important to look for evidence of the client's ability to modify or change his or her experience or behaviour.
- Contraindications are only indicators: there are no sharp boundaries or operational criteria that can be used to distinguish clearly between clients who are suitable and those who are unsuitable for brief counselling.
- Many of the contraindications will be evident at some time or other in most clients, and it is their degree and persistence which is important in interpreting them as valid contraindicators.

- Identifying certain characteristics may help you to adjust your expectations of what might be achieved with the person in a limited period, rather than necessarily assessing him or her as unsuitable for counselling.
- Some contraindications might actually provide an initial or continuing focus for the counselling itself.

The following characteristics raise questions about a person's suitability for brief counselling, subject to the caveats discussed above:

- **Unrealistic expectations which persist:** some people expect counselling to give them immediate solutions to their problems, to be told what to do, to be given advice and direction. It is when such unrealistic expectations persist that they become a contraindication.

- **No real desire to change:** clients need, at some level, to want to change if counselling is to be effective. Most clients are in some way resistant to change; despite the pain and distress, they find it hard to give up troublesome aspects of their behaviour, perhaps because of hidden 'pay-offs' or because they give expression to unheard parts of themselves. Some clients, especially but not necessarily involuntary clients, may show little if any willingness to change. You might find it useful to explore how and why such clients came to counselling.

- **No clear problem:** it is hard to discover what some people want from counselling.

- **Long history of seeking psychological help:** some clients have seen numerous helpers over many years and tend to have had only a few sessions with each. Typically, they may also be seeing someone else for counselling or therapy. It may be evident that they habitually talk about their problems to everybody and anybody but are reluctant to enter into any form of developing relationship. You may find it useful to start by exploring their views on why the other forms of helping were unsuccessful.

- **Unresponsive clients:** counselling is based on talking and cannot make much progress, certainly in the short term, with clients who have great difficulty in talking about their experiences and in putting their thoughts and feelings into words.

- **Avoiding emotions:** some clients talk a lot about what they have done or are going to do, about their experiences and behaviour and, more especially, other people's experiences and behaviour. It is as if the preoccupation with the story is a way of avoiding their emotions and feelings. If clients sustain a cool and rational view of themselves and their problems and the counselling is devoid of emotion, change may be less likely. On the other hand, some issues are more amenable to problem-solving techniques than others and may be satisfactorily resolved by thinking them through.

- **Inability to relate to others:** most approaches to counselling place a high value on the need to establish an effective working relationship. You can look for evidence of a capacity to relate to others, irrespective of whether the relationship was experienced as positive or negative. It is unlikely that clients who have found it very difficult to relate either well or badly to others will find it possible to form a working relationship with you.

- **Lack of capacity to trust:** people vary in the time it takes for them to learn to trust others. The capacity to trust is essential in order for the client to be open and revealing of very personal problems and concerns. Clients will test whether they can trust you in a variety of ways – often by asking questions – but may not be consciously aware of what they are doing or why they are doing it. While counsellors should not want to foster a dependent relationship, clients need to place some reliance on the counsellor and counselling. Fiercely independent clients will not stay long. Indications of this are the request for only occasional counselling sessions, or clients who persistently say 'yes but'. Other clients find any face-to-face relationship too intimate and threatening; they also tend to drop out of counselling.

- **People who are too dependent:** people who depend on a high dosage of drugs to carry on with their day-to-day routine are unlikely to benefit from brief counselling. Another form of dependence is on the counsellor and counselling. Clients need to be able to tolerate painful feelings and feel secure enough to be able to cope with life between sessions.

- **Reluctance to accept responsibility:** while many people come to counselling wanting other people or their circumstances to change, counselling can only work towards helping them change the way they themselves feel, think or behave. Some people seem unable to see the ways in which they might be contributing to their own difficulties, or the ways in which they might change, and typically lack empathy with others.

- **Out of touch with reality:** disturbing and irrational thoughts and behaviour which make it difficult for a person to manage everyday life are a further contraindication. The key criterion is the extent to which the client is actually aware of what is going on. Some people with these characteristics are quite unaware of the implications of their behaviour and the havoc caused in their lives and in the lives of those around them. Others seem unable to tolerate their disturbing thoughts and feelings and seriously fear that they are 'going mad'. A sometimes related pattern of behaviour is the way some people flit from one subject to another.

CORE CONDITIONS

See also: Acceptance, Change, Common factors, Congruence, Counselling, Effectiveness of counselling, Empathy, Power, Respect

The term 'core conditions' is generally associated with client-centred (or person-centred) counselling. Rogers (e.g. 1957, 1980) believed that effective counselling is most likely when the counsellor is able to offer clients a relationship rich in the qualities of empathy, congruence and unconditional positive regard. Most forms of counselling agree that these three counsellor qualities are necessary but only client-centred counselling regards them as sufficient.

COST-EFFECTIVENESS OF COUNSELLING

See: Brief counselling, Common factors, Effectiveness of counselling, Evaluation, Evidence-based practice

COUNSELLING

See also: Beginnings, Change, Core conditions, Frameworks, Integration and eclecticism, Multiculturalism, Psychological type, Readiness to change, Referral, Relationship between counsellor and client, Rewards of counselling, Specialisms in counselling, Theories of counselling, Writing (expressive)

Most counsellors would probably agree that 'helping people to help themselves' is a useful starting point for a definition of counselling, but agreeing a fuller definition can prove problematic. The BACP's definition (see the Association's website) describes the roles of client and counsellor and something of the process and possible content of sessions. The BACP argues that it is not possible to make a generally accepted distinction between counselling and psychotherapy, and this is the approach that we follow, using the terms interchangeably as we believe that they refer to an overlapping spectrum of activities. Another approach to defining 'counselling' is to distinguish between different kinds of counselling, for example between counselling for personal growth, with people who are functioning well in most respects, and counselling with severely distressed people. Other systems for describing counselling are based on theories or kinds of problem (e.g. Dryden, 2007; Feltham and Horton, 2006). Such systems can help to clarify what counselling is and is not, both for yourself and for others, and therefore when to offer counselling to someone and when to suggest referral.

An example of an integrative process model of counselling or psychotherapy follows. It is similar to the approach described by O'Brien and Houston (2007), consistent with the work of Egan (1975, 2007), Hill (2003) and others, and is of the 'open-system' type.

The model is intended to provide both a conceptualisation of the counselling process and a direction for practice that does not undermine the integrity of different approaches. Alternatively, it can stand alone as an integrative skills approach to counselling. The model includes a map of the process through which the counsellor and client work together, which can be shared with the client. It helps counsellors articulate what they are doing and why they are doing it. There is strong emphasis on reflexivity, and it is seen as important that both client and counsellor reflect on what they are doing. It is hoped that clients will not only address their current issues but also gain skills and understanding which they can apply to new issues arising in the future. The model does not imply any one theory of personality or human development.

Table 2 Summary of the integrative process model

Theme	Stage 1 tasks	Stage 2 tasks	Stage 3 tasks
1 Relationship	Establish	Maintain and use	End
2 Content	Identification and exploration of issue(s), client resources and needs, focus for change	Exploration of wants, developing realistic goals and commitment	Development of strategies and action plans
3 Planning	Assessment, therapeutic planning, and reflection	Monitoring and revision; reflection on process	Evaluation of process and outcomes

The model is a matrix of three themes (relationship, content and therapeutic planning) each of which is sequentially developed through three stages. The stages of each theme are intended to guide the process of integration and are characterised by the need to achieve particular process tasks for each stage. These tasks can be facilitated by specific skills and by the adoption of a wide range of ideas, strategies or techniques from different approaches when appropriate to the needs of the individual client.

The first theme is the developing *relationship* between the counsellor and client. In Stage 1, the tasks are to establish rapport and the working alliance, facilitate client self-disclosure and clarify boundaries and roles within the relationship. (The following example shows the model as integrating framework: in this stage the counsellor is likely to use the skills of active listening, empathic responses, etc. to develop rapport; can adopt the person-centred perspective that being empathic, accepting and genuine is therapeutic and sometimes sufficient; but may also use other techniques designed to achieve the tasks identified.) In Stage 2, the therapeutic climate and working alliance are maintained. Work continues within the boundaries and contract to develop and, where appropriate, to use the dynamics of the relationship as a window for learning and continuing motivation. Stage 3 is concerned with seeking resolution of issues around ending.

The second theme is the *content* of the client's presenting issues and the process of working with these. In Stage 1, the initial task is to understand the client's experience and world view. The counsellor and client then explore various possible perspectives on the client's issues and affirm the client's unique strengths and preferred ways of coping. A focus for the work to be done or a target for change is identified. Stage 2 is concerned with shifting the focus from how things are or have been to what the client wants. The tasks are to develop a detailed picture of a possible future, focusing on different ways of thinking, feeling and behaving; to identify realistic and meaningful goals arising from this; and to consolidate the client's commitment to change. Note that change may be any combination of 'externally focused' (focus on new behaviours/experiences) or 'internally focused' (focus on thoughts/feelings or deeper self-understanding and acceptance). Stage 3 focuses on developing a range of strategies to achieve the identified goal(s): selecting strategies best suited to the client and their circumstances; and planning effectively for change, thereby helping the client to apply and integrate change into new ways of being or living.

The third theme is *therapeutic planning*. Stage1 is initially concerned with assessment and with clarification of the therapeutic and business contract. The counsellor and client develop a tentative formulation of the nature, possible origins and ramifications of the client's issues, clarify aims for therapy, and explore and agree the ways they might work together. (Aims for therapy may on the one hand include the client discovering solutions or ways of managing immediate problems more effectively; and/or on the other a desire for a stronger sense of identity, insight, growth, self-actualisation, etc.) In Stage 2, the tasks are to monitor and where necessary revise therapeutic plans in consultation with the client, and to reflect on and evaluate progress. The final stage is concerned with ending and evaluation. The tasks are to clarify and contract ending procedures; to review what has been achieved, why change has happened and what still needs to be achieved; and to consolidate what the client has learned that may be useful to her or him in the future.

Using this model requires an understanding of the counselling process, a range of communication skills and an awareness of when to use specific strategies and skills. The stages are not intended as a rigid structure, and the stages of each theme are not necessarily co-occurring (e.g. the relationship may have moved into Stage 2, while the content theme is still concerned with Stage 1). As new needs or different aspects of the problem emerge, the actual process, especially around the content theme, will continually move backwards and forwards within the organising framework.

The model's rationale is based on assumptions in two areas: human development and the counselling process. Six key assumptions are as follows:

- Psychological problems are regarded as multidimensional and seldom attributable to one source, situation or factor. It is assumed that people are too complex to be explained by any one theory and that social context plays an important part.
- The client's readiness to change and psychological type may influence the way in which the counsellor works.

- It is possible to identify common steps and stages in the counselling process, irrespective of the counsellor's theoretical orientation.
- It is essential for counsellors to develop the necessary personal qualities and skills to counsel effectively. To have a map of the process is not enough; counsellors need to be able to select appropriate strategies and explanatory concepts for assessment and change and have the skills to implement them.
- Counselling is culture bound, class bound and monolingual. These generic characteristics may clash with the cultural values of various minority groups (see entry on Multiculturalism).
- Some styles and approaches to counselling may be more effective with some clients than with others.

Our experience suggests that this model provides an open framework that allows flexibility in approach, including the incorporation of new research findings, is readily adapted to diverse client populations and can be developed by individual counsellors to fit their own personal styles.

COUNTER-TRANSFERENCE

See also: Emotions, First impressions, Process, Self-awareness, Sexual attraction, Supervision, Transference

'Counter-transference' is a psychoanalytic term, referring to the counsellor's largely unconscious reactions towards a client, confusing the client with someone else, and thus distorting the counsellor's judgement and ability to empathise. Five types of counter-transference suggested by Hawkins and Shohet (2006, pp90–91) are:

- reactions to the client that originate from the counsellor's past (situations or relationships with other people) or are an aspect of the counsellor projected by the counsellor onto the client
- the counsellor's reactions that arise out of taking on the role transferred onto the counsellor by the client (e.g. if the client treats the counsellor like a parent, the counsellor may feel critical or angry with the client, in the way the client's parents did)
- the counsellor's reaction used to counter the client's transference (e.g. the counsellor becomes overly friendly or casual about time in response to being treated as an expert or authority figure by the client)
- the counsellor feels like an 'emotional skip', taking on projected material from the client
- the counsellor wants the client to change for the counsellor's sake, perhaps as a response to demands for results (e.g. to demonstrate effectiveness).

Stewart (2005, p512) suggested several indicators of counter-transference, including preoccupation with a particular client in the form of daydreams or fantasies, behaving differently towards the client (more leniently, more strictly), and not wanting to end counselling with him or her. Whatever your theoretical orientation, and whether or not you use the term counter-transference, it is important to explore your reactions to clients in supervision and in this way to make more space to respond appropriately to clients. For discussion of a possible place for counter-transference in integrative counselling, see O'Brien and Houston (2007, pp150–154 and 164–165).

CRISIS COUNSELLING

See also: Crying, Emotions, Empathy, Literal description, Loss, Referral

The word 'crisis' is usually applied to immediately threatening and highly stressful situations that seem to demand some urgent response or action. People typically feel overwhelmed, unable to cope and often angry, fearful and despairing. In a crisis, people face a situation that upsets their characteristic patterns of thought and behaviour. Their habitual ways of responding to and dealing with problems are insufficient.

The goal of crisis counselling is to resolve the immediate crisis and restore, as far as possible, the client's normal level of functioning. Problems not directly related to the crisis are put aside. The counsellor often takes a more active and directive role than usual: in terms of Egan's (2007) model, which is consistent with the integrative model discussed in the entry on Counselling, there is a '*rapid* application of the three stages of the helping process to the most distressing aspects' (p225, our italics). The action stage is emphasised.

Crisis counselling tends therefore to be intense, brief, and practical. Four major goals and three 'balancing factors' are prominent in the literature (e.g. Moos, 1991). In crisis counselling, the counsellor aims to accomplish the goals by helping the client with the three balancing factors. The relative presence or absence of these factors seems to determine an individual's ability to deal with crisis and whether his or her return to equilibrium is likely to result in a healthy or a problematic adaptation. The goals are:

- to understand the personal meaning and significance of the situation
- to preserve or encourage a positive self-image by confronting and accepting the reality of the situation
- to experience the painful emotions and re-establish a reasonable emotional balance
- to maintain a sense of competence by adjusting to the environment and responding to the crisis.

The related balancing factors are as follows:

- **Realistic perception of the situation:** if someone has a realistic perception of what has happened and can recognise the relationship between the crisis and the feelings of stress, then attempts to manage the problem and reduce the level of stress are more likely to be effective.

- **Adequate coping resources:** throughout their lives people learn to cope with difficult situations in many different and individual ways. These skills and strategies can focus on finding meaning and coping with the practical aspects of dealing with the emotions linked to the crisis.
- **Basic human support:** humans are social beings and there is good evidence to suggest that the existence of a natural support network of family and friends, and the person's ability to make use of it, has a vital role in outcome.

Crisis counselling may also involve helping the client understand the nature of the crisis. Parry (1990) and others have identified several variables that help define a crisis and the nature of its impact on the individual:

- **Focus:** was the person directly involved or did the crisis happen to someone else?
- **Predictability:** was the event unexpected or was it possible to predict that it was going to happen?
- **Intensity:** how suddenly did it all happen? Was there any warning? How long did it last?
- **Choice:** did the person voluntarily enter the situation that resulted in a crisis? For example, choosing to separate from a partner may end up as a traumatic situation.
- **Pervasiveness:** does the crisis permeate many different areas of the person's life or is it contained within one area?
- **Magnitude:** how unfamiliar or different was the new situation? To what extent did it disrupt the routine pattern of living?
- **Controllability:** once the crisis happened, did the person feel able to do anything at all that might help in some way?
- **Risk:** was there any threat or danger?
- **Distress:** was there any pain, suffering or humiliation?
- **Revelation:** was anything negative revealed during or as a result of the crisis?
- **Loss:** loss is part of all crisis situations, i.e. the loss of things as they were before the crisis. 'Loss' here is a very general term (e.g. of status, independence, role or relationship, identity, valued possession or ideal, a loved person, and so on).

The basic steps in crisis counselling are assessment, planning and intervention:

1. **Assessment:** the first clinical judgement is whether the person should receive immediate and intensive support. This decision is based on an assessment of, first, the likelihood of any imminent danger to the person or other people and, secondly, whether the individual is able to maintain normal responsibilities and obligations or whether these should be temporarily and explicitly transferred to others.

The assessment then moves on to examine, often in detail, the precipitating event and the effects of the resulting crisis. The purpose is to understand what has happened and assess the person's ability to cope with the situation. It is often some time before the precise nature and full extent of the crisis is recognised. It can be useful to encourage the client to talk through what has happened over the previous 48 hours or so. Assessment is basically concerned with gathering information.

2. **Planning:** this step is about identifying the central issues. Priorities and goals are decided. Alternative strategies and solutions to reduce the effects of crisis are generated and the best options chosen. Tentative explanations are put forward to account for the individual's reaction.

3. **Intervention:** after the necessary data are collected, the focus is on the immediate situation and possible ways forward. The client needs to leave the first session with some positive guidelines for coping. These are evaluated and revised in subsequent sessions. Some people need to be reassured that they are not losing their sanity. An acute sense of distraction, total preoccupation with what happened and hallucinations are examples of common and normal responses to a crisis. It is also important to allow for a very wide range of individual reactions. Counsellors should also remain alert for chronic or pathological reactions and the possible need for referral. Later sessions work on anticipatory planning and developing realistic goals for the future. The counsellor and client continue to work towards resolution of the crisis and may, at least initially, meet several times a week.

CRISIS FOR THE COUNSELLOR

See also: Action planning, Burnout, Congruence, Core conditions, Referral, Self-disclosure, Stress, Supervision, Support groups

Counsellors often feel that, no matter what they are going through in their personal lives, they should always be available and helpful to clients. There is an expectation that counsellors can leave their personal concerns behind when they enter the counselling room and, to a great extent, this expectation is a reasonable one. But counsellors can experience problems in their own lives, and if very difficult or even overwhelming these are very likely to affect the counsellor's ability to give full attention to the concerns of others. At such times, counsellors can feel uncertain about whether they should say anything about their personal troubles, perhaps in the name of congruence, or the point at which it is advisable to cease counselling until their personal problems have been resolved.

Some approaches, particularly those with a psychodynamic orientation, suggest that there should be very little self-disclosure or none at all. Client-centred counsellors tend to be more self-disclosing, but even so would not wish their self-disclosure to shift the focus of counselling away from the client to the counsellor. The most unhelpful thing of all would be to draw clients into your personal life and problems so that they became distracted from their own concerns. This would also be unethical.

In times of crisis, the strength of your support network becomes crucial. If immediate colleagues are not approachable or are unavailable, your supervisor would usually be the first person to whom you turn for professional advice and support. She or he should be able to help you separate those issues that are of a personal nature and best dealt with through your own counselling (or by other means) from professional and ethical issues. Any decision about whether to take a break from counselling also needs to be explored in supervision.

CRYING

See also: Catharsis, Counselling, Emotions, Immediacy, Nonverbal communication, Paraphrasing, Self-disclosure, Touch

When clients cry, it is tempting to distract them with a cup of tea or other form of comfort or sympathy; however, even though this is a natural response to people in distress, it is of course unhelpful. Counselling helps people explore the depth of their present emotions, however distressing and painful they are. Yalom (2001, p164) writes that he often uses the question, 'If your tears had a voice, what would they be saying?'

Even so, it is also unhelpful to believe that people *should* cry and that if they do not there must be something wrong either with them or with you as a counsellor. People vary considerably in emotional expressiveness, and it is disrespectful to expect everyone to be emotionally expressive (Kennedy-Moore and Watson, 1999, p59). Kennedy-Moore and Watson further argue that it is unhelpful when a client cries and cries because such 'flooded expression' interferes with thinking and making sense of one's emotions. Rather, counsellors should first accept and empathise with a client's tears, then help the client by suggesting deep breathing, attention out, or saying to oneself, for example, 'Getting worked up like this isn't helpful'. When clients put their emotions into words, it can increase their understanding and sense of control, for example 'I've felt guilty about this for years, but it's not my fault'.

Some counsellors feel very uncomfortable or embarrassed with clients who cry, or who begin to express very deep or powerful emotions, and some have different expectations of women and men in these respects. It can be difficult to stay with someone in very deep distress without wanting to interfere, and you can sometimes begin to feel very distressed yourself. If this does happen, you could be overidentifying with your client, or some deep emotions in you may be being restimulated. Some tearfulness on the part of the counsellor may be completely appropriate (see the whirlpool metaphor in the entry on Paraphrasing). Either way, discussion in supervision is probably the best action.

DEMENTIA

See also: Ageing, Multiculturalism, Specialisms in counselling

There is likely to be an increasing role for counsellors in working with people who are in the early stages of dementia and their families (Weaks *et al.*, 2006). This is because of earlier diagnosis and new drugs that may delay dementia.

Weaks *et al.* reviewed the few research studies so far and summarised some of the results of their own continuing study in terms of several therapeutic tasks:

- exploring the possibility of life as normal
- evaluating the usefulness of different sources of information
- understanding the changing roles within their relationship(s)
- understanding the emotional process
- addressing deep philosophical questions
- embracing stigma
- creating a different identity
- telling and retelling the diagnosis story
- finding a way through the healthcare system.

They also raise but do not discuss the issue of who is best placed to work in this developing field: 'Would it be a CPN with counselling training, or a counsellor with specialist knowledge of dementia?' (Weaks *et al.*, 2006, p15).

Cheston and Bender (2003, p17) also approached the person with dementia as 'an active and interactive being operating within a social context'. They focused on a 'troubled person rather than a diseased brain' and discussed offering therapy at various stages of dementia and how the forces of 'money, politics and power' influence the quality of treatments which are offered.

There is useful information on the websites of University College London's Institute of Neurology's Dementia Research Centre, where there are also links to Counselling and Diagnosis in Dementia (CANDID), the International Psychogeriatric Association and the Alzheimer's Society.

DENIAL

See also: Abuse, Avoidance, Challenging, Collusion, Emotions, Empathy

Some parts of each of us are difficult to look at or 'own', and we may therefore deny their existence or their full significance. Usually, there is a fearful or upsetting experience behind the denial; particularly painful times may have been suppressed beyond easy recall. If you think a client is denying something it is better not to be too persistent in trying to unearth the problem, as the client may become more defensive and put up further barriers.

Prevention is probably the best approach to conscious denial, through helping clients feel safer and less threatened, listening to the underlying sense of what is said and reflecting back any unease. Part of the contract between you and your client can include an agreement that the client can say if there is something that she or he does not want to talk about and that you will respect that wish. By feeling safe, clients are able to face up to and talk about the subject that they at first wanted to avoid, without being pushed into a situation of denial. Some clients are helped by exploring their difficulty in talking about a topic rather than exploring the topic itself.

Sometimes a client denies a gentle challenge (e.g. 'It sounds as though you find endings difficult?' 'No, I don't.'); they may be right or may be denying the loss and pain in ending. In either case, although it is usually best to accept what the client says, it can be helpful to outline the evidence on which your challenge was based. The challenge might, however, have triggered something in the client (as they reflect, they realise that endings *are* difficult for them). The topic of difficult endings might surface again during another session and the counsellor could link the two incidents, perhaps enabling the client to explore further.

DEPRESSION

See also: Bibliotherapy, Crying, DSM-IV, Exercise (physical), Loss, NICE, Psychodiagnosis, Self-awareness, Suicide, Supervision, Thoughts, Trust

Feeling 'down', unhappy and sad (and perhaps melancholy) are parts of life and can therefore be accepted and understood rather than treated or numbed. It is not realistic to expect to feel happy all the time. 'Depression' may mean anything from temporarily feeling 'down' to being so debilitated as to be unable to move or speak. In major depressive disorder, the person feels persistently very low in mood, lacks interest in social interactions and other activities and suffers from physiological symptoms such as sleep disturbance, lack of energy, changes in appetite, impaired concentration and feelings of low self-acceptance and hopelessness. Usually, a number of the above symptoms need to occur for a period of two weeks or longer to receive a diagnosis of clinical depression (DSM-IV).

Depression appears to be on the increase and around 20 per cent of all people will experience a period of depression at some time in their life, with more than half of us having to deal with depressive symptoms from time to time (Segal *et al.*, 2002). Furthermore, there is strong evidence that depression is a recurrent condition (Hollon *et al.*, 2006) and in its worst manifestation can lead to suicidal thoughts. Of the 5,000 people who commit suicide every year in the UK, most will have been depressed.

Treatment for depression usually involves counselling or antidepressant medication or both. Cognitive-behavioural psychotherapy (CBT) was identified by the NICE guidelines (NICE, 2004b) as the first line of treatment for depression and anxiety, and NICE recommended that it should be available promptly from appropriately trained and supervised therapists.

Interventions include increasing the client's activity levels to re-experience pleasure and achievement; exercise; increasing social interactions; changing diet (e.g. more omega-3 oils); challenging unhelpful thinking styles; and becoming aware of one's own 'depression signature'. These warning signals – the signature – can include becoming irritable, decreasing social participation and exercise, changing sleep and eating habits, procrastinating and feeling depleted (Segal *et al.*, 2002). Segal *et al.* discuss mindfulness-based cognitive therapy (MBCT) for clients who have suffered more than three episodes of depression and judge it to be an effective tool to prevent relapse. A review by Hollon *et al.* (2006) of research on CBT in the treatment of depression concluded that the effects tend to last longer than psychoactive medication, which they see as 'largely palliative'.

Exercise is effective for mild and moderate depression. See the websites of the Mental Health Foundation and Green Gym. In many areas of the UK, GPs can 'prescribe' exercise, supervised by qualified trainers.

Two forms of computerised CBT for treating mild to moderate depression were approved by NICE in 2006: 'Beating the Blues' and 'FearFighter'. A combined CBT and group therapy (using transactional analysis) approach over eight sessions also seems promising for people who are 'neither too depressed and out of reach, nor too well: distressed and disturbed but able to talk about themselves to a moderate degree and reach out to others' (Hayman and Allen, 2006, p45).

A useful recent finding (one which emphasises the contribution of the client as more than the holder of the diagnosis and the receiver of treatment) is that symptoms are often concealed from therapists. Hook and Andrews (2005) surveyed people who had received therapy for depression; many had not told their therapist about symptoms such as suicidal thoughts, drug misuse and aggression, and the main reason given was shame. Moreover, those people who had withheld information were more depressed at the end of their therapy than those who had been open. Knowing that shame is likely to be a barrier can help you to empathise with and challenge your clients more effectively. Other reasons given for concealing symptoms included lack of trust in the therapies, fear of rejection, guilt and the issue being too painful.

Seligman *et al.* (2006) discussed some encouraging but preliminary research on 'positive psychotherapy' for depression. The approach focuses on positive emotion, encouragement and meaning. Seligman *et al.* think that an absence of these factors may cause depression rather than be symptoms or consequences of it. For example, and apparently very simply, they ask clients to do the 'three good things' exercise: 'Before you go to sleep, write down three things that went well today and why they went well'.

There is a vast literature on depression and its treatment. We think much of it is superficial and even exploitative. Some stimulating exceptions are Gilbert's (2006) overview; King *et al.*'s (2000) comparison of CBT and client-centred therapy as treatments for depression, which showed that both were equally effective; Storr's (1990) view that depressed people need to 'disinter' the active, aggressive elements of themselves, for example by discussing their feelings towards their parents, whom they are likely to see as perfect; the Bugentals' argument (1980) that a period of depression can be healing and a valuable signal that change is needed – it helps clients rest, patiently and acceptingly, simplifying their life and treating their depression as important to their wellbeing; Sutherland's (1998) vivid account of his own depression, with an abrasive critique of a wide variety of treatments; Brown and Harris (1978) who found that depression usually happens because of severe adversity and lack of a protective factor, and Leahy and Holland's (2000) treatment plans.

Finally, a trap for counsellors is to take on to themselves the feelings of despair in the client (whether expressed overtly or not) to such an extent that they too feel hopeless. Supervision may be used to help the counsellor separate her or his feelings from the client's.

For up-to-date information, see the websites of the Depression Alliance, Mind, the Royal College of Psychiatrists, and Students Against Depression; the last has detailed self-help strategies and, centrally, accounts by students of low mood depression and suicidal thoughts and what they did about them.

DIAGNOSIS

See: Assessment, DSM-IV, Psychodiagnosis

DIFFERENCE

See: Alexithymia, Autistic spectrum disorder, Dementia, Dyslexia, Love (styles of loving), Multiculturalism, Psychological type

DIFFICULT CLIENTS

See also: Assertiveness, Collusion, Contraindications for brief counselling, Drama triangle, Empathy, Games, Personality disorders, Psychological type, Referral

Care needs to be taken in applying a label such as 'difficult' to a client. It could be argued that there is no such thing as an inherently difficult client, merely difficulties in the matching of client to counsellor or clients who do not easily adapt to the conventions of the counselling relationship because of some combination of their personality type, culture, previous experiences, etc. Such difficulties present a challenge to the counsellor who may have to work harder, differently, or with more creativity or commitment in order to engage the client. So for the purposes of this entry, 'difficult clients' are those whom you find particularly challenging. Specific difficulties are covered elsewhere, but the following are some general strategies for coping with difficult clients:

- Present your difficulties openly to your supervisor or supervision group.
- Ask yourself what, exactly, you find difficult about this client, why it is a problem, and whose problem it is.
- Explore the extent to which this client reminds you of people you have found difficult in the past.

- Reflect on the quality of the relationship that you are able to offer to this client.

- Make a distinction between what clients say to you and the ways in which they express themselves. For example, you might 'switch off' to clients who swear or who repeat themselves a lot, but they are still expressing themselves, perhaps in the best way they can, and you should try to focus on that, rather than on the language itself.

- Similarly, make a distinction between clients whose values are unacceptable to you and professional responsibility (Walker, 1993). The professional responsibility of a counsellor is to work with a client within the client's values, not to try to change the client's values to be more acceptable to the counsellor. You may have to consider the relationship you can offer to the client, accepting his or her current values, and consider referral if you are unable to offer a sufficient level of acceptance. Within established therapeutic relationships, it may useful to challenge clients' values (in their interests and at the service of their goals) but the right to challenge needs to be earned through empathy, acceptance and genuineness.

- Look to see if the clients you find difficult have features in common or if there are recurring 'themes'. Again, these are issues that may be explored with your supervisor or in personal counselling.

- Try to distinguish between the person and the quality or behaviour you find difficult.

You might find it very difficult to counsel some clients, however hard you try. In such circumstances, it may be better to refer them. It is, of course, advisable to discuss how to do this in supervision, so that you do it as constructively as possible.

DIFFICULTIES IN BEING A CLIENT

See also: Avoidance, Beginnings, Contract, negotiating a, Distress at the end of a counselling session (clients'), Expectations (clients'), Fees, Multiculturalism, Psychological type, Respect, Trust

Many clients come to us at times when they have difficulties in making any decision, including the decision to seek help. Some clients feel a sense of failure, that they ought to be able to take care of themselves, and this in itself may lower a client's already threatened sense of self-esteem. Your client may have had to overcome much resistance and prejudice about counselling before coming to see you, and this makes the first few minutes of your first session even more important. Treating any expression of fear or anxiety with empathy will help your clients feel that you respect their doubts, and will also help to establish trust in your capacity to understand.

People from some cultural groups can find it especially difficult to talk in personal terms to complete strangers; you need to be patient and understanding here, particularly if you are not familiar with your client's cultural traditions and norms. Some clients also have to overcome strong feelings of guilt or disloyalty to members of their families before they can talk openly. Other factors that can be put forward as difficulties include time commitment and travelling distance. These may be a sign of avoidance, which you can offer to help the client explore; otherwise, there is not much you can do, and the final decision about whether or not to continue will have to be left to your client.

The key question is 'What could make counselling easier for my client?' It may help greatly if you arrange to see clients at times when they do not have to walk far after dark or spend time alone in dark railway stations or at bus stops. Similarly, people who cannot negotiate stairs or who are in a wheelchair obviously find access to many buildings and streets difficult. What you can do to an old building or to a private house to make access easier will be limited, but removal of obstacles from hallways and provision of a wooden ramp to help negotiate steps will help.

Once a client has decided to start counselling with you, he or she may find difficulties in continuing. Finance could have a part to play in this, and, if you operate a sliding scale according to clients' ability to pay, your client might ask to renegotiate this part of the contract. How you respond to this is up to you, but decisive factors could include your own income level, a point below which you are not prepared to go, and a point at which you feel exploited.

DISTRESS AT THE END OF A COUNSELLING SESSION (CLIENTS')

See also: Crying, Difficulties in being a client, Frequency of sessions, Length of sessions, Suicide, Time boundaries

In deep personal exploration of the kind that can occur within a counselling session, clients can often become aware of painful emotional material that has been buried or half-forgotten for a long time. It is often the case that such material surfaces towards the end of a session, and the counsellor may have some concerns about whether or not there is time to resolve the problems before the client has to leave. Some counsellors, if they become aware that deep material is surfacing with little time remaining, prefer gently to remind the client of the time and suggest that it might be better to take this exploration further in the next session; the risks here are that the opportunity might be lost for good and that the client may never return to the painful experience. Other counsellors view the use of time as entirely the responsibility of the client and prefer not to direct sessions in any way; with this approach, there is the chance that clients may leave the counselling room in a distressed state and be at some risk in 'the outside world', especially if they are driving or going back to work in a dangerous environment.

Your experience with a client will help you decide what course of action to take if you think that he or she is likely to be very distressed at the end of the session. For example, how does this person usually manage distressing experiences?

Does the person become disoriented and unable to make rational decisions, or does he or she have strong personal resources and coping mechanisms? Will the client be returning to a relatively safe place, among friends or family? Is there is a history of suicide threats or self-harming? You need to balance this risk assessment against your respect for your client's autonomy and right to manage his or her own affairs. You are not there to make your clients feel good at the end of each session, and distress is often a part of the process to which your clients have committed themselves. An attempt to avoid painful experiences on the grounds of lack of time could be counterproductive and might reflect your discomfort rather than any real risk to your client.

An ideal situation is to have somewhere where a very distressed client can rest and regain composure before leaving, but for many counsellors this is not a possibility. Nor is extending the time of the session likely to be possible as other clients may be waiting to see you; in any event, you need to consider the disadvantages of running over time and make it a rare exception rather than the rule. If you think the situation warrants it, you have the option of ringing a friend or family member or the client's GP (all with your client's permission) or, in *very* exceptional circumstances, taking the client to his or her home if you can – even though this may mean postponing other appointments or keeping other clients waiting.

If you work in a team or as part of an organisation, it is a good idea to establish a strategy for what to do in the event of an emergency, so that you can minimise disruption and inconvenience to other clients whilst taking proper care of someone who may be at significant risk. If you work on your own, it is useful to contact other counsellors in your area in a similar position and agree a method of mutual support and cooperation in times of difficulty. This form of networking and mutual support could also be useful in other ways.

DISTRESS AT THE END OF A SESSION (COUNSELLORS')

See also: Counter-transference, Crisis for the counsellor, Crying, Stress

Counselling can be a risky activity for counsellors if emotional material brought up by clients is particularly distressing or touches on areas of personal pain for the counsellor. Counsellors can feel a range of emotions at the end of a session, from exhilaration to sadness, depression and, occasionally, distress. Clients sometimes have very distressing stories to tell, and different counsellors are vulnerable to different levels of distress. Some counsellors are particularly open to feelings of personal distress if their clients are exploring issues of child abuse or violence; others find issues to do with, for example, isolation, loneliness or suicide particularly difficult.

You should remember that it is not a sign of personal or professional weakness to be touched, or even deeply moved, when clients are exploring painful or distressing emotions. Your approach to counselling will guide you as to the degree of openness you can allow yourself during a counselling session, and you can explore in supervision situations that you find particularly moving or personally upsetting.

You might encounter problems if, at the end of a session, you feel more deeply distressed than can be accounted for simply by feelings of sympathy or compassion for your client. Something in the client's material may be touching you in an area where you have unresolved or strong feelings. Again, this is not necessarily a matter for alarm, but it could be a sign that you have some work to do on this material for yourself.

If you are feeling deeply distressed, it may be ethical and professional to postpone other appointments until you have regained your equilibrium. It is also sensible to organise your counselling appointments to give you a break between clients: even 10 minutes can be enough to clear your mind in readiness for your next client. Some counsellors find relaxation and breathing exercises useful; others recommend a short walk or finding something to do that marks the temporary end of your contact with a client, such as writing, telephoning a friend or even making a cup of tea.

There are two longer-term strategies to consider. First, you need to talk over the situation with your supervisor or a trusted colleague, focusing on your reaction to your client rather than on the client personally. Your discussion might lead to the second strategy, which is to consider going into personal counselling yourself or, if you are already in counselling, to bring up the distressing experience at your next session.

If your feelings of distress happen more often with particular clients, or are connected with particular issues, you have some indication of a pattern that needs to be explored in some way. You should view this as an opportunity for personal growth in yourself rather than as a 'problem' to be overcome. The worst thing to do is stoically 'grin and bear it': this is not only unhelpful, and perhaps damaging, to you but also unhelpful to your client, and you may miss an opportunity for both you and your client to move on.

DNA (DID NOT ATTEND)

See: Clients who don't come back, Missed sessions

DRAMA TRIANGLE

See also: Assertiveness, Challenging, Collusion, Games, Immediacy, Self-awareness

The 'drama triangle' (Karpman, 1968) is a model that some counsellors and clients find useful in explaining certain patterns in behaviour, especially between two people. It suggests three complementary roles: Victim, Rescuer and Persecutor. Here are two examples of the roles as brief, normal responses: first, seeing pictures on the television of starving children (victims) and immediately writing out a cheque to help their cause (rescuer); secondly, being ill (victim), which may bring someone to look after us (rescuer) and lead to a colleague being angry (persecutor) because of having to do our work. These examples show normal behaviour; the people concerned do not carry on and on in the same roles and therefore do not become caught in the drama triangle.

Problems occur when people are stuck, either in one of the roles or going round and round the triangle, drawing in others. A classic Victim role is taken by someone who feels, or actually is, hard done by and seems to be constantly being put upon. Some people get angry with the Victim (Persecutors); others might try to help (Rescuers); but nothing seems to change matters. The original Victim might then alternate to Persecutor, blaming the others, who could then become Victims.

People who get caught in the triangle, in whatever role, tend to have low self-esteem and see themselves as having little control over their lives. Others may view them differently and perceive them as being very powerful or frustrating as they stay firmly in their role in the triangle. Counsellors can try to help them increase their self-esteem, become more self-sufficient and escape from the trap. However, the more deeply the client is stuck in his or her role in the triangle, the easier it is for the counsellor to become trapped too. Some clients make it very difficult for the counsellor to resist telling them what to do or doing things for them, while others leave the counsellor feeling angry. If the counsellor is unaware of this and gets caught in the triangle, the client is again pushed into the Victim role, the place that is so familiar to him or her. So the triangle continues, even within the counselling relationship.

DRAWINGS

See also: Exercises, Homework, Intuition, Life-space diagram, Metaphors in counselling, Nonverbal communication

Not all clients find talking the most effective mode of communication at all times or the best way to reflect and get in touch with their experiences and feelings. You may find that some clients are able to gain new understandings or get in touch with feelings more effectively by taking time to make a drawing. Making a drawing can create a space for reflection and enable the client to approach an issue from a different angle, engaging his or her capacity for imagery and creativity in a way which talking may not. We have found the following examples of drawing exercises useful:

- Draw your public and private face.
- Make a picture of your family (or other significant group).
- Draw an image to represent anger (or sadness or other significant emotion).
- Make a picture of yourself in a better future, assuming things are going well.
- Draw a tree (or animal etc.) that represents you.
- Make an image of a place where you could feel relaxed (or happy etc.).

You may also find it useful to suggest drawing after an activity such as guided imagery to help clients capture images that they have experienced.

It is important to take time to reflect on drawings and explore clients' responses to what they have drawn. You may need to avoid the temptation to interpret clients' drawings for them; take care to focus on what the drawing means to them and what feelings it generates. If given the space to reflect, clients can often find more in their drawings than they were aware of as they made them.

Obviously, not all clients will be keen on drawing as an activity. Some may have inhibitions about their ability or negative experiences from school which make them reluctant. As always, the client should be actively engaged in therapeutic planning, and you should offer therapeutic activities such as drawing to clients for whom they have some appeal and do not create undue stress. In such circumstances, drawing can provide a valuable opportunity to explore an issue in a creative way and perhaps gain new insights and perspectives or a deeper awareness.

DRINKS/REFRESHMENTS

See also: Nonverbal communication

The way you establish or fail to establish a concentrated and 'focused' mood may affect the counselling process significantly. Offering drinks and other refreshments to clients can cause problems in this respect. If you work in a place with a waiting room and/or receptionist, it is possible to supply refreshments in a way that is unobtrusive and does not interfere with the counselling process. However, if you work on your own, and your refreshment facilities are in your counselling room, it can be quite distracting for the client if the counsellor spends time filling kettles, washing cups, etc. There is also the problem of what to say while this process is going on. Do you start 'counselling' while making drinks, or do you engage in 'small talk'?

A further problem is that on the one hand a drink can help clients to relax, but on the other it can become something to hold and 'hide behind', with clients feeling exposed when they put the cup down.

However, if you can prepare a drink with the minimum of fuss, there seems to be no real reason why you should not offer one to your client, especially on a very cold or hot day or when the client has had a long journey. Having drinking water readily available is a helpful idea, especially as increases in adrenaline levels can make the throat very dry.

DROPOUT

See: Brief counselling, Clients who don't come back, Expectations (clients'), First session, Missed sessions

DRUGS (PSYCHOTROPIC)

See also: Assessment, Contract, negotiating a, Depression, Drunk and/or drugged clients, Giving information, Intake interviews

Psychotropic drugs act on the brain by altering its chemistry. Three major categories of these drugs are antipsychotics, antidepressants and tranquilisers. Up-to-date information on their side effects, interactions with other drugs, etc. is available on the website of NWMHP Pharmacy Medicine Information. Assessment interviews often include questions about medication because it can interfere with counselling, for example by numbing emotions or through side effects like confusion, headaches and aggression. However, in some people, psychotropic drugs reduce symptoms enough to make counselling possible. For general discussion, see Daines *et al.* (2007).

DRUNK AND/OR DRUGGED CLIENTS

See also: Anger, Boundaries, Contract, negotiating a, Drugs (psychotropic), Emotions, Violence and its prevention

If you work for an agency that specialises in treating people who misuse alcohol or other drugs, it will probably have a clear procedure for dealing with a client who is drunk or has obviously recently taken a drug other than alcohol. A problem for the generic counsellor is to be confronted with a client who is drunk or drugged when this is not a familiar state to the counsellor. The behaviour of a drunken person or a person under the influence of other drugs can be unpredictable, threatening and frightening. If your client does become aggressive or threatening or behaves unpredictably, get help if necessary, as calmly and quietly as you can.

All drugs affect a person's behaviour and perceptions to some degree (Daines *et al.*, 2007). Some prescribed drugs may, for some people, reduce anxiety sufficiently to allow counselling to take place. On the other hand, a client who is obviously drunk or drugged is unlikely to be in a suitable frame of mind for counselling. If you have reason to believe a client is affected by drugs, you can try to explain that counselling is unlikely to be effective under such circumstances and that it is better to postpone the session rather than to continue. If your client is not receptive to this advice, you may decide to try to continue, even though any counselling is likely to be a waste of effort. You can discuss the issue later with your client when he or she is not influenced by drugs. It is probably advisable to be clear at this point that you will not attempt to continue with counselling whenever the client is using any drugs, including alcohol. A further consideration is that you may be open to prosecution if you knowingly allow your premises to be used for taking controlled drugs.

DSM-IV (DIAGNOSTIC AND STATISTICAL MANUAL OF MENTAL DISORDER)

See also: Assessment, Contraindications for brief counselling, Counselling, EAPs, Mental health and mental illness, Psychodiagnosis

DSM-IV is the fourth edition of the widely used American Psychiatric Association handbook for diagnosing 'mental disorders' (APA, 2000). 'It describes more ways to go psychologically wrong than you would have thought possible,' writes Funder (2007, p626), who also finds it 'surprisingly readable'. The manual does not focus on treatment. One issue is the overlap (or 'excessive diagnostic co-occurrence') of symptoms, which may be a result of treating the disorders as qualitatively distinct conditions, in the spirit of a traditional medical model. An alternative view is that the disorders may be more usefully thought of in dimensional terms; the fifth edition, which is being prepared, may reflect this (Funder, 2007).

On a pragmatic note, private health insurance and Employment Assistance Programmes (EAPs) now expect a written diagnosis based on DSM-IV criteria before agreement to fund psychotherapy is given.

DYSLEXIA

See also: Contract, negotiating a, Immediacy, Loss

Dyslexia is a controversial diagnosis (Nicolson, 2005) that generally refers to an inherited inefficiency in memory and information processing. This may affect verbal and written communication, organising oneself, sense of time, adaptation to change, and other aspects of behaviour and experience; and the number and type of difficulties and their mildness or severity vary from one dyslexic person to another. It also seems to be quite common: 4 to 10 per cent of the UK population (McLoughlin *et al.*, 2002). Dyslexia can occur at any level of intellectual ability; many people with dyslexia have successful careers.

There are numerous implications for counselling (Grande and Bayne, 2006), e.g. people with dyslexia may have problems with completing consent forms, submitting homework punctually and having a sense of when a session is over. Such problems can be misinterpreted as defensive. For example, one client's elaborate system of checking, which enabled her to cope well with her memory problem, was misinterpreted by her counsellor as obsessive-compulsive disorder (OCD).

Discovering that you are dyslexic, and integrating this information into your identity and life, is usually emotionally challenging. Relief may be the first reaction: at last labels like 'stupid' and 'lazy' can be replaced. Anger may follow, and there may be frustration at wasted years of education and missed opportunities. Clients may *know* that they are intelligent and capable, yet continue to *feel* stupid. They may be troubled about who to tell about their diagnosis and how best to do it.

Orenstein (2001) suggested a shame–cognitive freeze pattern in people with dyslexia. Her interviewees described it as being 'stuck in a place of nothingness' – the 'chasm' – and 'numb', and they withdrew into depression or distracted themselves with humour or rebellion. To break the pattern, Orenstein suggests learning to recognise the shame and vulnerability, accepting it and waiting for it to pass.

Another generally useful approach is to help clients have a realistic and balanced view of their strengths and weaknesses. Numerous practical strategies (e.g. Reading Pens and text-to-speak software) are reviewed by Packwood (2006).

The Disability Discrimination Act requires employers to help people with dyslexia work in ways that suit them, and financial support may be available from the Department of Work and Pensions (see the website for JobCentre Plus). The British Dyslexia Association's helpline is 0118 966/8271; there is useful information on its website and on the website of the Dyslexia Research Trust.

EAPs (EMPLOYEE ASSISTANCE PROGRAMMES)

See also: Assessment, Evidence-based practice

Employees are facing increasing pressures to be effective at work while maintaining a quality home life. Modern business demands high performance, long working hours and heavy workloads. At home, people face money pressures, family demands, education concerns, high lifestyle expectations and limited time with loved ones.

When an employee has an issue, whether the origin is work or home based, performance in the workplace is likely to be affected. Sickness and absence can increase, while concentration and efficiency may decrease. According to the CBI, millions of working days a year are lost through stress, anxiety and depression, with sickness absence costing billions of pounds a year.

Workplace stress is thus becoming a major health and safety concern for employees and employers alike. It makes sense, therefore, for organisations to take the best care of their employees, not just to comply with legislation, but to inspire greater commitment, efficiency and productivity. Moreover, the number of workplace-stress litigation claims is on the increase.

The Health and Safety at Work Act 1974 requires employers to secure the health (including mental health), safety and welfare of employees whilst at work. Equally, the Management of Health and Safety at Work Regulations 1999 require employers to assess the risk of stress-related ill health arising from work activities and to take measures to control the identified risk, and the Health and Safety Executive includes stress as part of its workplace assessments. The courts have acknowledged that an organisation with an EAP has gone a long way in fulfilling its duty-of-care responsibilities. Employees or their family members will usually be offered a limited number of counselling hours (four to eight sessions) through the EAP. Thus an EAP can:

- reduce employee and organisational stress
- provide a confidential and free service for employees who feel unable to turn elsewhere

- improve productivity and efficiency (a distracted employee does not work efficiently)
- combat or manage harassment and bullying
- assist employees in achieving a harmonious work–life balance
- reduce staff turnover and absence rates
- support employees facing psychological challenges
- support an individual or team through a difficult period.
- demonstrate a duty of care to employees
- minimise the risk of litigation for the organisation

ECLECTICISM

See: Integration and eclecticism

EFFECTIVENESS OF COUNSELLING

See also: Common factors, Counselling, Evaluation, Evidence-based practice, Good counsellors, NICE, Research

It is now firmly established that counselling is effective (Barkham, 2007; Lambert, 2004; Stiles *et al.*, 1986), although this statement needs qualification. First, the degree of effectiveness is generally seen by researchers, perhaps unfairly, as modest, in tune with Freud's remark about transforming 'neurotic misery' into 'common unhappiness'. The unfairness lies in expecting radical change, as if counselling was like reprogramming a computer or washing out a test tube. Secondly, there are problems with measuring 'success' in counselling: some changes in behaviour are relatively easy to measure (e.g. smoking less); others, such as deeper self-awareness, are more difficult. Reliance on self-report measures is another problem (McLeod, 2001), although brain imaging research is becoming more widely used. Also, NICE tends (so far) to weight evidence from randomised controlled trials much more heavily than evidence from other sources, however strong that evidence appears to be (e.g. Elliott *et al.*, 2004; Stiles *et al.*, 2006).

It has been argued that the effectiveness of counselling only *appears* to be modest, that it depends on what you compare it with. For example, Rosenthal (1990) discussed an acclaimed study of the effects of aspirin on reducing heart attacks. The reduction in number of heart attacks was 4 per cent: four people in a hundred, on average, improved (i.e. avoided suffering a heart attack) by taking aspirin. He then pointed out that the average effect size for counselling is about 10 per cent and that this effect size is, by these standards, considerably better than 'modest'. Even if the benefits seem small – months rather than weeks between periods of depression and two weeks more at work a year – economically and personally they can be very worthwhile.

Relatively little is known about *why* counselling is effective. Radically different techniques seem to be equally successful. One explanation is in terms of common or non-specific factors such as support ('warm involvement') and challenge ('communicating a new perspective on client or situation') (Stiles *et al.*, 1986). Another possibility is that different approaches – techniques, counsellors – 'fit' different clients best.

A final, major point about effectiveness is that it is very easy to believe that a particular method 'works' when it is actually irrelevant. This is partly because what we see and remember are open to bias but also because many people (perhaps 40 per cent) improve, or report that they have improved, without counselling. If they had been in counselling they would probably have improved anyway, and they and others might well have inferred that the counsellor or technique was effective. This does not detract from the general conclusion that counselling helps people change more quickly and perhaps more substantially than no counselling.

E-MAIL COUNSELLING

See: Online counselling

EMOTIONS

See also: Alexithymia, Catharsis, Collusion, Empathy, Feeling, Literal description, Mindfulness, Paraphrasing, Process, Self-awareness, Thoughts, Two-chair technique

> The advantage of our emotions is that they lead us astray. (Oscar Wilde)

Most counselling and psychotherapy is based on the idea that we need to be aware of our emotions and feelings, and how they affect us. The difficult part is usually in identifying and owning them. One obstacle is that emotions are often confused with thoughts. As a rule of thumb, emotions usually come directly after a verb: for example, 'I am happy'; 'I feel sad'. Exceptions include 'I feel thirsty' (a sensation) and 'I feel cheated' (an experience about which people feel a variety of emotions). However, when the word 'that' can be inserted after the verb, what is denoted is a thought: for example, 'I feel all is lost', and 'I feel that all is lost'. The real emotion here remains unstated: it could be fear, anxiety or another emotion; we don't know. It is at this point that the counsellor may need to help clients become aware of the emotions underlying their statements and of the difference between thoughts and emotions.

Sometimes, clients have great difficulty in expressing emotions, or a particular emotion, and counsellors may be unaware of this or even collude with it, because they also do not want to talk about the subject. One way of picking up unspoken emotion is by becoming aware of your own emotions. If there is a strong emotion or feeling around, checking it out with the client may increase his or her awareness of these feelings. An example of this is a trainee counsellor who in supervision complained of feeling hopeless and useless as the client had said very little. She was encouraged to check these emotions out with the client in the next session, and the client confirmed that this was just how she (the client) felt. On the other hand, the much-used question 'How do you feel about that?' is often unhelpful, because the client is unsure. It also tends to make clients think, which takes them away from emotions and feelings. Instead, an empathic statement like 'You sound worried' may help clients' awareness of their emotions.

Some counsellors find Greenberg and Safran's (1990) distinction between primary, secondary and instrumental emotions useful. Greenberg and Safran argued that it is only working with primary emotions that leads to change. Primary emotions are typically referred to as 'authentic' or 'real', while secondary emotions are a response to them, or to thoughts, and are ways of coping with primary emotions rather than experiencing them. An example is being angry (secondary emotion in this case) as a reaction to feeling afraid (primary emotion here). Instrumental emotions have been learned and are used to influence or manipulate other people. For example, some people have learned that if they get angry others tend to give way to them.

Table 3 provides one way of helping clients find the right or most accurate words for their emotions by choosing the general category or categories first, then narrowing the search down. Yalom (1989) used the memorable and resonant terms 'mad', 'sad', 'bad' and 'glad' for the general categories but mad and bad are too easily misinterpreted, hence our use of angry, sad, afraid and glad. The subcategories of high and medium intensity are very rough guides; what matters is that the client (or counsellor) finds the right word or words, modified perhaps by 'very' or 'a bit'. A word like 'jealous' might be helpful in its own right but also a combination of, say, 'angry' and 'sad', so that sometimes words from these categories will be clearer still. Another way is to assign 10 'units', with a miscellaneous option, as in 'I'm three parts happy, five parts confused and two miscellaneous' (Green, 1964).

The four-category system assumes that there are basic emotions and that these four terms describe them. Both assumptions are disputed by researchers (Oatley et al., 2006). One line of evidence is the high level of agreement across cultures in selecting emotion words that fit facial expressions.

Emotions can be talked about in a distant, unemotional way. In counselling, particularly, this is often not helpful and there are many approaches for encouraging clients to make greater contact with their emotions and experience them more clearly and deeply. These approaches include asking clients to go through their reactions to an event more slowly; to repeat a word or gesture; to use the word 'I'; to say something louder or in an exaggerated way. Or you could exaggerate it yourself; use literal description (also called evocative unfolding); agree with your client a way of expressing emotion that is right for them; check your client's beliefs about expressing emotions (and challenge them if necessary); use immediacy, to try to 'ground' an emotion, sensation or thought in the person's body (e.g. 'Where do you feel empty?' 'Can you describe your sense of empty?'), or use the two-chair technique. It seems to be particularly

Table 3 Four categories of emotion, with examples

Category	High	Medium
Angry	Disgusted Furious Bitter Seething	Angry Exasperated Frustrated Miffed Sore Annoyed Fed-up
Sad	Depressed Defeated Devastated Empty Worthless Hopeless Crushed Battered	Discouraged Unhappy Low Bruised Disappointed Hurt Ashamed Upset Guilty Gloomy
Afraid	Petrified Terrified Deeply shocked Horrified Panicky Frozen	Anxious Insecure Nervous Shaky Cautious Unsure Muddled Confused Lost Apprehensive Threatened Vulnerable Scared
Glad	Ecstatic Elated High Delighted Strong Enchanted Powerful Dynamic Loving Devoted Enthusiastic Proud Inspired	Pleased Happy Cheerful Confident Contented Calm Affectionate Trusting Friendly Peaceful Hopeful Relieved Interested Alert Determined Excited

helpful (in clarifying thoughts and wants as well as emotions and in making more sense of things) to experience emotions as they feel at that moment.

'Emotional blocking' is the term for when clients feel externally threatened by their emotions. Indications are sudden changes of topic and freezing or tension. Kennedy-Moore and Watson (1999, pp216–218) suggest not *pushing* for emotional expression; using a technique (e.g. one of those listed in the previous paragraph); or saying that you notice the change of topic or the tension and wonder if it might be a sign of 'something going on'.

However, most clients express their emotions without the need for techniques like these, and the techniques may even be unhelpful. Instead, it is a matter of listening and noticing!

EMPATHY

See also: Core conditions, Counselling, Frame of reference, Intuition, Metaphors in counselling, Paraphrasing, Questions

In the everyday sense, empathy means the ability to understand how another person is feeling and experiencing the world from that person's point of view. In client-centred counselling, empathy is seen as one of the most important concepts and the communication of empathic understanding as one of the core conditions without which personal change in counselling is unlikely to happen. Barrett-Lennard (1993) described empathy as having an 'aroused, active, reaching out nature'. To Rogers, empathy meant:

> entering into the private perceptual world of the other and becoming thoroughly at home with it. It involves being sensitive, moment by moment, to the changing felt meanings which flow in this other person, to the fear or rage or tenderness or confusion or whatever that he or she is experiencing … It includes communicating your sensings of the person's world as you look with fresh and unfrightened eyes at elements of which he or she is fearful … You are a confident companion to the person in his or her inner world. (Rogers, 1980, p142)

Rogers' concern with his clients' inner, subjective, experiencing meant that it was most important for him to achieve as complete an understanding of a client's personal world as possible.

The place of empathic understanding is not restricted to client-centred counselling or even to the various humanistic approaches. In psychodynamic counselling, for example, in particular that based on the 'self-psychology' of Kohut, empathy is regarded as an important 'ingredient' of counselling. 'It seems to me it is the essence of the science of psychoanalysis to have harnessed empathy to the slow and careful approach of science. We are not empathic in sudden intuitive flashes' (Kohut, 1987, p275). Kohut viewed empathy as a means of information gathering to enable him to make more accurate interpretations, but he also stressed the value of empathy as a means of letting his clients know that he was doing his best to understand them.

In attempting an integration of the approaches of Rogers, Kohut, Gill and Freud, Kahn remarked:

> Thus our job is not to give advice, opinions, or answers, but continually to do our best to *understand* the client: To understand what clients are experiencing and what they are feeling at this moment. To understand the gradually unfolding coherence of the themes of their lives ... What therapists need to learn is less a technique or a group of techniques than ways of opening themselves, first to their clients' experiences and then to their own spontaneity. That spontaneity will reveal their own special, idiosyncratic way of communicating empathy at that moment. (Kahn, 1991, p168)

See also Kahn (1997).

Almost without exception, counsellors from any school of thought would agree that empathy is an important characteristic of effective counselling. However, Rogers went further: noticing the therapeutic benefits of listening and understanding, he concluded that this form of listening, when communicated to the client as empathic understanding, was helpful in its own right, not as a preparation for other counselling techniques:

> To my mind, empathy is in itself a healing agent. It is one of the most potent aspects of therapy, because it releases, it confirms, it brings even the most frightened client into the human race. If a person is understood, he or she belongs. (Rogers, 1986, p129)

Empathy is not sympathy or identification. Counsellors should guard against their responses being sympathetic at the expense of being empathic. Identification – where you feel a client's situation is familiar to you – can lead you to respond from your own experience rather than from your client's frame of reference. Your client may find this either helpful or distracting, but it is not empathic.

Empathy involves a process of being with another person; that is, attempting to 'step into the other person's shoes' and 'see the world through the other person's eyes' and laying aside your own perceptions, values, meanings and perspectives as far as possible. However, two other aspects of empathy deserve to be emphasised here. The first is the *as if* quality of empathic understanding. This refers to the idea that one can enter the frame of reference of another person to the extent that events, feelings, etc. can be experienced, to some extent, *as if* those events were one's own – but without losing the *as if* quality. In other words, empathically understanding someone does not imply 'getting lost' in their world. The empathic counsellor maintains his or her separate identity and does not become overwhelmed by what may be strong or frightening feelings.

The second aspect for emphasis is that empathy needs to be communicated if the other person is to become aware of being understood. This communication is usually, although not exclusively, verbal; holding someone's hand, or even shedding a tear, may be equally as empathic as anything said. An empathic response would capture the content of the client's words but, more importantly, it would also capture some, at least, of the emotion that lies behind those words.

Responding empathically is a way of showing your clients that you understand something of their inner or subjective worlds and what it means to be them.

Empathy: example 1

A client says, 'I don't know what I feel towards my father. There are so many layers of feeling, some really deep, but one minute I seem to hate him, and the next to love him. I wish I could sort out what my real feelings are.'

If the counsellor responds, 'You just don't know what you feel', this would be accurate in part, but not very empathic. However, if the counsellor responds, 'There are so many mixed feelings, you get really confused. But you would like to get clear what are the real and deep feelings you know are there somewhere,' this would be more empathic because it responds both to the other person's confusion, and to their desire for clarity.

Barrett-Lennard (1993) suggested several 'channels' for empathy: sensitive restatement, metaphor and imagery (both as reflections and when they form spontaneously and intuitively in the counsellor), some actions, and sometimes a question 'pops forward', which 'could not be asked – would not occur – without an empathic awareness of the other's experiencing' (p8). (See also Mearns and Thorne, 2007; Merry, 1995, 1999.)

Paraphrasing is not the same as experiencing empathic understanding, although it is a useful skill for communicating the empathy you experience. Rogers in particular was keen that empathic understanding be regarded as a valued 'way of being' with clients (and others) rather than as a technique.

A major review of research on empathy concluded that the 'lack of specification and organization of different views of empathy has led to theoretical confusion, methodological difficulties, inconsistent findings, and neglected areas of research' (Duan and Hill, 1996, p269), but Elliott *et al.* (2004) and Bohart *et al.* (2002) see it as an empirically well-supported element of the counselling relationship.

Empathy: example 2

The client says, 'When I took my new boyfriend home for the first time, it was quite a big risk for me. I thought about it for ages, but I thought I'd give my Mum the benefit of the doubt, but she went absolutely spare. I was so embarrassed, and I thought, why is she doing this? This is a big mistake. She doesn't trust me to know my own mind at all. I was furious.'

Response 1: 'Mmhmm.'

Response 2: 'I guess you felt hurt and discounted after plucking up the courage to do this. It sounds like you gave it a chance, but got really badly let down, and you're just so very angry with her.'

Response 3: 'How did your father take it?'

Response 4: 'Has your mother always been like this with you?'

Response 5: 'You thought about it for a bit, but you took him home anyway. Your Mum was upset about it, and this annoyed you.'

Response 6: 'Is this the same kind of thing as before? Like when you were telling me that your mother always disapproved of your friends at school?'

Response 1 has been wrongly described as 'empathic, showing understanding, and that I was with my client and listening', but it is *not* empathic.

Responses like 2 are by far the most empathic.

Responses like 3 have been described as 'an open question or probe inviting my client to explore the situation further' but are not empathic.

Responses like 4 have been described as 'trying to look for patterns' and are not empathic.

Responses like 5 (which has some content accuracy but little empathy) have been described as 'empathic', with no awareness that the emotions have been diluted from 'absolutely spare' to 'upset' and from 'furious' to 'annoyed'.

Responses like 6 have been described as 'making links with things from the client's past which she has already mentioned', and again are not empathic.

ENDINGS

See also: Clients who don't come back, Contract, negotiating a

Ending counselling with a client is perhaps ideally a process which is planned with the client so that a number of relevant issues can be addressed. However, it can often happen by default, with the client failing to turn up or leaving a message about not wanting to continue. Clients are often clear about how much counselling is enough and how they want to end (Manthei, 2007). You may negotiate at the start how long counselling will last and even specify the end date. More usually, however, the idea of ending will be put forward by you or your client when it begins to feel appropriate and will be negotiated at that time.

In CBT, the ending of therapy starts right at the onset when negotiating a contract with the client (Wills and Sanders, 1997). Moreover, most sessions start with a review of homework and progress, which keeps reminding both therapist and client of how much time might still be required to reach a satisfactory outcome. As CBT aims to teach clients to become their own 'therapist', it is also made explicit that therapeutic progress is probably going to continue after the termination of sessions. Thus, one of the most important themes covered with regard to 'ending therapy' is the client's ability to help him- or herself during future difficulties. Often, one way of beginning to end therapy is to increase the intervals between sessions to two or even three weeks. In addition, CBT encourages clients to come to follow-up sessions approximately every three months.

Peake *et al.* (1988) suggested that counsellors may find it helpful to reflect on three questions about ending, concerned with explicitness, flexibility and the client's needs.

- **How explicit is the issue of ending?** Should you make use of the fact that counselling will end or give way to the temptation to let it pass without any mention, inwardly promising to deal with it when it happens? Knowing that 'the end is near' can enhance motivation; it helps some clients to concentrate their efforts on making the best use of the time available. It can work against the procrastination and resistance to change that can accompany a sense of counselling as open ended and everlasting. The loss, whether it is real or symbolic, embodied in ending the counselling relationship can be a very potent force for positive change.

If you use ending to try to stimulate change the next question is when to raise it. At the beginning, many counsellors will have discussed the client's expectations of how long it may take and there may be at least some implicit understanding that it will be a matter of so many sessions or so many weeks, months or years. After that, unless there is an explicit time-limited contract, it would probably be premature to raise the issue until counselling is firmly under way and some real sense of progress has been achieved. A question such as 'How will you know when you're ready to think about ending?' is often useful. In brief counselling, some counsellors find it useful to remind clients during each session how many sessions have gone and how many remain.

- **How firm is the decision about ending?** There are several related questions here. Should counselling finish on the agreed date, or can it be allowed to continue if the client wants it to do so? How flexible should a counsellor be about ending and what are the ramifications? What circumstances justify an extension? The answers to these questions depend on the nature of the counselling goals and on your philosophy and theoretical model.

  Some counsellors favour a staggered ending, increasing the time between sessions towards the end of a contract. This may be useful with a client you have seen for a long time or where the client's issues are ongoing (e.g. bereavement). Another option is to offer a follow-up session some three to six months after the counselling has ended, to review and consolidate progress made.

- **What are the needs of your client around ending?** Many clients experience little if any difficulty, seeing the end of counselling as an inevitable and natural event. This may be more likely when the counselling is relatively short term, where there was not a strong attachment, or where the focus was on problem management. However, other clients find ending very difficult. They feel that they will not be able to cope without the counsellor, and ending may stimulate earlier painful experiences of loss and separation. You may need to help these clients cope with ending by talking through their existential or developmental needs, acknowledging their achievements and resources, and deciding on particular strategies.

Some practical suggestions for endings

The aims of spending some time on ending are to help clients to sustain any changes they have made and to look forward to a new beginning. The following questions provide a flexible framework:

- **How does the client feel about ending?** Encourage clients to talk about ending. Sometimes, it is helpful to reassure clients that ending can produce feelings of loss and that this is a normal and natural part of the process. It may be helpful to be congruent in sharing some of your own feelings. Hopefully, any negative feelings the client has can be expressed and resolved, and the ending of the counselling relationship can be a model of a more positive ending than she or he may have experienced in other relationships.

- **What has this counselling relationship been like?** Help clients evaluate helpful and difficult aspects. It may also provide you with valuable feedback on your approach.

- **What has been achieved?** Try to consolidate learning by examining the initial goals and the changes that have occurred. Further changes may be anticipated and it may be appropriate to review and celebrate the client's strengths and achievements.

- **How has it been achieved?** Help your clients identify the ways in which they have contributed to, or are responsible for, what has been achieved and the positive aspects of their relationship with you. If clients attribute responsibility for any gains to the counsellor, they might find it difficult to sustain and build on any useful changes beyond the ending.

- **What still needs to be achieved?** It may be useful to identify unmet goals, relative weaknesses and aspects that clients feel they still want to develop. Many counsellors believe that a lot of learning and change goes on not only between counselling sessions but after counselling has ended. It can be useful to examine your client's available resources, support network and other options for maintaining and developing the gains achieved in counselling.

- **What have you learned that will help you in the future?** Hopefully, as a result of effective counselling clients have not only addressed the issue they came with but have also acquired insights, skills and techniques that they can apply as new challenges occur in their lives. Encourage clients to make this learning explicit. Some clients develop an internal model of their counsellor during therapy and find that they can refer to this 'internal counsellor' when new situations arise.

- **What might happen in the future?** Ideally, clients end counselling looking positively towards the future, while not ignoring the possibility that problems or symptoms could return. Help clients to anticipate potential stresses and 'rough spots', and develop contingency plans to deal with them.

This might include returning to counselling. Many people go in and out of counselling rather than having only one continuous period. A good ending makes it more likely that clients have positive feelings about this prospect rather than feeling like a failure or seeing counselling as a waste of time for not 'curing' them.

The framework outlined above focuses on the client. You may also wish to reflect on your own experience, to review what has been achieved and how, and to work through your own reactions to an ending.

END OF INDIVIDUAL SESSIONS

See also: Exercises, Mindfulness

It is desirable for counsellors to close each client session mindfully, so as to avoid transferring any residual concerns, thoughts and emotions into the next session. This is particularly important if there is just a brief break between sessions. Rituals that seem to work for some counsellors include removing the client's notes from sight or storing them immediately; opening the window; using aromatherapy sprays to 'refresh' the energy of the rooms; thinking 'closure' thoughts; and committing to focus on the new 'now'. Alternatively, one could simply stretch, take a brisk walk or take deep breaths.

ETHICAL DILEMMAS

See also: Boundaries, Codes of ethics, Complaints, Ethical Framework

The following process for resolving, or at least clarifying, ethical dilemmas is adapted from Bond (2000):

1. Describe the ethical problem or dilemma briefly.
2. Ask whose dilemma it is. Consider in what way it is a problem for the client, counsellor or for other people.
3. Identify all your options for action and their probable consequences.
4. Evaluate these options in relation to available ethical principles and guidelines. The BACP *Ethical Framework* (2002) identifies the following principles to be applied in deciding on the appropriate course of action:
    - **Fidelity: honouring the trust placed in the practitioner**
      What course of action is most in accordance with the trust placed in the counsellor?
    - **Autonomy: respect for the client's right to be self-governing**
      Which option is most in keeping with the client's wishes?
    - **Beneficence: a commitment to promoting the client's wellbeing**
      Which option is most likely to benefit the client?

Ending

- **Non-maleficence: a commitment to avoiding harm to the client**
  Which option is least likely to bring harm to the client (or others)?
- **Justice: the fair and impartial treatment of all clients and the provision of adequate services**
  Which option best satisfies the needs to consider any legal requirements and obligations (to the client or others), to appreciate differences between people, and to ensure a fair provision of services?
- **Self-respect: fostering the practitioner's self-knowledge and care for self**
  Which option best takes into account the needs and welfare of the counsellor?

5. Where possible discuss in supervision, and if appropriate seek legal advice.

6. Select the best course of action. It is unlikely that all of the above principles will point to the same course of action and careful thought should be given to which principles might take priority in relation to a particular dilemma. Negotiate with the client if there is joint responsibility.

7. Evaluate the outcome.

ETHICAL FRAMEWORK

See also: Codes of ethics, Complaints

In its *Ethical Framework for Good Practice in Counselling and Psychotherapy*, the BACP (2002) provides guidance on the values, principles and personal moral qualities which it sees as appropriate in defining ethical practice in counselling and which should be applied to the resolution of ethical dilemmas. It extends previous guidance given in the *Code of Ethics and Practice for Counsellors* (BAC, 1998), in particular by explicitly stating the values and personal moral qualities upon which the training, development and practice of a counsellor or psychotherapist should be based. This is seen as an alternative to providing a comprehensive set of rules applicable in all circumstances, and it provides guidance above and beyond principles (which may be particularly useful in the resolution of dilemmas) to take account of other approaches to ethics and recognise the contribution of values and personal qualities to ethical practice in general.

The Framework also offers more general guidance on good practice in counselling and psychotherapy, and it details the BACP's Professional Conduct Procedure. For further details see the BACP's website.

ETHNICITY

See: Multiculturalism

EVALUATION

See also: Beginnings, Contract, negotiating a, EAPs, Effectiveness of counselling, Ethical Framework, Evidence-based practice, Feedback from clients to counsellor, NICE

Evaluation can be either formal or informal. A counsellor may arrange an informal verbal review with a client to evaluate progress and discuss whether the counsellor is meeting the needs of the client. For example, a series of simple questions such as 'Where did you feel you were when you started counselling?', 'Where are you now?' and 'Where would you like to be in terms of the work still outstanding?' may be enough to stimulate a useful evaluation. Evaluation with the client helps to foster a cooperative relationship and can imply a shared responsibility for monitoring progress and effectiveness and reviewing therapeutic plans. It is good practice to evaluate at regular intervals during counselling as well as upon ending.

Within the growing field of workplace counselling, many EAPs insist on a system for evaluating and auditing the counselling service. There is increasing pressure for services to evaluate practice (Mellor-Clark and Barkham, 2006). Evaluation differs from research in that its primary purpose is to assist decision making and it is usually written up for local consumption. In addition, evaluation may prove a useful tool for helping counsellors consider further their individual training needs and meet existing ethical requirements for continued professional development as outlined by professional bodies such as the BPS, BACP and BABCP. For example, the BACP includes the 'systematic monitoring of practice and outcomes' as part of the principle of 'beneficence' (actually doing good).

Clinical Outcomes for Routine Evaluation (CORE) is a system for measuring the outcomes of counselling and psychotherapy; service evaluation and performance management. The system includes a range of forms to measure progress and outcomes in therapy, gather evaluation information from clients and therapists, and monitor other aspects of the service such as administration; it also includes IT tools for collating and presenting the information gathered. See the CORE website and, for detailed, practical discussions of the benefits and dangers of CORE, see Mothersole (2004, 2006).

An example of a simple evaluation form is shown in Figure 2 (p84).

EVIDENCE-BASED PRACTICE (EBP)

See also: Common factors, Effectiveness of counselling, Evaluation, Giving information, Good counsellors, NICE, Research

Evidence-based practice (EBP) has had a dramatic rise in a number of disciplines, including counselling and psychotherapy. The book *Evidence-Based Medicine* by Sackett *et al.* (1997) has been particularly influential; the authors defined evidence-based medicine (EBM) as 'the conscientious, explicit and judicious use of current best evidence in making decisions about individual patients'

CLIENT SATISFACTION QUESTIONNAIRE

Your views are very important in helping monitor the quality of the counselling work offered. Please return this questionnaire in the s.a.e. provided. As with your counselling work, any information you provide will be treated as confidential.

Using a scale of 0–8 (0 = very poor, 8 = excellent), please rate the following.

Pre-counselling contract:

1. How well was your initial enquiry dealt with?
   0 1 2 3 4 5 6 7 8
2. How useful did you find the client information sent to you?
   0 1 2 3 4 5 6 7 8

The counselling environment:

1. How would you rate the counselling facilities offered?
   0 1 2 3 4 5 6 7 8

The counsellor:

1. How helpful did you find your counsellor?
   0 1 2 3 4 5 6 7 8
2. What did you like most about your counsellor?
   _____
   _____
   _____

3. Was there anything your counsellor could have done differently that would have been helpful?
   _____
   _____
   _____

Your progress:
Using the rating scale 0-8 (0 = 'feeling really awful', 8 = 'feeling really good'), please rate the following:

1. At the beginning of your counselling, how would you have rated yourself?
   0 1 2 3 4 5 6 7 8
2. After the counselling, how would you rate yourself?
   0 1 2 3 4 5 6 7 8
3. What did you find most helpful about the counselling offered to you?
   _____
   _____
   _____

Thank you for completing this questionnaire.

Figure 2 Example of a client evaluation form

(p2). They also emphasised the roles of patient choice and clinical expertise. Substitute 'client' for 'patient' and at first sight – in counselling as in medicine – EBP seems obviously to be a good idea. *Of course* counsellors should take into account the 'best evidence', rather than relying primarily on their training, expert opinion, fashion or their own, necessarily limited, experience, and should avoid using ineffective or even harmful approaches and techniques.

However, applying EBP is not so straightforward. Geddes and Harrison (1997) usefully contrasted two positions on EBM, which also apply to EBP: critics of EBM caricature its opponents as 'evangelists who fail to appreciate the complexity of everyday medical practice and who overlook the wisdom of experienced clinicians' (p220); advocates of EBM view the critics as 'Luddites who have an overvalued opinion of their clinical acumen'. They also point to the risk that EBM can be used as an excuse to cut services. A further risk is finding 'certainty' where it does not exist: 'EBM, if used well, maximises the evidence but does not necessarily reduce the fuzziness – the danger is that we assume it does' (Anderson, 1997, p226).

There are problems at each of three main stages of EBP: producing the evidence; making it accessible to counsellors; and implementing it. First, for many aspects of counselling, the evidence does not exist or is unclear. Moreover, counselling is a particularly complex field in which to do good research, and even the most rigorous research methods have significant limitations. For example, randomised controlled trials (RCTs), regarded as the 'gold standard' method in medicine, look for *overall* effects, when these sometimes conceal *opposing* effects. Real clinical excellence, in contrast, tailors treatment to individuals. Nevertheless, RCTs have been extremely valuable in medicine, showing, for example, that some medical procedures, at one time standard, killed more patients than they cured (Wessely, 2001). A more fundamental problem with RCTs in counselling research follows from the common factors finding, i.e. that the major approaches have broadly equivalent outcomes. In other words, it is not so much comparing CBT and person-centred counselling as treatments of anxiety (say) as comparing counsellors. Not surprisingly, individual counsellors vary in their effectiveness (Beutler *et al.*, 2004; Okiishi *et al.*, 2003), quite possibly with different kinds of client and problem. Moreover, as the different mainstream approaches are generally equally effective (e.g. Lambert, 2004), and NICE recommends CBT, the other approaches should be recommended too.

Secondly, there are problems with making the evidence available. Because there are sometimes hundreds of studies on a particular question, keeping up with the research literature is impossible for a single person. In addition, assessing the quality of each study's methodology is a highly skilled activity. This problem can be solved to some extent with systematic reviews and guidelines, as NICE has shown. However, two systematic reviews of ostensibly the same literature often reach different conclusions (Mackay *et al.*, 2003).

The third main problem with EBP is implementing it: for example, how best to tell a client about relevant research, and the question of how to use practice guidelines (Rowland, 2001). Where your practice differs from such guidelines, you may be asked to explain why; however, like RCTs, they are focused on treatments rather than on individuals.

There are counter-arguments for each of the problems but also some more fundamental criticisms, for example Marzillier (2004) and subsequent letters. Marzillier argued that evidence-based psychotherapy is a myth, because the medical world is irrelevant to psychological problems. He is not against research itself. Rather, it is outcome research that he sees as 'misleading and simplistic', as not doing justice to people's complexity and psychotherapy's intricacy. However, qualitative research methods do attempt to do justice to complexity and are used and recognised more than they were (McLeod, 2001, 2003b). The notion of 'evidence' needs to be broadly defined.

Finally, it seems very likely that the skills and knowledge of counsellors will remain crucial and that EBP will help us compare competing claims, consider guidelines like those from NICE, and be able to give reasons for the decisions that we make. The term 'evidence-informed practice' reflects this emphasis more accurately than the widely used (in 2007) EBP.

EXERCISE (PHYSICAL)

See also: End of individual sessions, Stress

Some counsellors and clients survive well without coming close to the current main recommendation for physical exercise, which is to accumulate about 30 minutes of 'low intensity' activity each day. This means walking fairly briskly or its equivalent, rather than getting sweaty and out of breath. The opposite question – how much exercise is too much? – seems to be a problem for only a few people (Cockerill and Riddington, 1996).

If you do want to exercise, it is generally best to become more active *gradually and comfortably*, with more than 30 minutes a day or more vigorous exercise giving a reserve of fitness and greater protection against some illnesses (Seligman, 1995). Also, check with your GP if you have chest pains, are not used to exercise, have joint problems, or if there is any other reason why exercise may be risky for you. Other fairly standard pieces of advice are to remember that rest (at least one day a week) matters too, to find a form of exercise that suits you and that you enjoy (Bayne, 2004) and that 'gradually' varies for different activities (although it is probably best to base this on your own self-awareness rather than on an external criterion like number of minutes). For some people who are already used to vigorous exercise, interval training, for example jogging now and again during a walk or alternating high-intensity short bursts (15 seconds to a minute) with two-minute rests, for about 10 minutes each session and three times a week seems to be effective (Coyle, 2005), but the evidence so far does not really match the enthusiasm of the recommendations.

Exercise provides an outlet for the psychological effect of negative emotions and improves mood by producing positive biochemical changes in the body and brain. It reduces the amount of adrenal hormones your body releases in response to stress and increases the release of greater amounts of endorphins – pain-relieving, mood-elevating chemicals. Depressed people often lack these neurochemicals. The positive mood states associated with frequent exercise are so significant that 'exercise therapy' may be a more effective treatment for depression than either psychotherapy or antidepressants.

Thayer's research (e.g. 1996) on mild exercise and its effects on mood supports the effectiveness of fairly brisk five-minute walks; they increase energy and reduce tension for the next two hours on average. Music was reported as quite effective too, so dancing might be particularly beneficial. Thayer's main theme was that the results of accurate, systematic self-observation can be useful to regulate moods and cope with stress. For example, he suggested trying brisk five-minute walks at various times of the day and then rating your levels of energy and tension. This needs to be done several times and the results averaged, because the effects are subtle (several factors affect energy and tension). A scale for measuring level of energy is shown below.

Tired out	Average amount of energy (for you)				Lots of energy
1	2	3	4	5	6

EXERCISES

See also: Drawings, Homework, Giving information, Nonverbal communication

The idea of inviting clients to try an exercise is a common strategy in co-counselling, Gestalt and CBT. As a general principle, we strongly advise that you offer to clients only those exercises that have a clear purpose, and that you have experienced yourself as a client or in training.

If an exercise is approached as an invitation to try something and see what happens, clients can reject the idea more easily. If they do, it may be useful to talk about what it is that they find difficult.

Some clients find eye-to-eye and/or face-to-face contact threatening, especially when talking about some issues, and may find it easier to focus on a form of writing or drawing shared with the counsellor. Paper-and-pencil exercises can represent or summarise in words, diagrams or pictures what the client is saying, or be a way for the counsellor to explain or challenge.

EXPECTATIONS (CLIENTS')

See also: Common factors, Contract, negotiating a, Effectiveness of counselling, Giving information, Intake interviews, Psychological type

Clients do not usually enter counselling in complete ignorance of what to expect or of how counselling might help them. Some clients, however, have unreasonable or mistaken ideas about counselling: for example, they expect to be given helpful advice or to be told how to overcome their problems. Others expect to *have* to talk about childhood memories, or to lie on a couch and be 'analysed' (McLeod, 1990). If you do an intake interview or contract-setting interview, you will be able to explore these expectations and be clear with your clients what is expected of them and what they can reasonably expect of you. Launching straight into counselling without exploring expectations can store up problems for later, particularly when clients feel disappointed or let down because they had unrealistic expectations to start with.

Reasonable (and common) expectations held by clients include confidentiality (within appropriate limits); the chance to be listened to; to be treated with respect; the possibility that painful memories or feelings may be stirred up; the probability that counselling will have a positive effect on their lives; that they will feel differently after counselling than they did before it; and that they will gain fresh insights and perspectives on themselves and their lives.

Unrealistic expectations include instant 'results'; the solving of financial or social problems such as bad housing or unemployment; that they can change other people's behaviour; that the past can somehow be changed; and that they will supply the problems and you will supply the solutions. People whose expectations are low or nonexistent very rarely enter counselling voluntarily, and if they do they tend to leave early. Clients with very high expectations may be disappointed when changes do not happen overnight and may also leave counselling early. Other clients need time to adjust their expectations gradually; for them the process of induction is partly about learning what is realistic.

The degree of faith that the client has in the effectiveness of counselling (in the presence of reasonable expectations) is known to influence strongly the likelihood of success (Hubble *et al.*, 1999). The fact that counselling exists at all points to the notion that people do believe that change is both possible and desirable, and that it can be accomplished through a relationship with a skilled and trained counsellor. This expectation is supported by research (see entry on Effectiveness of counselling), and therefore it is a matter of being optimistic about the *possibilities* without exaggerating them.

The following ideas about 'basic principles of counselling' may be a useful resource. They were developed by the BAC in 1993, mainly with clients in mind but also as a statement representing BAC members' very diverse approaches to counselling.

- The aim of counselling is to provide an opportunity for a client to work towards living in a more satisfying and resourceful way.
- Counselling is voluntarily and deliberately undertaken by counsellor and client. It is different from other ways of helping.
- Before counselling starts, the counsellor clarifies with the client the basis on which counselling is to be given, including method, duration, fees and confidentiality; changes can subsequently be made only with the agreement of the client.
- In counselling the right of the client to make his or her own decisions is respected.
- Counsellors continually monitor their own skills, experience, resources and practice.
- Counsellors will be properly trained for their roles and be committed to maintaining their competence.
- Counsellors will not misrepresent their training or experience.
- Counsellors have regular and appropriate supervision/consultative support.
- Counsellors do not abuse their position of trust financially, emotionally or sexually.
- All that takes place between counsellor and client is treated with respect and discretion.

FEEDBACK FROM CLIENTS TO COUNSELLOR

See also: Clients who don't come back, Evaluation, Immediacy, Relationship between counsellor and client

It is important that you remain open to feedback from your clients, to help you check the extent to which you are enabling them to move towards more fulfilling or effective ways of living. In counselling sessions, you will get feedback from your clients concerning the extent to which they feel understood and valued, both indirectly, through comments like 'Yes, that is how things feel at the moment', and directly, i.e. what clients actually tell you about their experience of you. Some counsellors invite feedback as part of regular review sessions and in a final evaluation session.

Whether or not the client continues to attend counselling with you is a form of feedback. It is possible, however, for clients to continue with counselling even though they do not seem to be deriving any benefit from it, or for clients to drop out for their own reasons, quite separate from the counselling or you. If you have a client who is often late, or often wishes to leave early, or who misses sessions regularly, she or he could be making an indirect statement about the counselling itself. It is usually helpful to find a way of bringing this indirect form of communication out into the open, perhaps by sharing your feelings of concern about it.

The things clients say about their lives in general may contain important indirect feedback for you as a counsellor. For instance, someone who reports having a wider circle of friends and acquaintances than before may in effect be providing some positive feedback. Likewise, someone who reports more isolation from others may be providing useful feedback. Related forms of feedback are, for example, how far your clients are able to speak about themselves and their feelings more directly than before, how far your clients seem to be less dependent on other people for their sense of self-esteem and how far your clients are becoming more proactive and 'in charge' of their lives. It is helpful to become sensitive to these kinds of 'clues' about how your client is making use of counselling and, where appropriate, to incorporate them into the relationship you have with your client. However, it is important to interpret these clues cautiously: they may say more about the client or the client's need for a particular response from you than about you.

FEELING

See also: Emotions, Mindfulness, Psychobabble, Psychological type, Self-awareness, Support groups, Values

The term 'feeling' is sometimes used to refer to the general 'atmosphere' of your body (e.g. calm or restless) and sometimes to a way of making decisions, one which is based on values. Rogers' term 'organismic valuing process' has a similar meaning. 'Feeling' and 'emotion' are used by different people in different ways, as are' think', 'intuition', 'sense', and many other counselling terms.

FEES

See also: Assertiveness, Boundaries, Client information handout, Collusion, Contract, negotiating a, Giving information

Apart from inviting clients to pay a donation, which is common practice in some agencies, there are three main ways of setting fees: a fixed fee for a session; negotiating a lower fee in certain circumstances; negotiating with each client an agreed point on a sliding scale (e.g. a 50-minute counselling session for 1/40 of the client's weekly income or, more simply, whatever your client earns in an hour). In addition, some counsellors offer the initial interview free of charge, and part of this interview is concerned with agreeing fees. An underlying principle, which may appeal, is that neither you nor your client feels exploited.

There are various options for when payment should be paid: at the beginning or end of each session; in advance for a fixed number of sessions; or by invoice every month or so. If you choose the first option, you are likely to lose the fee for a missed session. If you choose the second option, you need to discuss with your clients the consequences of missing sessions. A good way forward is to establish with your clients a minimum period of notice for missing sessions, after which the fee will not be refunded or carried over. Some counsellors ask for a set reduced fee for cancelled sessions. The same period of notice – typically not less than 24 hours – can apply if the counsellor postpones a session. As a general guide, typical fees in 2007 ranged from £30 to £50 a session. Not many counsellors in private practice can afford to have more than one or two clients at the lower end of this scale. Not charging some clients a fee at all, or charging a low fee, can be seen as a generous and just decision or as a betrayal of other counsellors whom you are undercutting.

That still leaves the question of what to charge. Comparisons may be useful: for example, what do 'alternative health' practitioners charge? But then there is essential work which is not paid or is very low paid. On the other hand, there is the view cited by Hawley: 'I have worked with many clients who would simply not take seriously or even trust someone calling themselves a qualified professional and charging £35 per hour' (2003, p17). Feltham (2002) contrasted two modes, the anarchist and the 'conscienceless entrepreneur', but saw most counsellors as moderates and realists.

A business-like approach is to calculate overheads; time for CPD, holidays, resting and supervision; how many clients you can counsel a day; and what you consider to be a fair income for you as a full-time counsellor or pro rata. Possible overheads are heating, lighting, decorating, etc.; marketing; tax; fees for other professionals; training and membership of organisations. Bartering (of services or goods) may be an attractive possibility, although maintaining boundaries is the primary consideration. Moreover, if your 'income' in this form is regular and can be defined by HM Revenue and Customs as coming from a business, then you may still be liable to tax on the monetary equivalent. HM Revenue and Customs requires accurate records of all payments made to you and of all expenses incurred as a result of your practice. You may wish to consult an accountant about what expenditure can be offset against tax.

Feltham (2003), Tudor (1998), and Tudor and Worrall (2002) discuss counsellors' fees in depth. The main principle seems to be that you should talk about them with your client straightforwardly, sensitively and calmly, as with any other topic.

FIRST IMPRESSIONS

See also: Beginnings, Furniture, Intuition, Nonverbal communication, Self-awareness, Transference

First impressions can have a disproportionate power. We tend to form them very quickly and almost automatically and then interpret later information in terms of these impressions: i.e. to treat our first impression as accurate and any later information that conflicts with it as untypical. This is likely to lead to bias; accurate judgements are more likely if equal weight is given to equally important pieces of information, whether these come first or later. Good counsellors do this anyway, treating impressions (which are probably inevitable) as hypotheses but being ready to revise them. Intuitions and first impressions are thus neither ignored nor believed but checked.

Bayne (2005) provides useful strategies for being more accurate:

- Look for patterns, over time and across situations.
- Therefore, treat first impressions as hypotheses.
- Look for evidence against your first impression, as well as for it.
- Take the situation into account (some situations, such as selection interviews or first dates, tend to constrain behaviour much more than others).

Similarity is the strongest general source of bias in first (and later) impressions. We tend to like people who are like ourselves. Physical attractiveness is also potent: we tend to believe that 'what is beautiful is good'.

Compelling first impressions are particularly likely to be wrong, because there has not been time to gather enough evidence and because their strength must come from something in you. Co-counselling refers to 'restimulations' and suggests a procedure for dealing with them. A version of this is to ask yourself the following:

1. 'Who does this client remind me of'? (It could be an actual person or a stereotype, e.g. a teacher.)
2. In what ways? (Be as specific as possible and persistent: repeat the question until all the possibilities seem exhausted.)
3. What do I want to say to this person? (What haven't I said that I want to?)
4. In what ways is this client *not* like this other person? (Again, repeat the question as often as necessary and be persistent.)

Sometimes, of course, clients may be restimulated by you, and you can ask them the set of questions above.

FIRST SESSION

See: Assessment, Beginnings, Client information handout, Clients who don't come back, Contract, negotiating a, Contraindications for brief counselling, Difficulties in being a client, Expectations (clients'), Fees, First impressions, Furniture, History taking, Giving information, Multiculturalism, Referral, Relationship between counsellor and client

FORCE-FIELD ANALYSIS

See also: Counselling, Exercises, Goals, Sealing

Force-field analysis is a generic technique for helping clients to explore the factors likely to influence their progress, perhaps in relation to a goal, or the implementation of an action plan (e.g. see Egan, 2007). Part of its value lies in actually writing things out, externalising them instead of churning them around in your head. The client explores the factors (or *forces*) likely to be around which are facilitative of success (helping forces) and those likely to inhibit progress or lead to failure (hindering or restraining forces). The relative strengths of the identified forces are assessed, and contingency plans can be developed to strengthen the helping forces and weaken the hindering forces.

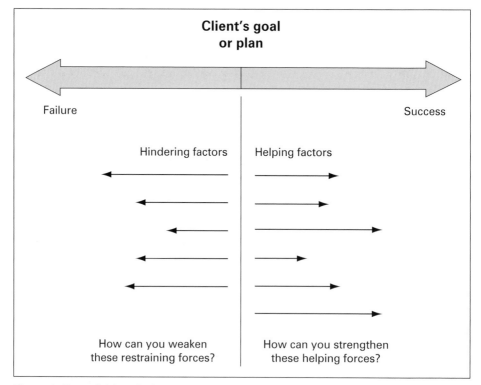

Figure 3 Force-field analysis

Force-field analysis can be used as a way of analysing the landscape in relation to an identified goal, as a way of preparing to develop an action plan; or it can be used as a check step once an action plan has been developed, to raise awareness of influencing factors and help the client refine their plan.

In more detail, the procedure is to work through the following steps:

1. First state the goal – what the client wants to achieve and, if known, the strategy for achieving it.

2. Generate a list of forces that might contribute towards achieving it (things that might help), and a list of obstacles or forces against achieving the goal (things that might get in the way). Encourage the client to think about possible events, people, internal forces such as his or her own feelings and motivation, potential distractions, rewards, interruptions, etc. that may have an influence. Not every positive force will have a corresponding negative force. It is important not to censor at this stage, but to record all ideas as they come.

3. Analyse the forces. The forces on each side could be graded on a scale of 1 to 10 for likely power and impact. Perhaps circle the most significant helping and hindering forces. This analysis may show up gaps in the client's awareness of his or her situation or indicate a need for further information or exploration.

4. Identify ways to strengthen the positive forces and weaken the forces against achieving the goal. Focus on the most significant forces. Encourage the client to be specific and relate specific actions to particular forces. Make a note of significant forces for which no action is possible. Develop contingency plans for forces which are uncertain.

5. Assess the feasibility of the stated goal. Does the action substantially offset the obstacles? Overall, does the strength of the positive forces outweigh the obstacles? If so, go ahead. If not, go to Step 6.

6. Reconsider the goal. The goal might be too general or vague, too ambitious, not reflect the real problem, or not be within the client's control. It may also contain more than one goal: if so, try to break it down further.

In force-field analysis there is a 'battle' between restraining forces, which might include guilt, irrational beliefs and practical problems on one 'side' and, on the other, positive forces, say a strong desire, a sense that things could be much better, support and some opportunities. Analysis of the forces can lead to a more comprehensive and better-thought-out action plan which takes account of the realities of the client's situation.

FRAME OF REFERENCE

See also: Active listening, Empathy, Nonverbal communication

'Frame of reference' is another way of expressing the idea of empathy. To stay within the client's frame of reference is to be empathic in a sustained way.

An accurate paraphrase is, by definition, in the client's frame of reference. By consistently listening carefully to clients' verbal messages and being aware of their nonverbal communication, you develop a more comprehensive sense of their experiences, perceptions, feelings, etc. and can respond to them from the basis of that understanding. Conversely, in your own frame of reference, you see the client from your own viewpoint (e.g. 'It doesn't look that bad to me', or 'I don't think you're overweight').

FRAMEWORKS

See also: Counselling, Theories of counselling

Frameworks are working maps, designed to help counsellors make sense of, or offer plausible explanations for, aspects of clients, counselling and themselves. Frameworks are therefore similar in purpose to theories and models, and indeed the three terms often seem to be used interchangeably. Some people seem to be drawn to very simple frameworks, which they may then complicate when trying to understand a person or a process; others seem to be drawn to initial complexity, from which they then select to clarify or 'get hold of' particular instances. An example of a simple framework is 'support and challenge'. You can ask during a counselling session, or later, 'At this point am I supporting or challenging, and which do I want to be doing? And why?' A simple framework can quickly lead to quite complex considerations.

FREEWRITING

See also: Assertiveness, Self-awareness, Stress, Writing (expressive)

Freewriting (Elbow, 1973, 1997) is a way of exploring inner experience. It is also a technique for tackling writer's 'block'. There are three steps in the following variation:

1. Write *without stopping* for several minutes (e.g. 10) either on a particular subject or on anything that comes to mind. If you are stuck, write something about that (e.g. 'I'm stuck' or 'I'm fed up with this. It's stupid') again and again if that's what comes to mind. Write anything, but keep writing.
2. Underline significant/useful bits.
3. Freewrite about them.

Freewriting thus replaces 'Think clearly and then write' with 'Write to find out what you mean, feel and want'. Essentially, writing and editing are separated by lots of writing and lots of discarding.

If you use a word processor, Elbow (1997) suggests turning the screen down so that you cannot see your words. For some people the effect is to focus on their thoughts rather than on the sometimes off-putting words. Elbow calls this 'invisible writing'.

Freewriting can also be a group activity. In one kind of group, members write for themselves about their reaction to something for five minutes and then discuss their reactions in pairs, or in the whole group, revealing as much or as little of their freewriting as they choose (Murray, 1997, 1998). This method is rated as particularly enjoyable and could easily be used in personal development and supervision groups.

FREQUENCY OF SESSIONS

See also: Contract, negotiating a, Contraindications for brief counselling, Endings, Length of sessions

In psychoanalysis, it is not unusual to see the same client three times a week or more, but most counsellors see clients only once a week. Once a week seems to be acceptable to most people (it is convenient and not too costly) but there is no real reason why it should be a 'golden rule'. For example, if a client is in a deeply anxious or very vulnerable state, it can help to meet more often than once a week, although most counsellors would see such a contract as temporary. It is probably better to have more frequent meetings in the early stages, and then to settle on once-weekly meetings later on, rather than the other way round.

After a while, some clients prefer to meet once a fortnight if they feel they have made a lot of progress and only need support now to consolidate the changes that they feel they have made. Once a month may be too infrequent, and, if a client asks for this, we advise you to check out the reasons and perhaps ask whether he or she should leave counselling entirely. Monthly meetings may tend to become reports on what has happened since you last met, which is unlikely to be useful. A compromise is to have a batch of weekly meetings, then a break of two or three months, followed by weekly meetings if necessary.

FRIENDSHIP WITH CLIENTS

See also: Boundaries, Endings, Ethical dilemmas, Sexual attraction, Supervision

Counselling is a formal relationship, and its boundaries and limitations need to be respected and maintained. This is helpful and reassuring to both counsellors and clients. Sometimes clients ask for a relationship outside counselling, but it is not ethical to allow this whilst counselling is continuing. You can explain that it is not possible within your professional ethical framework and that you can be of more help if the counselling relationship remains protected and uncomplicated by outside situations. Any changes in the relationship should be discussed in supervision and discussion should take into account the issues and power dynamics present in the relationship. Blurring of relationship boundaries into areas more normally associated with friendships and social relationships (such as regular acceptance of gifts, doing favours for clients or vice versa) may have unforeseen consequences and are often a feature of professional conduct hearings when the therapeutic relationship has become compromised (see the BACP's website for more on professional conduct hearings).

Once the counselling relationship is over (and the proper ending of the counselling relationship is important in this respect), there are still problems in becoming socially involved with clients, at least until some time has elapsed. This does not have to be seen by your client as rejection, but rather as a way of ensuring that you are available to help in the future, which might be impossible if you have become involved in some other role. If you do become friends with an ex-client, and this does sometimes happen, you are no longer available as that person's counsellor. Some organisations and codes of ethics prohibit social contact with all former clients, while others take the view that a genuine, accepting and empathic relationship developed in counselling can, and sometimes will, develop into a genuine friendship (Mearns and Thorne, 2007).

FURNITURE

See also: Drinks/refreshments, Nonverbal communication, Power, Privacy

Your furniture contributes to your clients' initial impression of you. If the impression is a negative one, you must be correspondingly more effective to compensate. In part, your choice of furniture depends on your approach to counselling (e.g. couch or not, cushions or not), but there are some general guidelines. If you take the view that the disparity in power between counsellor and client should be reduced as much as possible, then chairs and seating positions should be equal. Across the corner of a desk is the position sometimes used, although this is not equal: the counsellor, seated in front of the desk, can write on it more easily. Most counsellors prefer no desk.

Perhaps the most practical suggestions are to role play being a client in your own room, and to seek the views of colleagues and perhaps clients (near or at the end of their time with you). Some personal things in the room and an intermediate degree of tidiness seem to be interpreted by most people as welcoming, but some counsellors prefer a plain room with no distracting objects. The balance sought may best be seen as one between not deterring or inhibiting clients – for example, family photos may discourage some clients – and being consistent with yourself and therefore more at ease.

GAMES

See also: Assertiveness, Challenging, Drama triangle, Immediacy, Paraphrasing

The term 'games' is used to describe some forms of interaction between people: ones with an ulterior motive. Berne (1973, p83) thought that 'The meaningful part of most people's lives is mostly made up of games' and that games are an obstacle to real intimacy.

Numerous 'games' were first suggested by Berne (1964) (e.g. 'If it weren't for you'; 'Why don't you – yes but'; and 'Ain't it awful'). They are played at different degrees of intensity and can be very serious indeed. When something is 'going on' between two people, a game may explain it, especially if it keeps happening. You can then offer to explore the possible game or decline to play it, by paraphrasing, or by using an assertiveness skill or a challenge. For example, in 'Ain't it awful', you are asked to be sympathetic and agree, and some declining responses are 'I see you as emphasising the negative'; 'It sounds as if you've decided it's hopeless'; 'I see things differently', and 'What might you do about it?'

GENDER

See: Multiculturalism

GENUINENESS

See: Congruence

GIFTS

See also: Assertiveness, Boundaries, Immediacy, Nonverbal communication

There seems to be nothing inherently wrong with accepting gifts from clients from time to time, particularly as tokens of appreciation when, for example, counselling is coming to an end. The occasional small gift need not be any cause for concern and can be enjoyed, but the client who is forever bringing or sending unwanted or expensive gifts can be a problem. Inappropriate gifts are a challenge to boundaries, and your client may be in counselling partly because he or she is confused or unaware about appropriate boundaries; accepting gifts from such clients can create further problems.

It can be difficult to refuse a gift. Some people can be very hurt or embarrassed by a refusal, so it needs to be done with great sensitivity. Moreover, gifts have different significance in different cultures. It may be better to risk hurt or embarrassment by confronting the issue directly, but how you do this will depend on the approach you take generally to counselling. In psychodynamic counselling, a client offering a gift may be thought of as exhibiting transference, and you will deal with this in the same way that you deal with all forms of transference. A person-centred counsellor might appreciate the sentiment behind the gift but want to express his or her own mixed feelings about accepting it. Whichever form of counselling you prefer, it is better to incorporate the 'gift giving' into the counselling directly than to ignore the significance that it may have, particularly if it happens often.

GIVING INFORMATION

See also: Advice, Bibliotherapy, Challenging, Process, Psychobabble

There is some confusion about the difference between giving information and giving advice. We suggest that *information* is intended to help clients decide for themselves, whereas *advice* tells clients the best thing to do. There is also disagreement among counsellors as to whether giving information is appropriate. On the one hand, some counsellors give information because they believe that it helps clients to understand themselves better and make decisions. On the other hand, there is the view that counsellors should never give information, usually on the grounds that clients will tend to construe it as advice, because the counsellor is in a position of power, and may blame the counsellor for any wrong decisions they take. A further argument is that giving information interferes with clients doing things for themselves.

Four types of information giving (in the sense defined above) are:

- **challenge:** e.g. 'I have heard you call yourself silly on three different occasions'
- **reply to a request for feedback:** e.g. when the client asks, 'Do other people behave like me?' (sometimes it is appropriate to ask clients to check out for themselves whether this is so, or to ask them to try to answer the question; at other times it may be appropriate to say, 'Yes, they do and there are many different ways of behaving')
- **enlarging the field of knowledge:** e.g. informing a bereaved client about the different stages of loss and the wide variability in experiencing them or not
- **helping clients to obtain information:** e.g. from a relevant book or an organisation.

Ley's (1988, p179) recommendations on giving information (mainly of the third and fourth types listed above) include:

- find out what the person wants to know
- check for jargon
- use short words and sentences
- be specific
- categorise
- summarise
- check understanding.

An additional recommendation is 'be positive (where possible)'. (See the entry on Ageing: in one example, preventing falls in older people was more effectively presented as improving balance.)

GOALS

See also: Action planning, Endings, Evaluation, Force-field analysis, Scaling, Therapeutic planning

Many approaches to counselling view goals as an important way of determining and maintaining a sense of direction in therapeutic work, and indeed agreement between therapist and client about goals is seen as an important component of most formulations of the therapeutic alliance. However, some might see an overemphasis on goals as potentially constraining in terms of freedom to 'go with' whatever arises in a session or allowing the counselling to develop in an 'organic' way. Nevertheless, it is our experience that, whether or not goals are addressed early in the therapeutic process, clients do tend to develop them as the work progresses, and it is useful to explore these and make them explicit.

Two types of inter-related goals can be addressed. First, it is useful to know the client's goals for therapy: what she or he hopes to get out of the counselling. If discussed and made explicit, these goals can be a useful tool for evaluation and for the process of ending. Secondly, clients will often have, or benefit from developing, goals which they hope to achieve in their life outside of counselling.

The mnemonic SMART is often used to help clients develop workable goals from initial hopes or broad aims. This refers to goals ideally being:

- Specific (expressed in clear, concrete and positive terms)
- Measurable (stating clear criteria for success, so that the client will know when the goal has been achieved)
- Appropriate (adequately addressing the issue at hand and appropriate to the client's values, culture, etc.)
- Realistic (achievable and within the client's control)
- Timed (some target timeframe is attached).

Some flexibility is needed if goals are not to be constraining. New issues may arise in therapy; new priorities may develop in the client's life, and influences may emerge which make established goals unrealistic or no longer relevant. However, attention to goals can be valuable in providing a sense of direction and momentum to therapy; achievement of goals can be a boost to a client's self-esteem and encourage further work; and both therapeutic and life goals provide a focus for hope and motivation.

Feltham (2006) illustrated the range of goals in contemporary approaches to counselling with this provocative list:

- support
- psychoeducational guidance
- adjustment and resource provision
- crisis intervention and management
- problem solving and decision making
- symptom amelioration
- insight and understanding
- cure
- self-actualization
- personality change
- discovery of meaning and transcendental experience
- systemic, organisational or social change.

GOOD COUNSELLORS

See also: Core conditions, Effectiveness of counselling, Mistakes, Psychological type, Referral

Ideas about 'good counsellors' are usually expressed in terms of the personal qualities of the counsellor, although, from the client's point of view, a good counsellor tends to be one he or she likes and feels comfortable with. Perhaps the most likely characteristics of good counsellors are the 'core qualities' emphasised in client- or person-centred counselling: empathy, respect and genuineness. Brenner (1982) suggested five qualities: empathy; composure; readiness to discuss everything ('Open, precise communication about each topic that the client introduces – directly or indirectly – is the heart and soul of successful psychotherapy and counselling' (p7)); encouragement, or belief in the client's potential to function more fully; and purposefulness. The *Ethical Framework for Good Practice in Counselling and Psychotherapy* (BACP, 2007) lists virtues such as integrity, resilience, wisdom and courage. McLeod (2003a) discussed several qualities, including personal 'soundness', mastery of technique and ability to understand and work within social systems.

Reddy (1987) recognised the core qualities and suggested others but added, tartly, that 'Taken together these qualities seem more like a preparation for sainthood than for a job' (p43) and that a particularly necessary quality is 'freedom from the need for perfection' (p44). Fortunately, most clients do not expect or want perfection (e.g. Manthei, 2007). Moreover, psychological type theory suggests that counsellors of each personality type are likely to have characteristic strengths and weaknesses (Bayne, 2004). There is no one 'right' way to be a good counsellor.

Empirically, there have been a few studies of 'master therapists', as nominated by their peers. For example, Jennings and Skovholt (1999) found that those identified in this way were, among other characteristics, emotionally receptive and with excellent relationship skills. No surprises there! And such qualities may reflect why they were nominated more than why they are effective with clients.

It seems very likely that some counsellors are generally more effective than others, and that some are even generally harmful. However, the personal qualities involved are unclear so far (Lambert and Ogles, 2004; Okiishi *et al.*, 2003).

GROUP COUNSELLING

See also: Assertiveness, Referral, Self-awareness

This is a very broad term, covering all types of counselling for more than two clients. There are many different ways of running groups, but, in most cases, the idea is that the members listen to, support and challenge each other. Members can thus learn to be assertive and to experience how other people see them. They can benefit from being able to experiment with new ways of communicating and behaving in a safe environment. Members can also receive support and experience empathy, offer support and help to others (with potential benefits to self-esteem), and can learn from hearing about the difficulties and successes of others. Many clients gain a valuable experience of belonging and solidarity from being part of a group. The leader of the group may facilitate in a variety of ways: some make process comments; others facilitate interactions between the members. Some clients find it useful to move from individual to group counselling. Corey (2006) and Yalom and Leszcz (2005) have written major texts on group counselling.

HIDDEN AGENDAS

See also: Collusion, Drama triangle, Empathy, Games, Immediacy

'Hidden agenda' is the term used when somebody has a concealed purpose, of which she or he may or may not be aware. For example, clients might come for counselling with a hidden agenda of just completing a required number of sessions without really looking at themselves, or someone in a group might be there only because they are attracted to someone else in the group.

Hidden agendas can be quite disruptive, as it usually soon becomes apparent that things are not as they seem; something is not right, but the reason can be hard to discover. Empathy or immediacy may be the best ways of sorting out the impasse.

HISTORY TAKING

See also: Assessment, Evidence-based practice, Intake interviews, Psychodiagnosis

A client's history is a systematic collection of facts about the client's past and current life. Some counsellors do not take any form of client history, as they feel not only that much of the information will be irrelevant but also that it may simulate the medical model in which clients, after responding to requests for information, may expect a diagnosis and a solution to their problem. Perhaps a more important objection is that the whole process of history taking can set up a relationship pattern which interferes with establishing an effective working alliance with the client. Attitudes vary with theoretical approach. History taking is generally seen as more important in more structured approaches (e.g. transactional analysis, Adlerian therapy and some cognitive-behavioural approaches) and less so in person-centred and experiential approaches and those whose focus is more on the present and future (e.g. problem management, solution-focused therapy).

The purpose of a client history is to gather information about the client's background, especially as it may relate to current problems. A clinical history is not sought as an end in itself or because the counsellor will use it to structure the counselling or to explore and focus on the client's history. Rather, it is used as part of the overall assessment process that may help the counsellor to understand the client's presenting problem. The assumption is that current problems are precipitated and maintained by events and experiences in the client's history.

Some counsellors prefer to collect some or all of the information in a brief questionnaire that is completed by the client. Others ask clients to write autobiographies, keep personal journals, write poetry or draw lifeline diagrams (time graphs in which key life points are marked along a time continuum), all of which can be used to supplement interview data.

Various kinds of information can be obtained during a more formal history taking; a list of areas which might be addressed includes:

- identification and contact/biographical data
- presenting problem(s)
- previous counselling/psychiatric help
- education/work history
- health
- social history
- key developmental experiences
- family, marital and sexual history.

The sequence in which this information is obtained in the interview is important. Generally, the interviewer begins with the least threatening topics and leaves the more sensitive areas until nearer the end of the session when there is likely to be a greater degree of rapport. The nature of the presenting problem will determine the extent and depth to which each area is covered with each client.

HOLIDAYS

See also: Boundaries, Burnout, Contract, negotiating a, Stress, Suicide

We suggest giving your clients as much notice of your holidays as you reasonably can, being clear about how long you will be away and what arrangements need to be made for 're-entry' into counselling when you get back. If you will be away for long, your clients may like you to arrange for them to see a colleague meanwhile. A phone number where they can contact someone else is also helpful. Their counsellor's holiday can be a difficult time for clients. Clients with suicidal ideas are more likely to act on them during holidays and breaks from counselling. It is wise to discuss this with such clients and try to agree strategies by which they can access support, perhaps developing a contract to cover the period of the break.

HOMEWORK

See also: Bibliotherapy, Brainstorming, Dyslexia, Exercises, Imagery, Life-space diagram, Psychological type, Thoughts, Writing (expressive)

The term 'homework' refers to specific activities that clients undertake to complete between counselling sessions. Some counsellors prefer to call these activities tasks, assignments, practice or work between sessions (Feltham and Dryden, 2006). Homework is an integral feature of cognitive-behavioural approaches to counselling and, in particular, the brief therapies. It is not, however, exclusive to these approaches and can encourage clients to recognise their own ability to initiate change and to make connections between counselling and the rest of their lives. Trying out new behaviours may also consolidate learning and reinforce commitment to change. The various types of homework are listed below:

- **Reading (bibliotherapy):** the client may be invited to read about some aspect of counselling theory or about someone else's experience and ways of dealing with the client's problem.

- **Writing:** this may be anything, from a very simple account of what the client wants from counselling, or a description of a particular situation or experience, to a full life story. Writing may also take the form of lists: of things to do, of issues or problems, of things the client is afraid of or anxious about. Making lists may be a way of generating ideas or brainstorming ways of coping more effectively with a problem. Another form of writing is a letter to or from a real or imagined person. A letter to a real person is not usually sent to that person but is used as a vehicle for exploration or catharsis.

- **Diagrams:** clients might prepare a life-space diagram or genogram.

- **Questionnaires:** these might include self-descriptive checklists, evaluation questionnaires, or inventories designed to elicit specific information, e.g. psychological type, anxiety or depression inventories.

- **Recording:** this is a written form of monitoring the occurrence of particular situations, feelings or behaviours. It may be done by keeping a diary or daily log and may also incorporate rating scales to record levels of anxiety or other feelings, or evaluations of progress.

- **Practical exercises:** these may involve the client in trying out a new or different activity or behaviour, such as some kind of physical exercise, being more assertive in a particular way, initiating a dialogue with a particular person or implementing a rehearsed action to interrupt negative self-talk or obsessive behaviour. It may also involve the use of relaxation exercises.

- **Creative exercises:** these may involve writing short poems, drawing or painting pictures or collages of special significance to the client. They are brought to a session and explored with the counsellor. Some clients may be able to use guided imagery and visualisation rehearsed during the session.

The following guidelines are adapted from Feltham and Dryden (2006):

- Explain the rationale behind any task.
- Avoid appearing to 'set homework'; negotiate and encourage the client to offer alternative ideas and modifications.
- Make sure that the task relates directly to the client's problem.
- Listen for and challenge any ambivalence and encourage commitment.
- Take the client's abilities and circumstances into account.
- Discuss when, where and how the client will attempt the task.
- Establish with the client the criteria for evaluating the outcome.
- Explore any possible obstacles.
- Help clients to prepare by mentally rehearsing what they are going to do.
- Emphasise that, whether clients feel that they do it well or badly or do not actually do it at all, something valuable is likely to be gained from discussing their experience.
- Before the end of the session, check that clients really do understand what to do and why they are doing it.

At the next session, it is usually essential to follow-up the task:

- Discuss what has happened.
- Discuss any reasons for not attempting the task.
- Explore what happened if the task was attempted but not completed.
- Invite clients to take increasing responsibility for setting their own tasks.

Feltham and Dryden also advise that counsellors might well learn how to help clients with homework assignments by first setting some for themselves!

HOOKED

See also: Challenging, Drama triangle, Emotions, Games, Process, Transference

This rather jargonistic term is used in an interactive sense when the 'process' of one person catches – or hooks into – the 'process' of another person. This is most clearly seen in the drama triangle or in very emotional interactions when the emotion aroused seems out of proportion to the incident. It is also sustained in a compulsive way. For example, if someone is in a Victim role, others try to do too much for them or get angry with them, thus getting 'hooked' into their process. If you avoid being hooked, you can encourage other people to develop their own sense of worth and self-esteem, and to free themselves, at least to some extent, from their self-defeating pattern.

HOT FLUSHES

See also: Ageing, Giving information, Immediacy, Mindfulness, Self-disclosure, Stress

Frost (2006) discussed the problem for counsellors of having hot flushes during counselling. The risks include the client thinking that you are embarrassed or anxious – and therefore not 'containing' them – and your being distracted. Frost experimented, apprehensively, with telling her clients and found that their responses were helpfully revealing (about them) and were an opportunity to say to some clients that she was not too shocked by what they said, and that counsellors should be open to discussing anything.

There is only a little formal research on hot flushes at work (Frost, 2006; Reynolds, 1999) and it suggests that stress and anxiety increase their occurrence, and that therefore relaxation exercises may help, as well as such measures as opening windows, not drinking tea and coffee, and freezer packs under loose-fitting clothes. Verbally, the best options seem to be including the information that you are menopausal as part of the contract (and saying why as part of explaining the nature of counselling) or self-disclosing if a client says something or reacts nonverbally when you have a hot flush (see Immediacy).

In terms of physiology, it may be useful to know that body temperature can rise by up to 3 degrees Fahrenheit during hot flushes and the person may sweat profusely and feel very uncomfortable.

HUMOUR

See also: Challenging, Empathy, Immediacy

Clients who use a lot of humour, who try to 'entertain' you, who laugh too much at difficult situations, or who make too many jokes about themselves and their experiences, may be communicating an inability or reluctance to face difficult circumstances openly. We suggest treating excessive displays of humour, or hostile humour, with caution. You may need to confront or challenge your clients with their behaviour and explore what it might mean for them. This does not, of course, mean that every joke or laugh need be treated as a 'cover-up'.

As a counsellor, using humour can be useful to offer a new perspective: seeing the absurd aspect of something and thereby gaining some control over it. However, too much or inappropriate humour can deflect the client from exploring difficult or painful experiences.

HUNCHES

See: Challenging, Intuition

ILLNESS/DISABILITY

See: Multiculturalism

IMAGERY

See also: Exercises

Many schools of counselling use imagery in some form or another to supplement or bypass words or the 'thinking' mind (Hall *et al.*, 2006; Payne, 2000). For example, in psychosynthesis counselling it is used to integrate subpersonalities and heal past traumas, to help a client deal with his or her inner world. In CBT, imagery is used to help clients recreate past situations and thus access related negative beliefs, which can then be challenged; to rehearse new ways of behaving; in relaxation training; to prepare for change; to manage pain; and so on.

Imagery is not recommended for people who have a severe mental illness or who find it difficult to create images (Payne, 2000). Other practical guidelines are to warn participants that strong emotional reactions may be experienced and to end gently and positively, referring to feeling alert and refreshed. Hall *et al.* (2006) similarly emphasise the importance of the counselling relationship, the role of trust and the pitfalls of interpretation.

People who visualise weakly or not at all may *feel* people, objects and scenes in their minds instead. Most people do both. Those who do not visualise can practise it if they wish and may develop the ability quickly. Use a simple image at first, for example a candle; study it closely, then close your eyes and see how long you can 'hold it'. If the ability to visualise does not develop, the imagery exercises can be tried in a feeling way.

Lazarus (1989) outlined six ways in which imagery can be used:

- anti-future shock imagery (preparing oneself for a feared future event)
- associated imagery (using imagery to track unpleasant feelings)
- aversive imagery (using an unpleasant image to help counter an unwanted behaviour)
- goal rehearsal or coping imagery (using images of being able to reach a goal or manage a situation)
- positive imagery (using pleasant images for relaxation purposes)
- the step-up technique (exaggerating a feared situation and using imagery to cope with it).

The following exercise is one which uses the client's imagination to create a state of relaxation. The counsellor says:

> I would like you to sit as comfortably as possible and close your eyes [short pause]. Imagine yourself in a beautiful walled garden at the time of the year you like the most [short pause]. As you are walking around you notice a door in one of the walls of the garden and as you walk closer towards it you see it is a rather splendid arch-shaped wooden

door with a large black wrought-iron handle [short pause]. You decide to open the door and, as you go through the door, you arrive in a wonderful special place [short pause] somewhere safe [short pause] that only you know about [short pause] your own very special place.

The counsellor says nothing for a few minutes, leaving the client to gain the benefits of the exercise. Then, the exercise continues:

You now slowly begin to say goodbye to your special place and in your own time make your way back to the door [short pause]. Now you go back into the garden and close the door firmly behind you, knowing that your special place is always there for you whenever you want to return to it [short pause]. In your own time, walk slowly around the garden and open your eyes feeling alert and refreshed.

IMMEDIACY

See also: Assertiveness, Challenging, Self-awareness

Immediacy can be defined as 'direct, mutual talk': for example, 'I see us as going round in circles and I'm confused. I wonder if you feel the same way.' Immediacy is about sharing something of your own thoughts, feelings and process with the client as a way of enabling discussion about some aspect of your relationship, the work you are doing or the communication between you. As such it is an expression of the counsellor's willingness to be genuine or congruent in the relationship. It should be used when there is a likelihood that it will be of benefit to the client. You should communicate in a way that is appropriately tentative and does not impose your perspective on the client. Skilled use of immediacy maintains focus on the client's issues and agenda and does not divert attention onto the counsellor, and it can be a way of acknowledging a sticking point, discomfort, or resistance and enabling discussion (Egan, 2007). The following checklist defines immediacy in more detail. It is a set of guidelines rather than a prescription.

- Decide whether you have a sufficiently strong relationship with your client.
- Give some indication that you want to talk about some aspect of the relationship between you.
- Describe (rather than evaluate).
- 'Own' what you say by using personal pronouns (I, my).
- Use the present tense; emphasise the 'here and now' (e.g. 'At this moment I feel …').
- Say something about some combination of:
  - how you feel
  - how you sense the other person is feeling
  - what you think is happening between you

- how you think it might be affecting what you are trying to achieve together.
- Ask for your client's view, and listen carefully to the response.

INSURANCE

See also: Complaints, Ethical Framework, Legal system

Indemnity insurance policies offer indemnity for liability at law for damages – claimant's costs and expenses in respect of claims for breach of professional duties made against a counsellor as a result of alleged neglect, error or omission in the provision of counselling services. Some policies also provide cover for potential liabilities incurred outside the counsellor–client relationship, including approved research projects, teaching or seminars and written reports. However, most policies list exclusions from legal liability.

Under 'Guidance for good practice', the BACP (2002) states: 'Practitioners are strongly encouraged to ensure that their work is adequately covered by insurance for professional indemnity and liability.' For current recommendations of insurance brokers, contact a membership organisation like the BACP. Counsellors who work in the NHS or in schools or colleges should check whether they have indemnity cover from their authority or organisation. This may depend on whether 'counselling' is specifically mentioned in their contract of employment.

The case against

Mearns (1993) first pointed out that so far there have been no significant claims in the UK against counsellors for professional malpractice, negligence, errors or omissions, which as far as we know is still the case. The key concept is 'reasonable behaviour'. However, he had other, less obvious, reasons for regarding indemnity insurance 'with considerable derision':

- If insurance exists, claims are more likely.
- As a consequence, insurers tend to advise not saying that you are insured or admitting responsibility, which is dishonest.
- Indemnity insurance assumes that counsellors are *responsible for* their clients (as a medical practitioner is for a patient), rather than responsible *to* their clients.

INTAKE INTERVIEWS

See also: Assessment, History taking

When an intake interview, sometimes called an initial assessment interview, is carried out, it is viewed as primarily informational rather than therapeutic. For this reason, and/or because it is sometimes thought that an experienced or more senior person should be responsible for initial assessment and subsequent allocation to the most appropriate counsellor, the intake interview can be conducted by someone other than the counsellor who will work with the client.

INTEGRATION AND ECLECTICISM

See also: Common factors, Counselling, Personality, Theories of counselling

There has been a strong trend towards integrationist and eclectic approaches to counselling for many years, and this seems likely to continue (Lambert, 2004; McLeod, 2003a; O'Brien and Houston, 2007). In broad terms, eclectic counsellors choose the best techniques and ideas from a variety of sources and may do so by applying their judgement and experience in the moment, or according to a system, while integrative counsellors try to form a coherent, harmonious whole either from combining two or more theories or parts of theories or by having an integrating framework within which a range of approaches and techniques can be applied (e.g. the integrative process model described in the entry on Counselling). The idea of 'common factors' is, in various forms, an attempt at theoretical integration.

The merits of 'pure' approaches versus integration or eclecticism are arguable, as is how best to develop a personal integration (Horton, 2006; McLeod, 2003a). Horton (2006, p236) argued that most counsellors, including those who espouse pure models, 'tend gradually to develop their own personalized conceptual systems and individual styles of working'.

INTERPRETATION

See also: Challenging, Power

Different theoretical approaches take different positions on the issue of interpretation, which might be defined as sharing your own version of the meaning of some aspect of the client's experience. From a humanistic perspective, this is generally to be avoided, and exploration should take place from within the client's frame of reference or by encouraging clients to try out other perspectives for themselves with skilled facilitative interventions (see Challenging). However, from the psychodynamic point of view, certainly historically, interpretation has been one of the cornerstones of the therapist's approach and a core way of trying to bring unconscious or unacknowledged material into awareness.

This has been criticised as contributing heavily to an uneven power relationship and casting the therapist in an 'expert' role, telling clients how to make sense of their experience. Many psychodynamically oriented therapists now attempt to use interpretation in a more tentative way than might have been the tradition and owned as one possible perspective for the client to consider.

We consider that interpretation should be approached with great caution if it is to be employed at all. You need to be clear that the possible meaning you are intending to share with the client is relevant to him or her (and does not arise from your own issues, biases, or values), that it will not overshadow any emerging insight that the client may be developing for him- or herself and that it is owned as your own interpretation, not presented as definitive fact. Interpretation should be an offer to the client and a basis for consideration. It should open up discussion and reflection, rather than close it down.

INTUITION

See also: First impressions, Imagery, Mindfulness, Psychological type, Self-awareness

Intuitions can be defined as 'insights without deliberate effort or thought'. They can be encouraged, but not summonsed, by being relaxed and receptive (Charles, 2004; Claxton, 1997, 1998). Claxton suggested that sometimes the best strategy is 'daring to wait and to drift' (1998, p219). Charles recommended several ways of increasing intuition (in everyone, including the 'naturally intuitive'), for example developing an interest in the arts, sensory awareness exercises; and several applications in counselling, such as meditating to prepare for clients and taking time between sessions to 'ruminate'.

However, although intuition has been shown to be superior in some situations to conscious, analytic problem solving, it is also fallible. Counsellors relying on intuition risk introducing their own biases and preconceptions; operating from their own frame of reference; being unable to provide clients with a clear rationale for their interventions; missing opportunities for insight to be gained by analysing hunches and 'gut feelings'; becoming undisciplined in their practice; and disempowering clients by appearing as a therapeutic 'guru' or 'wizard'. Therefore, counsellors need to analyse their interventions and therapeutic strategies as well as develop their intuition: to treat their intuitions as meaningful, but to check them out.

JOURNALS, ACADEMIC AND APPLIED

See also: Continuing professional development, Professional development, Research

The main UK journals for counsellors are *The British Journal of Guidance and Counselling*, *Counselling Psychology Quarterly* and *Therapy Today*. There are also useful articles in many psychology journals.

KISSING

See: Nonverbal communication, Touch

LEGAL SYSTEM

See also: Complaints

Becoming involved with the legal system is likely to be a daunting experience and possibility for most counsellors. Bond and Sandhu (2005) discuss aspects of appearing in court (e.g. replying to solicitors' letters, appearing as a witness, writing reports for clients and the courts, and fees) calmly and systematically. In a wider-ranging book on legal issues, counselling and psychotherapy, Jenkins (2007) does *not* see the law as primarily a threat to counsellors, and he argues that ethics rather than the law should drive therapeutic practice.

LENGTH OF SESSIONS

See also: Boundaries, Contract, negotiating a, Time boundaries

Traditionally, sessions are 50 minutes long, and most counsellors have sessions of 50 minutes or an hour. The '50-minute hour' gives you a 10-minute break between clients if you have a full day of counselling, although many counsellors do not have practices that are as tightly organised as this.

It is, however, possible to contract for different session lengths. Some brief therapists prefer to work in short, focused sessions of perhaps half an hour or occasionally even less. Work with young people, or specific clients who have difficulty maintaining attention, may be more effective in shorter sessions. Some humanistic forms of counselling, particularly those involving a lot of body work, tend to work best in longer sessions of one and a half to three hours, or even all day. On occasion it may be useful to contract in advance for specific sessions to be longer, even when working with a norm of 50 minutes, for example if some cathartic work is planned. Most counsellors and their clients seem to find 50-minute or one-hour sessions about right.

It is important to be clear with your clients very early on (probably in your initial interview) about the length of sessions, and to stick to your agreement – neither letting sessions drift past the agreed time nor finishing early. If clients are late for sessions, they should not expect to be able to carry on past their allotted time other than in very exceptional circumstances. The way you use time is part of the way you protect boundaries in your counselling practice. Learning to use time effectively and function within appropriate boundaries is part of what some clients need from their counselling.

However, an alternative is to work with individual clients to discover what is best for them. Mountford (2005) discussed his experience of working in this way: he found that a good length of session for each client emerged naturally; his fee was calculated 'like a taxi, for the time actually spent with me'. He concluded:

> I find it easier to see four clients in a day and offer them, say, eight
> hours of counselling between them than see eight clients for 50
> minutes. What's more, because I am allowing room for the relationship
> to evolve in an unlimited way, and because I am allowing sufficient

time for process, I find the longer sessions a more satisfying way to work. (Mountford, 2005, p45)

LIFE-SPACE DIAGRAM

See also: Drawings, Emotions, Exercises, Life-space diagram using stones, Questions

The life-space diagram is a method of helping clients explore and clarify their relationships with others. One advantage is its immediate visual impact, another is its flexibility. Several steps are suggested:

1. Briefly describe the purpose of the exercise and invite the client to try it as a kind of experiment.

2. On a large piece of paper, although A4 would be adequate, make a list of all the people who in one way or another have real significance in the client's life. Some clients feel uncomfortable about writing while someone is watching: if so, it is a good idea for you to offer to do the writing, following the client's instructions and checking whether or not you are doing it correctly. Another practical point is that some clients equate significance with positive or friendly, or people with whom they have frequent contact. It may be necessary to explain that people they dislike, whom they hardly ever see or who are dead, can still be significant for them and can therefore be included in the diagram.

3. Print the word 'ME', which represents the client, in a small circle in the centre of the page.

4. Consider each person from the list in turn, placing them as near to (even actually touching) or as far from the ME as the client wants. Each has his or her own circle. The relative distance of each person from ME may represent the importance, closeness or intensity of feelings that the client has towards the individual. The client decides what the distance or space means. The visual impact can be heightened by joining the other circles to the ME with a broken or continuous line of varying thickness. This may add some meaning for the client. A thick heavy line may represent a particularly strong attachment, whereas a broken line may represent someone who is no longer alive, yet the client still feels close to them. It is important that the client decides the order and whom to include or leave out. This in itself may be worth exploring with the client.

As each person is added to the diagram, you can encourage the client to talk about the relationship with that person, for example by asking:

*   What do you think or feel about this person?
*   What do you want or expect from the person?
*   What do you imagine the person thinks or feels about you?

- What do you imagine the person wants or expects from you?

In a diagram which does not involve many people, a summary of the main thoughts or feelings could be written next to the appropriate circle.

As the life-space diagram nears completion, you could stimulate further exploration and discussion with a series of prompts, appropriate for the client and the presenting problem. For example:

- As you added new people did you want to move others nearer or further away from you?

- Is your relationship with anyone changing? Is that person moving closer or further away from you? What is happening between you at the present time?

- What might the diagram have looked like a month, a year or several years ago? What has caused any changes? What do you think it might look like in the future?

- How exact have you been in placing family and friends? Are they, or should they be, together in groups or more spread out, when you look at it carefully?

- Do you rely on certain kinds of relationships, e.g. friendship or work relationships? Does authority or power play a part in any of the relationships? What effect does this have?

- How do you feel about the way you are surrounded by your relationships? Is it a comfortable picture? How far is it a self-portrait? How would you like it to be different? What would you like to change? Can you see how you might take a step towards achieving any of those changes?

Some clients feel really good about what their life-space diagram represents for them. They may have many people touching the ME and have difficulty getting everybody they wanted close enough to them. However, for other clients the exercise causes great pain and distress. When they look at their diagram, they see in concrete visual form what at some level they know but have not wanted or been able to admit. The diagram may include very few people with none touching the ME and all spaced together around the edge of the paper. The empty space around the ME is seen and felt. It is important to be sensitive to the client's feelings and not to underestimate the power of this exercise.

LIFE-SPACE DIAGRAM USING STONES

See also: Drawings, Emotions, Exercises, Life-space diagram, Questions

An alternative form of the life-space diagram uses small stones. The next time you go to a beach where it is legal to do so, make a collection of pebbles of different shapes, sizes, textures and colours.

The exercise is approached in much the same way as the life-space diagram except that, instead of drawing names on a sheet of paper, pebbles are used to represent the people. You start by inviting the client to select a pebble to represent him- or herself. The pebble is placed in the centre of a piece of white paper or cloth and then other stones are positioned around the client's own stone to represent his or her life space. Each stone is carefully selected so that in some way it represents the particular person. The size, shape or colour of the pebble may be given a particular symbolic meaning by the client. You can encourage the client to talk about why each stone was chosen: the colourful and attractive personality, the big and strong personality, the small and dull personality, the beautifully rounded yet flawed personality.

An advantage of using stones or pebbles is that they can be held; their smoothness, roughness, size and shape provide a potent kinetic experience. They can also be moved about to change or adjust their position in relationship to others as new 'people' are added. Although the purpose and approach to the exercise are very similar to those of drawing a life-space diagram, the experience for the client can be very different. There are obviously many variations of this exercise, for example using different objects such as coins, buttons or the contents of a handbag. What is most important is that you recognise the potential impact of the exercise and allow plenty of time for it. The exercise is complete when the client wants to stop or has little to say. Although the exercise is usually part of the first phase of counselling, it can safely be done only when you have established a good relationship.

LITERAL DESCRIPTION

See also: Catharsis, Exercises

When clients talk about or 'talk through' painful and difficult experiences, they are naturally drawn into telling their story in the past tense. They also usually avoid aspects of the experience, search for reasons, explanations or justifications for their emotions or behaviour and are sometimes circular and repetitive, with a sense of getting nowhere. In these circumstances it can be helpful to encourage a client to intensify and expand their account, through literal description or 'evocative unfolding' (Kennedy-Moore and Watson, 1999).

The client is invited to describe the past experience in the present tense, to try to relive it in as much detail as possible, recalling colours, sounds, smells, position of objects, people, movements, and so on. Clients typically drift back into the past tense, often interpreting or evaluating what had happened, and you need to remind them to describe it as if it is happening now, or invite them to say it again in the present tense. For example, if the client says, 'Then I shouted at him', you might ask him or her to say, 'I'm shouting at him.'

Literal description is potentially a very powerful intervention and should be used with great care and sensitivity by counsellors who have experienced it themselves. It is best approached by asking clients if they would like to try something – a kind of experiment – to see if it would help them to get in touch with their feelings about what happened and to break through or disengage the storytelling pattern.

LITIGATION

See: Complaints, Insurance, Legal system

LOSS

See also: Bereavement, Crisis counselling, Crying, Emotions, Post-traumatic stress disorder, Stress, Suicide

Loss is a commonly presented counselling theme. Bereavement is a particular case of loss, but many of the principles which apply to bereavement (such as Worden's tasks model, 2004) can also be applied to more general cases of loss.

Loss takes many forms: for example, loss of youth, of children who leave home, of a job or status, of faith, of lifestyle, of friendship, of property, of a part of the body. In existential counselling, loss is one of the main themes that a counsellor looks for in a client's story (van Deurzen Smith, 2001). Loss can affect more than one individual: for example, major disasters may affect families, friends and whole communities. Many factors influence an individual's experience and ability to cope with loss. They include resilience, family background, hardiness, social support, and characteristics of the event (e.g. its predictability, intensity, how suddenly it happened, and its magnitude).

Wortman and Silver (1989, 2001) and Bonanno (2004) discuss several related myths about coping with loss: for example that distress and working through are necessary; that recovery or resolution are inevitable; that resilience in the face of loss and trauma is rare or pathological, callous or narcissistic; and that 'grief work' – 'working through' memories, thoughts and emotions about a loss – is usually desirable and effective. They stress the great variability in people's reactions to loss; on Wortman and Silver's review of the evidence, about 50 per cent of people do not experience intense anxiety, depression or grief after a serious loss; they continue to be psychologically well adjusted. Thirty per cent of people feel depressed and distressed after a serious loss; 18 per cent are 'chronic grievers' and 2 per cent appear well adjusted at first but are distressed a year later (Wortman and Silver, 1989) . Moreover, positive emotions may be experienced as well as negative ones, and people are sometimes surprised by how well they are coping (Bonanno, 2004).

Positive transitions can also involve an element of loss, as even desired changes often involve letting go of some things which are valued. In some cases, moving away and breaking off old friendships may be the only way that the client can maintain progress. The client then experiences a period of loss as he or she adapts to the new situation and comes to terms with ending friendships which may have begun in childhood.

Sugarman (2004) describes a general model for life transitions, which suggests that (despite significant individual differences and the fact that the phases overlap and repeat themselves) there is a generally recognisable sequence of responses accompanying a wide range of transitions, which includes elements of loss. The initial phases are concerned with attachment to the past, before a 'letting go' phase, which is followed by gradual adaptation to the new situation.

There are many other similar models relating to specific situations, and various 'pathways' to coping with them (e.g. Bonanno, 2004; Maddi, 2005).

LOVE (STYLES OF LOVING)

See also: Challenging, Emotions, Frameworks, Multiculturalism, Sexual attraction

> I do not like to work with patients who are in love. (Yalom, 1989, p15)

Lee's approach (e.g. 1988) to romantic love seems the most in harmony with integrative counselling and has some unusual strengths. For example, he distinguishes several kinds or styles of love and, in contrast to other typologies of love, sees all the styles as equally 'true'. This can be a challenging idea. His theory is also flexible as well as pluralistic: most people have a preferred style but each of us can love different partners in different styles or the same partner in different styles at different times. Thus, it suggests answers to questions like 'Does real love appear suddenly or gradually?', 'Do I love her more than she loves me?' and 'Do I really love him?'

Some key words for each style of loving (summarised from Lee, 1988) are:

- **eros** – ideal beauty, immediate physical attraction, delight
- **ludus** – playful, free of commitment, avoid intensity
- **mania** – feverish, obsessive, jealous
- **storge** – friendly, companionable, affectionate
- **pragma** – practical, realistic, compatible
- **storgic eros** – friendly intensity
- **ludic eros** – playful intensity
- **storgic ludus** – friendly and playful.

MARKETING

See also: Administration, Advertising, Fees, Private practice, Values

Marketing involves matching the resources being offered by the individual counsellor or counselling agency to those being sought by the client. The first part of any successful marketing strategy is to undertake market research: the process of finding out what people want. In business terms, this information helps to define the type of services offered (the product range); how best to communicate information about such services (advertising and publicity); how to present such services (professional image); and what fees to charge (McMahon *et al.*, 2005). Another way of expressing this is based on Townsend (1984):

- What are you selling? (What is *different* about it or you?)
- Who might want to buy it?
- How do you make contact with them?
- What is the fee?

One of the biggest challenges for counsellors in private practice is ensuring a regular 'supply' of clients. However, some counsellors (probably many) find the idea of selling themselves unattractive and consider the view that we all sell ourselves in one way or another all the time too cynical. It may help to think of it not as 'selling' but as 'telling people what I do', and then finding a way to do this that feels right for you.

MENTAL HEALTH AND MENTAL ILLNESS

See also: Anxiety, Contraindications for brief counselling, Depression, DSM-IV, Goals, Personality disorders, Psychodiagnosis, Referral, Teams (multidisciplinary)

With recent increases in the provision of counselling services via GP practices and referrals, counsellors are probably more likely than ever to be working with clients who have been, or might be, diagnosed as suffering from mental health problems. This can create philosophical difficulties in reconciling different approaches and working practices between professionals operating a 'medical model' (symptoms – diagnosis – treatment) and counsellors and psychotherapists who may be more inclined towards a positive health/wellbeing-based model and a holistic approach. There may also be differences in expectations in relation to sharing of information and confidentiality. Counsellors and psychotherapists can work effectively in collaboration with doctors and other professions allied to medicine, but it is helpful to ensure that there is clarity of expectations and of professional boundaries, record keeping, etc. when working in such a context. It is also helpful to have a working knowledge of the medical/psychiatric perspective on mental health and mental illness in order to appraise critically its value in individual cases, and to be able to communicate effectively with other professions. The book by Daines *et al.* (2007) is a useful resource for developing counsellors' awareness of these issues, and it would be instructive to familiarise yourself with DSM-IV as a way of understanding how psychiatric diagnoses are arrived at.

The person-centred model for psychological wellbeing can provide an alternative framework for understanding and working with mental health issues. This assumes that we all have an inherent tendency towards positive growth and fulfilment of potential, but that influences from the environment, relationships where positive regard is conditional, and conflicted or 'no-win' situations can frustrate this tendency and lead to psychological distress or dysfunction. The imposition of 'conditions of worth' ('you must be … in order to be accepted or valued') by the environment in general or by significant others can cause a splitting or incongruity between a person's concept of who he or she is, should be or want to be and how he or she experiences him- or herself on a moment-by-moment basis. This incongruity is seen as leading to depression, anxiety, psychosis and other psychological problems. Joseph and Worsley (2005) address the application of person-centred ideas to mental health and mental illness in detail.

There is increasing evidence that counselling can be helpful to clients who might traditionally have been treated by psychiatric services (see, for example, the entries on Anxiety and Depression). While a counselling approach may not be able directly to remove symptoms of mental illness and may not be feasible at times of extreme disturbance, it may be extremely helpful in addressing some of the underlying or associated issues in clients' lives, or in helping them to develop coping strategies for persistent symptoms, especially if care is taken to assess the client's needs and agree clear and realistic goals.

The benefits or otherwise of diagnostic labelling may be a useful topic to explore with clients. Some clients feel that psychiatric labels (such as 'obsessive-compulsive disorder', 'schizophrenia', 'personality disorder', etc.) are stigmatising and that they would prefer to be treated as a whole person without reference to diagnostic manuals (such as DSM-IV). Others find some comfort in the recognition that what they are experiencing is also shared by others, has a name, and that there are, perhaps, existing support networks that they can access. We suggest that where such issues arise they should be discussed openly with clients, and the therapeutic approach negotiated on the basis of the client's preferences. Helping clients to develop a framework for understanding their experience can be an important step in dealing with mental health problems, so that realistic goals can be established and action plans arrived at. Such a framework can be the medical model, or the cognitive-behavioural, or be based on a humanistic model of wellbeing, or indeed on a number of other perspectives (spiritual, interpersonal, skills, etc.). What is important is that individual clients have a framework which enables them to feel empowered, able to make choices, and take some control in their lives.

METAPHORS IN COUNSELLING

See also: Emotions, Empathy, Intuition, Questions, Self-disclosure

Metaphors are very common in everyday language, usually without our being aware of them, and they are central to the way we think, make sense of the world and make decisions (Tompkins *et al.*, 2005). They can also sometimes express emotions and beliefs better than more straightforward terms. If a client says, 'I feel like a coiled spring', this may be clearer than 'angry' and 'longing to do something'. Alternatively, metaphors are a step towards finding the emotion words that fit. Either way, a collaborative approach to concrete aspects of the client's metaphor and its meaning seems most effective: for example, 'Can I stop you? I wonder if it would be worth talking a bit more about the image you just used? For example, what does X look like?' Commonplace expressions, such as 'I feel like I'm in a tunnel', can have individual and useful meanings.

A key principle is that it is the client's metaphor, however vivid your own reaction! However, it may also be helpful to share your own interpretation or your own metaphor (see entries on Intuition and Self-disclosure). Metaphors can also be very subtle, or 'implicit'. Tompkins *et al.* (2005) give the example of a client who says, 'I need to find a purpose in my life'. The implicit metaphor there is 'find', rather than 'figure out', 'explore', 'uncover', etc. Tompkins *et al.* (2005) list several ways of using metaphors in counselling, depending on the counsellor's way of working, but concentrate on 'clean language questions' to help clients explore their metaphor. These are open questions which do not 'contaminate' the client's experience with your own metaphors and assumptions (see the Clean Language website). Examples are 'What kind of X?'; 'Is there anything else about X?'; 'Where is X?'; 'What happens just before?'; 'Next?'; 'What would you like to happen?'; 'Where does X come from?'

Two or three clean questions are sometimes enough, but Tompkins *et al.* recommend continuing to help clients develop their understanding of the attributes of their metaphor and the relationship between them 'for longer than you might think' and following:

> the natural direction of the metaphor as it evolves. While the nature of a client's metaphor may lead you down a few cul de sacs or round a number of circles, in the end the metaphor contains the seeds of its own transformation. (Tompkins *et al.*, 2005, p35)

Examples of a transformation are an insight or a nonverbal solution.

There is some research supporting the significance of metaphors. For example, McMullen and Conway (1996) found that metaphors for self-change, especially those for the whole self, were associated with positive change in counselling, and successful therapy has been related to use by counsellor and client of a few core metaphors (Angus, 1996).

METAPHORS FOR STYLES OF COUNSELLING

See also: Good counsellors, Psychological type, Relationship between counsellor and client, Theories of counselling

Metaphors can be used to describe general approaches to counselling. Which (if any) of the metaphors below is closest to your approach to counselling, and which are definitely not relevant to you?

They are adapted here for counsellors from the list of metaphors and questions for counsellor trainers provided by Inskipp (1996, pp87–88):

- **Guru:** does a guru always disempower?
- **Clown:** do you keep a clown hidden as not appropriate for counselling? Might it be useful sometimes?
- **Earth mother:** are you a safe harbour? Do you support more than challenge?
- **Patriarch:** do you enjoy power and creating order without being oppressive?
- **Whore:** do you use seduction to encourage clients to take risks, to empower or disempower?
- **Warrior:** do you enjoy conflict and challenge? Can you find the warrior when needed?

- **Magician:** the counselling is so beautifully done, clients are entranced, but are they empowered?

Other metaphors for style of counselling include terrier, teacher, surgeon, detective and companion.

MINDFULNESS

See also: Freewriting, Relaxation

Mindfulness is a technique in which a person becomes intentionally aware of his or her thoughts and actions in the present moment, nonjudgmentally. It plays a central role in Buddhism, with Right Mindfulness being the seventh element of the Noble Eightfold Path, the practice of which is considered a prerequisite for developing insight and wisdom. In a secular context, mindfulness is attracting increasing interest among Western psychiatrists as a nonpharmacological means of treating anxiety and depression (Gunarata, 2002; Hollon *et al.*, 2006; Segal *et al.*, 2002). By observing inner reality more closely, the person finds that happiness is not a quality brought about by a change in outer circumstances, but rather that it starts with releasing attachment to thoughts, thereby releasing 'automatic' reactions towards pleasant and unpleasant situations or feelings.

Many active people think the only way to release tension is by doing something: sport, cleaning, etc. This is true to some extent; however, we all need to find stillness at times too, to foster stability in the emotional brain. So people who are more active might need a little longer to reconnect to this state but will recognise it with relief and pleasure. This happens to most people if they give it a few tries. Mindfulness can be practised simply by doing something and totally connecting to it – staying in a state of awareness with it: when you walk, just walk; when you eat, just eat. The joy of the present moment is the time when our life is actually happening.

Mindfulness meditation comes in a variety of forms. One example of mindfulness is mentally to give a verbal label to each in-breath and out-breath during sitting meditation. So, each time one breathes in, one thinks 'rising', and each time one breathes out, one thinks 'falling'. In this type of meditation, the breath serves as an anchor which the practitioner uses to bring his or her awareness back to the present moment.

By residing more frequently in the present moment, practitioners begin to see both the inner and outer aspects of reality. Inner reality may unfold as one sees that the mind is continually chattering with commentary or judgment. By noticing that the mind is continually making commentary, one has the ability to notice carefully those thoughts – and decide if those thoughts have value. Most often, mindful people realise that 'thoughts are just thoughts' – the thoughts themselves have no weight. People are free to release a thought ('let it go') when they realise that the thought is not concrete reality. They are free to observe life without getting caught in the commentary.

Mindfulness does not have to be constrained to a formal meditation session. It is an activity that can be done at any time: it does not require sitting, or even focusing on the breath, but rather is done by bringing the mind to focus on what is happening in the present moment, while simply noticing the mind's usual 'commentary'. One can be mindful of the sensations in one's feet while walking, of the sound of the wind in the trees, or the feeling of soapy water while doing dishes. One can also be mindful of the mind's commentary: 'I wish I didn't have to walk any further'; 'I like the sound of the leaves rustling'; 'I wish washing dishes wasn't so boring and the soap wasn't drying out my skin', etc. Once we have noticed the mind's running commentary, we have the freedom to release those judgments: 'washing dishes: boring' may become 'washing dishes: washing dishes'. In this example, one may see that washing dishes does not have to be judged 'boring'; washing dishes is only a process of coordinating dishes with soap and water. Any activity done mindfully is a form of meditation, and mindfulness is possible practically all the time. (See the Wise Brain website.)

MIRACLE QUESTION, THE

See also: Action planning, Challenging, Goals, Questions, Scaling, Summaries and 'moving interviews forward'

The miracle question (de Shazer *et al.*, 2007) is a useful technique from solution-focused brief therapy. Various therapists have devised differing forms for this intervention, but in essence it takes the following form:

> Suppose you woke up tomorrow morning from a normal night's sleep, but overnight, without you knowing, a miracle had happened, so that the problem which brought you here had been solved [pause]. How would you become aware of this miracle? What would you notice that would begin to let you know that it had happened?

The intention here is to encourage the client to begin creating a vision of a future free of his or her problem, without becoming blocked by thinking about how this might be achieved. Additionally, it encourages thinking about specific details of a better life from within the framework of the current situation, and it may help to draw the client's attention to aspects of 'the solution' which are already present in his or her life. It is useful to encourage the client to generate some detail. Responses to the miracle question can be elaborated by asking for more detail and more specific examples of how things would be different. It can also be useful to ask what significant other people in the client's life would notice if the miracle happened. The picture generated can then form the basis for action planning or for the application of the scaling technique.

MISSED SESSIONS

See also: Administration, Assertiveness, Clients who don't come back, Contract, negotiating a, Expectations (clients'), Fees, Referral

When a client does not turn up for an appointment, you may be left wondering why and what to do. To some extent, this can be avoided by stating clearly in the contract what notice is expected and what payment is required if a client misses a session. The most straightforward situation is when clients have a regular time, pay in advance and know that if they miss a session they still pay. Other counsellors work with clients who come at varying times, who pay at the end of each session, or who may not be required to pay at all. The contract in these cases needs to be particularly clear. Whether or not to contact a client who has missed a session and how this is to be done can be discussed in supervision. Some counsellors phone clients after 15 minutes if they have not turned up, to see if they are all right or have just forgotten the session, although phoning can be intrusive, overprotective or put the client 'on the spot'. Others write a note or e-mail saying that they are sorry not to have seen the client today but hope to next time. Generally, respect for your client's autonomy means that you may not find out what has happened.

A preventive approach to reducing missed sessions was investigated by Reid *et al.* (2005) with striking results: their DNA (Did Not Attend) rate for first appointments improved from 31 per cent to 2 per cent. They achieved this by changing from offering clients a fixed day and time to offering them a choice of day and a time between 9am and 4pm.

Another useful perspective comes from a study of people's reasons for not taking up counselling appointments (Snape *et al.*, 2003): for example, many of the participants spoke about the courage it took to ask for counselling; some sought other sources of help (there was a waiting period). One of the researchers usefully contrasted the counsellor waiting for the client, and it being 'hard not to feel judgemental', with hearing the participants' 'tremendously complex and various reasons for not turning up' (Perren, 2003, p247).

MISTAKES

See also: Assertiveness, Good counsellors, Immediacy

Counsellors and psychotherapists, like all human beings, make mistakes from time to time: for example, there may be a failure to understand, a poorly chosen intervention, bad timing, a decision to adopt a particular technique or approach, a response based on one's own biases or arising from one's own issues, or any number of other choices which one makes in the course of work with a client. Within an empathic, accepting, and genuine therapeutic relationship, mistakes can be tolerated, provided that they are not too severe. If you are working in a collaborative way with a client, it should be possible, and is often useful, to acknowledge when a choice you have made has not worked out as you had hoped. You should respond with empathy for the impact this may have had on the client, be congruent about your own feelings and discuss how to move forward.

Mistakes can also have positive effects: unexpected insights can be revealed; new possibilities can emerge; the therapeutic relationship can become more 'real'. This is most likely to happen if clients are actively engaged in the process of therapeutic planning and evaluation, are able to relate to you as a collaborator in working on the problem, and trust you to have positive intentions and under-standing of their perspective, rather than seeing you as an infallible expert.

MODELS

See: Frameworks, Theories of counselling

MOTIVATIONAL INTERVIEWING

See also: Challenging, Counselling

Motivational interviewing (MI) (e.g. Miller, 1991; Miller and Rollnick, 2002) is an approach designed to help clients build commitment and reach a decision to change. The theoretical background of MI is contained in the principles of Egan (i.e. problem solving), Rogers (i.e. accurate empathy) and behavioural psychology (i.e. by changing what you do, you change what you think). Miller goes so far as to call it a non-directive approach (Miller, 1991, p54).

MI assumes that to motivate clients to change, you attempt to encourage them to make the decisions necessary to improve their life and avoid imposing change from without, as this often leads to rebellion. It therefore assumes that, unless people themselves see the need to change, no lasting change will ever be achieved.

Counsellors using MI have to be good listeners and interpreters, as they will feed back to the client in a structured and thus more potent form the reasons for change that the client has mentioned. At first, the client may be very reluctant to come forward with such information, so it is of utmost importance to read between the lines, to remember the little dissatisfactions that the client mentions and to tease out whether their importance has been undervalued.

The goal is to increase the client's intrinsic motivation, and in MI this is achieved by adhering to five general principles:

- **Express empathy:** accept people as they are and where they are. Ambivalence to change is seen as normal. The counsellor tries to elicit self-motivational statements.

- **Develop discrepancy:** 'Motivation for change is created when people perceive a discrepancy between their present behaviour and important personal goals' (Miller, 1991, p57).

- **Avoid argumentation:** start with where the client is. Avoid direct confrontation in order to avoid resistance and avoid labelling.

- **Roll with resistance:** reframe the client's statements to create a new momentum towards change. The counsellor invites the client to consider new information and perspectives. The client is actively involved in finding solutions for his or her problem.

- **Support self-efficacy:** the counsellor is an enabler to help clients to help themselves and have confidence that they can carry out the changes chosen (e.g. reduced drinking, occasional use or abstinence).

MULTICULTURALISM

See also: Ageing, Assertiveness, Autistic spectrum disorder, Dementia, Difficulties in being a client, Dyslexia, Immediacy, Personality disorders, Psychobabble, Psychological type, Specialisms in counselling

Multiculturalism emphasises a need for counsellors to be aware of and respect differences in ethnic origin, gender, social class, disability, sexual orientation, religion, age and other factors. There is a marked emphasis on inclusion and social justice. The very extensive literature on multiculturalism and counselling (e.g. d'Ardenne, 1993; Lago, 2006; O'Brien and Houston, 2007; Ponteretto, 2001; Ridley, 2005), contains numerous frameworks and models, and there is a corresponding danger of feeling overwhelmed by them and by the many multicultural factors which an 'ideal counsellor' would be familiar with and sensitive to.

One way of resolving this is to be 'curious about your clients' cultural backgrounds, not afraid to acknowledge your ignorance, and to ask about your clients' experiences of alienation within and beyond therapy. You are then half-way to dealing with the issues' (d'Ardenne, 1993, p6). Segal (1995, p66) refers to this attitude and skill as counsellors learning to 'use their own ignorance', and she gives the example of saying to a client with a disability, 'I don't know whether (you want me) to offer help or not' rather than trying to guess. She adds, 'The decision never to pretend to a client, however disabled they are, brings its own stresses, but in the long run strengthens the counselling process and the counsellor's confidence' (p66). Similarly, O'Brien and Houston suggest, pragmatically, that we should approach differences with 'respect and alertness, and at best with some knowledge' (2007, p143).

Ignorance about one's own cultural identity and associated assumptions about clients is much less reasonable. However, it is clearly desirable, up to a point, to know about a particular client's background and therefore not to ask questions about it (see entry on Specialisms). Your clients may be frustrated and impatient with this use of their time.

Another way of coping with the literature is to select those models and frameworks which seem most useful, while acknowledging that many others of value are therefore ignored. However, many of them also overlap and in addition include principles and recommendations that are part of an integrative approach to counselling anyway. We have chosen the frameworks developed by Bimrose (1996), Pedersen (1987) and Ridley (2005).

Three positions

In this framework, the traditional position is termed *Individualistic*. It emphasises the possibility of change and development for everyone, regardless of multicultural factors, and is an approach in which counselling qualities, skills and strategies are seen as generally applicable. Bimrose contrasts it with two others: the *Integrationist*, in which the counsellor is more ready to adapt to clients (e.g. by being active and directive or acknowledging the central role of oppression in a client's life) and the *Structuralist*, which focuses on social conditions as the major causes of individual distress. The framework can help counsellors locate and consider their own positions.

Ten assumptions

Pedersen (1987) identified 10 common assumptions that reflect a Western bias in counselling theories. He argued that in cross-cultural counselling these sources of bias may reinforce 'institutional racism, ageism, sexism and other forms of cultural bias' irrespective of the particular theoretical orientation being used. The assumptions are adapted and summarised below:

1. Definitions of normality

What constitutes 'normal' behaviour is not the same to people of different social, economic, political and cultural backgrounds. Use of a culture-bound definition of what is normal/abnormal with clients from other cultures risks assessment errors.

2. Emphasis on individualism

Many approaches to counselling emphasise individual self-awareness insight or self-actualisation. Empathic understanding may be offensive in some cultures. The tendency to focus on individual change serves to devalue the cultural norms that emphasise obligation and duty to family over individual interests that are so central to some cultural value systems. It also disregards the effects of individual change on the groups to which the client belongs.

3. Limited perspectives

Client problems tend to be assessed only from the limited perspectives of counselling or psychology. Academic disciplines such as sociology, anthropology, theology and medicine are often neglected.

4. Use of jargon

Most theories of counselling rely heavily on abstraction or jargon. Counsellors may falsely assume that their clients will understand this terminology when it is used outside the culture in which the theory was developed.

5. Overemphasis on independence

The high value often placed by counsellors on autonomy, self-direction and independence may devalue and neglect the functions of the healthy (and sometimes necessary) dependencies on family, community, church, etc. inculcated by some cultures.

6. Neglect of client support systems

The role of significant others in the client's life is often ignored and there is a tendency not to incorporate the client's natural support system into a therapeutic plan. In some cultures, talking to family or friends is more acceptable than disclosing intimate personal information to a stranger.

7. Emphasis on cause and effect

Many approaches to counselling depend on linear thinking that seeks to determine the cause of a problem. However, some cultures do not separate cause and effect; they think in terms of the interconnectedness of seemingly separate events.

8. Focus on individual change

Counsellors sometimes fail to acknowledge the often very real constraints that are placed on some clients' potential choices and actions, assuming a benign society. The assumption is that the locus of control and responsibility for change should always be on the individual client rather than the family, community or society.

9. Neglect of history

A focus on the 'here and now' and on the present behaviour or problem can neglect the relevance of the client's personal and cultural history, which in some cultures is seen as essential to a full understanding of current problems. Counsellors from the majority culture also tend to disregard their own history. This disregard is magnified when they work with clients from different cultures.

10. Lack of awareness of assumptions

Particularly harmful attitudes of counsellors are to think that they are aware of all their assumptions and to accept glibly the idea of equality and multiculturalism, without having given it serious thought.

Eight defences

Ridley (2005) describes eight culturally related defences that may occur to varying degrees when working with minority clients. These are summarised below:

1. Colour blindness

This is the illusion that clients from minority groups are no different from those of the majority culture and that cultural background is irrelevant.

2. Colour consciousness

This is the opposite of colour blindness and assumes that all the problems a minority client encounters stem from his or her cultural background.

3. Cultural transference

A client's (positive or negative) emotional reactions are transferred from parents or significant others, or from previous experience of someone of the same culture as the counsellor, and projected onto the counsellor.

4. Cultural counter-transference

The most important factor connected with positive outcomes in counselling is the relationship between counsellor and client.

5. Cultural ambivalence

Ridley suggests that, in order to be absolved from real or imagined guilt for being part of the potentially oppressive dominant culture, some majority group counsellors try too hard to gain a minority client's approval or respect. But some counsellors have ambivalent motives and enjoy the sense of power and control over their clients. They need to be seen as the expert helper and want clients to accept their approach to counselling, unconsciously becoming paternalistic or condescending and further reinforcing a client's learned helplessness.

6. Pseudotransference

This occurs when a majority group counsellor ignores the possibility that a cultural minority client's critical behaviour or apparent defensiveness is grounded in reality and labels the behaviour as pathological, problematic or simply as cultural transference.

7. Overidentification

Counsellors from ethnic minorities sometimes overidentify with clients of the same cultural group. They may collude with the client, express support or admiration for the client or even exhibit behaviour similar to that of the client, thereby gaining a sense of prestige, recognition or acceptance by the client. Although counsellors of the same culture as the client might find it easier to establish rapport rapidly and feel more deeply empathic, they risk getting caught up in the client's negative experiences, defining the client's problem too narrowly and unwittingly encouraging excessive or inappropriate exploration of cultural issues.

8. Majority identification

This occurs when minority counsellors deny their group identity, identifying more closely with the majority group culture as a way of dealing with the underlying resentment and psychological difficulties associated with racism and oppression.

Supervision provides the opportunity for counsellors to explore any cultural dynamics and what may be going on between them and their clients, and therefore to reduce the risks of either minimising or exaggerating their psychological significance and potential impact.

MUSTS

See: Thoughts

NARRATIVE

See also: Common factors, Counselling, Writing (expressive)

The concept of narrative as it relates to therapy has emerged as a helpful alternative framework in recent years (Angus and McLeod, 2004; Bolton *et al.*, 2004; McLeod, 1997b; White and Epston, 1990).

Narrative-informed therapy rests on the understanding that much of the knowledge and understanding that we carry with us is actually held in the form of stories we have been told, tell ourselves, or tell others, rather than as theories, principles and rules. Furthermore, the process of therapy can be seen as being about the sharing and elaborating of stories. When stories are shared in therapy, they can be explored in a way that they may not be in other contexts. Meanings, symbols, themes and metaphors can be examined; new perspectives and new understandings (about self, others, possibilities, etc.) can emerge, and stories can evolve and change as a result.

Clients often bring stories that are 'thin' in narrative terms. A 'thin' story connects a small number of events, lacks detail and depth, and leads to conclusions which are often simplistic and disempowering (e.g. 'I've been sacked from my last three jobs; I'm a failure at work; there's no point even trying'). The counsellor's job from a narrative perspective is to encourage the client to 'thicken' the story. This starts by developing the level of detail, but also involves exploring the narrative for alternative perspectives, key themes, possible meanings, and hopefully deeper and more sophisticated understandings.

It can sometimes help the client engage in the process to ask them to work on elaborating detail as if his or her story were going to be the basis for a film or novel. Key and minor characters, plot arcs, character arcs, subplots, the beginning/middle/end of the story and possibilities for resolution or for further developments can all be areas to explore in order to 'thicken' the story. (In the example given, exploring the story of the three sackings, and perhaps of other aspects of the client's life before, during and after these events, should hopefully lead to a better understanding of what happened and why, what it means and how the client can move forward from here.)

'Re-authoring' a story involves finding and emphasising different meanings, which can lead to different conclusions and a different future when extending the story forwards from the present. (Thus a story about victimisation might become a story about survival and inner resources and how these can be the basis for future development.) From a narrative perspective, the exploration and 'thickening' of clients' stories in therapy can lead to a greater sense of identity in terms of intentions, values, beliefs, commitments, hopes, and dreams; and this will equip them with better knowledge of how to go forward in their lives and the ability to create a more meaningful narrative for their future.

Narrative need not be seen as the basis for another distinct approach to therapy but as an alternative way of making sense of what happens in therapy and how it helps. Narrative concepts can shed light on the therapeutic process when working with a range of approaches, whether humanistic, psychodynamic, cognitive-behavioural, or any other approach.

NERVOUS CLIENTS

See also: Anxiety, Beginnings, Contract, negotiating a, Difficulties in being a client, Expectations (clients'), Nonverbal communication, Quiet clients, Respect, Silence, Warmth

Rapid speech, silence, shaking hands and difficulty in speaking may all indicate nervousness but could indicate something else. Being calm, establishing the client's needs, answering questions and empathising all usually help nervous clients to feel more relaxed. It may be useful to remember that for many people being a client is difficult.

NICE (THE NATIONAL INSTITUTE FOR HEALTH AND CLINICAL EXCELLENCE)

See also: Evidence-based practice, Research

This is an independent organisation responsible for providing evidence-based, clinical guidelines (CGs) on a range of health conditions. So far, those most relevant to counsellors are on anxiety (CG 22), depression (CG 23), eating disorders (CG 9) and self-harm (CG 16). The BACP was involved in developing these and others and has been a national stakeholder in NICE since 2002.

Four versions of each guideline are published on the NICE website:

- recommendations for the NHS
- a quick reference guide, outlining the key recommendations
- information for the general public
- the full guideline, which summarises all the evidence considered.

NONVERBAL COMMUNICATION

See also: Challenging, Crying, Drawings, Drinks/refreshments, Emotions, Empathy, Exercises, Furniture, Life-space diagram, Privacy, Silence, Touch

> He that has eyes to see and ears to hear may convince himself that no mortal can keep a secret. If the lips are silent, he chatters with his finger tips; betrayal oozes out of him at every pore. And thus the task of making conscious the most hidden recesses of the mind is one which it is quite possible to accomplish. (Freud)

Collett (2004) discusses 'tells' – small nonverbal clues – in detail, in the tradition of Freud and Sherlock Holmes (and, more recently, Dr House), but perhaps the most practical section comes near the end (pp350–351). Here, he is more cautious than in much of the rest of the book in his three principles to follow when interpreting tells:

- Look for multiple tells – resist the temptation to make an inference on the basis of a single tell.

- Do not jump to conclusions – resist the temptation to assume that tells always reveal the same things.
- Compare people with themselves in different settings and in the same setting with different people.

The following principles for interpreting nonverbal communications (NVCs) are consistent with Collett's:

- NVCs are ambiguous and can be faked.
- Changes are particularly likely to be meaningful (e.g. the person's face 'lights up').
- 'Mixed messages' or incongruence may also be meaningful (e.g. the person smiles when she says she feels sad). Incongruence may indicate conflict, embarrassment or a 'should'.

The most relevant tells for counsellors are probably those related to greeting, parting and anxiety. For example, Collett suggested that 'by watching how people greet each other it is often possible to see what kind of people they are and what their attitudes to each other are' (2004, p163). His analyses are complicated: for example, eight kinds of handshake with numerous other aspects of handshakes to take into account – who initiates them, how the hand is presented, accompanied by a smile or not. In particular, he sees handshakes as a good clue about whether or not one person wants to dominate the other.

On anxiety, Collett wrote that 'if we were more attentive to how people breathe we'd know a lot more about what they are feeling' (p224). Other tells for anxiety include posture, hand movements, smiles (anxious smiles lack the wrinkled 'crow's feet' round the eyes and an upward pull at the corners of the mouth), blinking, a dry mouth and swallowing.

Collett's chapter on sexual tells is less relevant to counsellors and would be most useful as a source of advice for people of a heterosexual orientation worried abut dating and flirting. However, flirting does of course happen in some counselling sessions.

There are many ideas in the counselling literature about NVC (e.g. Brems, 2001; Kennedy-Moore and Watson, 1999; Lago, 2006): for example, when clients are in touch with their emotions and making sense of them (creating or finding meaning), their voices tend to be hesitant, with 'ragged pauses' (Kennedy-Moore and Watson, 1999, p207) and unexpected emphases, and they often use vivid, alive language; conversely, less 'productive' expression is more rehearsed and distant.

A framework for interpreting NVCs

Stage 1

Observe NVCs. Four kinds of NVC can be distinguished:

- use of space (proxemics)
- movements, gestures, expressions (kinesics)

- aspects of speech other than words (paralanguage)
- other (e.g. clothes, physical attractiveness, furniture).

Stage 2

Separate interpretations from cues: for example, separate anxiety (interpretation) from restlessness (cue) or from twisting hands (more concrete version of cue).

Stage 3

Ask 'What other interpretations are there of this cue/set of cues?' (E.g. restlessness could be a full bladder, lots of energy, boredom, or fear.)

Stage 4

(a) Remember the NVCs and your interpretations for possible use later, or
(b) State your observation but not your interpretation to your client. e.g. 'I notice that you smile when you talk about …', or
(c) State your interpretation tentatively, or
(d) Ask your client to repeat the NVC, exaggerate it or stop it.

The techniques in (d) are Gestalt and co-counselling techniques. They can be powerful and need to be used sensitively. They assume that NVCs sometimes block awareness and that, if the movement is repeated, exaggerated or stopped, awareness will increase. For example, X flicked his head habitually when speaking. His counsellor held X's head (with permission) and X then shrugged. He asked X to exaggerate his shrug and the phrase 'Who cares?' came into X's mind.

'NO SHOW' CLIENTS

See: Beginnings, Clients who don't come back, Contract, negotiating a, Difficulties in being a client, Expectations (clients'), Giving information, Missed sessions, Multiculturalism

NOTE TAKING

See also: Assertiveness, Confidentiality, Contract, negotiating a, History taking, Immediacy, Record keeping, Self-awareness

Although some counsellors take full notes during sessions, most take none at all. Perhaps the question to ask is 'What do I need these notes for?' If they are to help you build up a picture of your client's concerns and progress, it might be better to write them up immediately after the session. The same goes if you are taking notes to help you make a presentation or write a case study.

In CBT it is very common to take notes on the content of the session while it is going on. In fact, recording sessions is an important ingredient with regard to structuring the session and collaborating with the client. As well as serving as a reminder to the counsellor, copies can be given to the client for learning and insight (transparency). Therapy notebooks are also recommended for the client to keep notes in (e.g. 'what do I want to remember of the session?' – specific insights, homework assignments, etc.) Some counsellors tape-record sessions and then give the tape to the client for homework to listen to later (Wills and Sanders, 1997).

A problem with taking notes during sessions is that they can distract your attention from listening and responding sensitively to your client. Taking notes during sessions could also make your client feel more like a 'case' than a person, although you can of course discuss this. However, if your approach to counselling involves asking many questions about family history, early relationships, etc., you might need to make a lot of notes, at least early on. Dalton (1992, pp16–18) discussed what happened when she agreed that a client could see her notes, written in a style she describes as 'telegrammatic' and 'unvarnished'. The client was furious with their 'coldness', a reaction which they later agreed was to do with the client's anxieties about being genuinely liked and about ending counselling. Dalton also discussed her motives for agreeing quickly to show the client her notes, and what she is likely to do in the future: slow down, discuss the client's reason for wanting to see her notes and explain her style of note taking.

OFFICE

See: Furniture, Nonverbal communication, Privacy

ONLINE COUNSELLING

See also: Common factors, Contract, negotiating a, Legal system, Relationship between counsellor and client, Website (personal), Writing (expressive)

Generally, new technology emerges; people adapt to it and use it; and the benefits and risks gradually become clearer. Online counselling, also called e-therapy, cybertherapy and webcounselling, is still in a fairly early stage but appears to work well for some people and to have some strong advantages: for example, wider accessibility; allowing close study of what was written; more control over pace for clients who like to take their time; the powerful effects of writing; less time travelling; anonymity (Anthony, 2006; Chester and Glass, 2006).

On the other hand, there are problems and risks: for example, no nonverbal clues (although video links may become more popular); e-mails seem to be permanently stored, so confidentiality may be compromised; legal and ethical complexities; and how does the client know the counsellor is trustworthy?

The BACP publishes guidelines, and there are also practitioner handbooks, such as the one by Goss and Anthony (2003). For training in online counselling, see the OnlineCounsellors website. In addition, some computerised CBT packages (e.g. for anxiety and depression) have been approved by NICE. The obvious advantages include starting earlier, lower cost, and greater control of the pace, but, as with all approaches, a large proportion of clients withdraw.

OPENNESS

See: Congruence

OUTCOME RESEARCH (ON COUNSELLING)

See: Common factors, Effectiveness of counselling

PANIC ATTACKS

See also: Anxiety, Assertiveness, Behaviour, Bibliotherapy, Post-traumatic stress disorder, Stress, Thoughts

Panic attacks are extreme and exaggerated fight or flight responses to stress (Donohoe and Ricketts, 2006). They can be terrifying. The symptoms include:

- palpitations, pounding heart or accelerated heart rate
- sweating
- hyperventilating and other incorrect breathing
- trembling or shaking
- sensations of shortness of breath or smothering, feeling of choking
- chest pain
- nausea or abdominal distress
- feeling dizzy
- fear of losing control
- fear of dying
- hot flushes or chills.

Panic attacks vary in frequency and intensity. One person may get a panic attack once in his or her lifetime and another will have up to 15 a day. For some people, panic attacks start after an obviously traumatic event; for others, they begin without any obvious trigger. It is quite common for doctors to prescribe drugs for panic attacks.

The NICE guidelines on treating panic attacks (NICE, 2004a) recommend CBT, i.e. some combination of:

- recognition and identification of triggers (e.g. when and where the panic attacks occur)
- consideration of lifestyle factors (e.g. caffeine intake)
- understanding the physiology of panic (e.g. the role of adrenaline)
- changing unhelpful cognitions (e.g. 'everyone will laugh at me')
- developing coping strategies (e.g. relaxation, breathing).

All these strategies involve taking control; as with all approaches, however, they do not work for everyone. Counselling can also help some clients come to terms with the reality of managing their panic attacks in the same way that someone with diabetes learns to manage that condition. The No Panic website has useful information.

PARALLEL PROCESS

See also: Challenging, Process, Supervision, Transference

The term 'parallel process' is used to describe a situation in which events in one relationship or situation seem to be repeated or mirrored in another. The idea has its roots in the concepts of transference and counter-transference, and the concept is primarily relevant to supervision. Parallel process can be both a trap for unwary counsellors and a possible way of understanding your relationship with your client. If parallel processes are occurring in a therapy relationship and in supervision, it may be possible to use the supervision relationship as a space to explore the difficulties or blocks, then take this learning back into the therapy relationship. For example, the supervisee might say, 'I really don't know how to begin' and the supervisor could work with this difficulty on the tentative assumption that it might also be a difficulty for the client. The supervisee might thus be able to develop better understanding of the client's experience and the supervisor might be able to model an appropriate response. In another example, the supervisor might feel blame or anger from the supervisee and could work with this as a feeling that the supervisee may have had during counselling. Some supervisors work most with the 'here and now' on the grounds that it will mirror the 'there and then' of the counselling session itself – an assumption that relies on the concept of parallel process (Hawkins and Shohet, 2006).

Parallel process can also be relevant to organisational settings, where counsellors may find themselves mirroring aspects of their clients' experiences in their relationship with their organisation. In particular, those working with particularly challenging or difficult clients may find that they themselves are being more challenging or difficult with their organisations and on examination become aware that they are, at some level, acting out patterns that they are experiencing from their clients. It is important to be aware that it is the process that is 'parallel' here, not the content. Insight is likely to come from exploring the feelings/emotional responses, rather than the specific issues.

PARAPHRASING

See also: Emotions, Empathy, Intuition, Metaphors in counselling, Questions, Self-awareness, Reflections of feelings

Paraphrasing is the main skill involved in being empathic. The main purposes of paraphrasing are:

- to help clients listen to themselves and clarify what they mean, feel and think (usually by putting it into words)
- to communicate acceptance and respect and therefore contribute (probably) to building a relationship.

When you paraphrase well you attempt to restate, freshly and concisely, the central, most alive part of what someone has said without adding any of your own ideas, feelings, interpretations, etc. Your tone is slightly questioning without being a question. It is tentative because you may be wrong. Being accurate (especially quickly) is much less important than trying to understand and to be empathic.

The most basic form of paraphrase is 'You feel [emotion] because of ...', but the focus can be on other elements of self-awareness than emotions, for example thoughts, needs and values. Perhaps most important is helping your client find the right words for emotions ('the Rumpelstiltskin effect').

A key aspect of skilful paraphrasing is being in close emotional contact with your client and also clearly separate: neither overidentifying (sometimes called 'fusing') nor being coolly distant. Davenport and Pipes (1990, p139) suggested the analogy of swimming close to a deep, powerful whirlpool: 'the challenge is to be close enough to the emotional energy to understand what the client must be experiencing without getting swept down into the action oneself'. Drowning with the client is not helpful, nor is viewing from too far away.

Paraphrasing is an art as well as a skill and therefore can be carried out technically well with poor results, or technically poorly with excellent results (or, of course, both skilfully and artistically, or neither). However, even technical paraphrases can be effective in the sense of encouraging clients to explore and clarify and allowing you to check your understanding.

How often do good counsellors paraphrase? It depends, but Rogers (e.g. 1987) believed in frequent checks, and Gendlin (1981, p19) suggested an *average* of every five or ten sentences, which is a guideline, not a rule. Gendlin made another specific suggestion about frequency: 'Don't let the person say more than you can take in and say back. Interrupt, say back, and let the person go on' (p20). If you dislike the word 'interrupt' in this suggestion, you might like to try replacing it with 'contribute'.

A flexible approach is also needed in choosing when to use your client's words in a paraphrase. Sometimes a word or phrase used by your client is very significant to that person and can be included by you (or noted for later).

The following suggestions about paraphrasing well and less well (adapted from Gendlin, 1981) are intended to help you check on and refine your own paraphrasing, not to replace the artistic element. They and the further elements of paraphrasing are the equivalent of coaching on a tennis stroke or a golf swing.

How do you know when you are paraphrasing well?

Your client is more likely to:

- say more, and go further 'inside' (may become more focused and intent) or
- sit silently, relieved that she or he has been understood and accepted (may become more relaxed).

And less well?

Your client is more likely to:
- try to paraphrase what you have said
- speak more superficially and continue to do so
- become tense, confused or annoyed ('I've just said that') or
- agree in a desultory way.

Some further elements of paraphrasing

- Simple words seem to capture meanings best (perhaps through discouraging intellectualising).
- The focus is on emotions etc. that are clearly expressed or close to the surface, not on daring intuitions.
- Pausing after clients have recognised or clarified an emotion gives them the space to feel it more and perhaps also to feel a sense of relief that someone has really listened.
- If you have understood (or think you have understood) only part of what your client has said, paraphrase that part and add that you do not understand the rest.
- Pause before you paraphrase or during a paraphrase, and trust yourself to find words which are good enough or better.
- Try including a *little* of your client's emotion or emotions in the way you say the paraphrase.
- Paraphrase present emotions too.

PEER SUPERVISION

See also: Supervision

Peer supervision is most appropriate for experienced counsellors and is probably best done in a small group. Each person takes a turn at presenting a case or theme for discussion by the group and is given the opportunity to explore particular aspects, as in standard supervision groups. Other group members can be supportive and challenging and offer alternative ways of thinking about particular issues.

A supervision group should be small enough, and meet often enough, to enable each member to have adequate time for case presentation. A group of four might need to meet every week for about two hours. Peer supervision in pairs, using a reciprocal model, can also be very useful.

The advantages of peer supervision groups include the opportunity to hear how others meet and overcome difficulties; to share ideas and information; and to practise being supportive and constructively challenging. Disadvantages include the fact that groups can find themselves short of time to include everyone fully, and that sometimes peer groups become collusive and find it difficult to be challenging. One way to overcome this second problem is for the group occasionally to ask an 'outside' facilitator to review its practices and the relationships that have built up among group members.

PERSONALITY

See also: Narrative, Personality disorders, Psychological type, Theories of counselling

Personality refers to 'an individual's characteristic patterns of thought, emotion and behaviour, together with the psychological mechanisms – hidden or not – behind those patterns' (Funder, 2007, p5). The most widely used theory in personality research is five factor theory, or the 'Big Five'; while in organisations and other non-clinical settings, it is psychological type theory in its Myers-Briggs Type Indicator (MBTI) sense. Both theories have sustained their popularity for many years and they also agree significantly with each other on the major personality characteristics, although with important differences, such as in language, tone and model of development (Bayne, 2005).

For example, one Big Five factor is called Conscientiousness, and each person is high, low or in-between on this characteristic. High Conscientiousness is associated with being well organised versus disorganised, careful versus careless, and self-disciplined versus weak-willed. The psychological type counterpart of Conscientiousness is *preference* for either Judging (organised etc.) or Perceiving (easy-going, flexible, adaptable): similar behaviours to those associated with Conscientiousness, but contrasting in evaluative tone and interpretation.

A broader framework for personality than either type or the Big Five has been proposed by McAdams (e.g. 1995). The framework's three levels are:

1. traits (or factors or preferences)
2. personal concerns or characteristic adaptations
3. integrative life stories.

To know a person well is to know them at all three levels. Personality measures and concepts as organised in McAdams's framework can inform each of these levels in a way that, in Singer's (2005) view, 'is at the heart of treating the whole person'. Singer (2005) structured his book *Personality and Psychotherapy* around the McAdams framework, which he applies in extended case studies.

An alternative view is that psychological type theory, used sensitively and perhaps with McAdams's framework in the background, can achieve the same outcomes more simply, constructively and economically (Bayne, 2004). Level 1 of McAdams's model is exemplified by the table in the entry on Psychological type. This level can be useful at all stages of counselling, but perhaps especially when building a relationship. The counsellor can adapt his or her behaviour accordingly and perhaps discuss this approach with the client. However, it is the 'frame of personality, not what fills out its picture, color, and, texture' (Singer, 2005, p45).

Level 2 includes motives, 'life tasks', etc., and the focus is more on *how* someone is (say) Conscientious (or prefers Judging or Perceiving), and on what they try to accomplish when they behave in these ways – on their characteristic adaptations to situations and roles. Level 3 of McAdams's framework is about how someone finds meaning: that person's identity, life stories or personal narratives. For example, a client sees herself as, among other themes, struggling for autonomy against men and against social pressures.

Personality at Level 1 is seen as stable and basic, both in Big Five theory and in the preferences of psychological type theory (Bayne, 2005). This stability could be seen as gloomy but it is part of having a core sense of self – life would be very different if people did not have some stable elements in their personalities – and it can also lead to realistic expectations of how much change is possible (Costa and McCrae, 1986). According to this view, people who are, for example, anxious as part of their personalities do not usually become calm people as a result of counselling or psychotherapy. Rather, they tend to become a little less anxious and to develop more effective ways of coping with their anxiety (Costa and McCrae, 1986; Miller, 1991).

Similarly, psychological type theory assumes that while our preferences remain the same throughout our lives, we do develop the skills and behaviours associated both with them and with our non-preferences. For example, an introvert usually develops the skills of introversion most while also developing some extrovert skills. Thus, preferences are both fixed and can also be developed. Aspects of personality and behaviour that are easier to change than factors or preferences include assertiveness, sexual problems and, probably, characteristics at Levels 2 and 3 of McAdams's model, especially beliefs about the world and oneself, and skills (Dweck, 2006).

Overall, the links between contemporary personality psychology and counselling practice look very promising, but much remains to be clarified and understood.

PERSONALITY DISORDERS

See also: DSM-IV, Mental health and mental illness, Personality, Referral, Specialisms in counselling

Personality disorder is a controversial term used to describe extreme and troublesome patterns of behaviour (BPS, 2006; Funder, 2007). About 10 per cent of the general population, and far higher proportions of other populations (e.g. 50 per cent plus of adult prisoners), meet the most widely used criteria for one or more of the disorders (BPS, 2006). They are 'heavy users of health services' (p35).

Many people meet the criteria for having four or more personality disorders (BPS, 2006, p6). Thus, they are categories of disorder, not types of people. However, some writers argue that personality disorders are really alternative philosophies or a moral problem rather than a mental illness.

DSM-IV suggests 10 personality disorders, although there is general agreement that these are 'no more than a crude first step in which abnormalities of personality lead to dysfunctional behaviour' (BPS, 2006, p8). For example, 'borderline personality disorder' is the term used to describe the behaviour and feelings of someone who has unstable, intense personal relationships, is very anxious about being abandoned, behaves very impulsively, and has a diffuse sense of identity. Such characteristics make building a therapeutic relationship difficult but not impossible. The publication by Bell (2003) is a self-help manual, written by a clinical psychologist for people diagnosed with this personality disorder.

The BPS report argues that the most effective treatments for personality disorders generally are 'intensive, long-term, theoretically coherent, well structured and well integrated with other services' (2006, p41). The report also recommends specialist training. Studies of focus groups of people diagnosed with personality disorders have identified several aspects of mental health services which they find helpful: for example, specialist services; being able to choose from a range of treatment options; a care team that listens to feedback; therapeutic optimism; expectations of positive change. The groups felt that many professionals did not understand the diagnosis and were unduly pessimistic about it (p54).

POST-TRAUMATIC STRESS DISORDER (PTSD)

See also: Abuse, Anger, Anxiety, Assessment, Crisis counselling, Depression, DSM-IV, Emotions, Loss, Panic attacks, Psychodiagnosis, Stress, Thoughts, Vicarious traumatisation

Post-traumatic stress disorder (PTSD) is a response to experiencing or witnessing a serious threat to life or wellbeing. The symptoms include re-experiencing the event (flashbacks), increased arousal around, and persistent avoidance of, stimuli associated with the trauma, or a sense of detachment from them. The trauma can range from crime and injury to armed combat and natural disasters.

Many people who survive major trauma (perhaps about 25 per cent) do not suffer from PTSD, while the symptoms disappear in another 25 per cent in a few weeks. In up to a third of survivors, symptoms become chronic (Hodgkinson, 2006; Scott and Stradling, 2006). People's resilience tends to be underestimated (Bonanno, 2004).

The NICE guidelines for treating PTSD were published in 2005 (see the NICE website) and endorse eye movement desensitisation reprocessing (EMDR) and trauma-focused CBT as the treatments with the strongest supporting evidence. However, the evidence reviewed is restricted, as discussed in the entry on Effectiveness of counselling. Trauma incident reduction is another deceptively simple technique; it belongs to the interventions used within the field of metapsychology (mindfulness-oriented exposure) and the facilitator guides the client but otherwise has a rather passive observer role. Training can be obtained from TIR[UK] (see website).

Clients who present with various forms of abuse from childhood could also be suffering from PTSD. In the case of sexual or physical abuse, the cause may be quite clear but there is no clear knowledge of what a child, particularly at preverbal stages, sees as traumatic. For some clients, the precipitating stressor is only the last in a long series of stressful circumstances and often the final stressor is quite minor.

Many clients with PTSD are also angry, anxious and/or depressed, so it is quite likely that the counsellor will be working with a variety of problems. Several approaches can help the client (Hollon *et al.*, 2006), for example peer-support groups, anxiety management groups, relaxation training, medication, and EMDR.

POWER

See also: Abuse, Assertiveness, Boundaries, Contract, negotiating a, Counselling, Endings, Expectations (clients'), Furniture, Immediacy, Multiculturalism, Questions, Respect, Role conflict, Sexual attraction, Trust

In most counselling relationships, the counsellor has more power than the client: counselling takes place in the counsellor's room; counsellors may be seen as an expert or authority; they know more about counselling than the client; clients disclose far more about themselves than counsellors do; and clients are often in a particularly troubled and vulnerable period of their lives.

An imbalance of power makes abuse more likely and can be an obstacle to the trust and clear communication at the heart of most approaches to counselling. Most counsellors try to reduce the power imbalance and to support clients' responsibility and autonomy. Listening hard to the client is deeply respectful in itself and so is the process of negotiating a contract. The general principle is to be aware of differences, or perceived differences, in power and to discuss them with the client if they are getting in the way of counselling (see entry on Immediacy).

It is also useful to adopt a collaborative and sharing position in relation to knowledge about counselling and the planning of therapy. The concept of 'informed consent' is useful in encouraging counsellors to share their approach with clients, helping clients to understand the models or techniques being offered and take full part in decisions about how to proceed. There are potential additional benefits here, in that if clients 'learn the model' they may be better equipped to deal with problems which arise subsequently.

PRIVACY

See also: Confidentiality, Furniture, Nonverbal communication, Violence and its prevention

Counselling is essentially a private activity not only in the sense that it is confidential but also in that it needs to take place in a private setting. An effective counselling relationship can be established only in a non-threatening environment in which the client feels safe and secure. Clients need to feel that they can talk about deeply personal and emotional issues without any risk of being disturbed, overheard or seen by others.

In many modern buildings with lightly constructed or poorly insulated partition walls, it is easy to hear doors banging and people talking and laughing or answering the telephone. This can be distracting at best and could increase a client's anxiety at a time when she or he already feels vulnerable. Clients need to feel that nobody will overhear them or come suddenly into the room. While you might have no, or only very limited, choice of where the counselling takes place, it is possible to take some steps to enhance the feeling of privacy:

- Put a clear 'PLEASE DON'T DISTURB' notice on the door.
- Ensure that the telephone is turned off or that calls will be automatically redirected.
- Make sure that clients sit where they cannot see or be seen by people passing by any window. Net curtains for windows and translucent self-adhesive sheets for glass door-panels can help with this. If fire regulations require that the glass panels can be seen through, you can leave a small gap, covering it temporarily when you are counselling.
- Inform other users of the building, especially of the corridor and adjacent rooms, of your need for privacy and seek their cooperation. If it is impossible to avoid hearing other people outside the room, it might help clients to tell them that other people are working in the building but that they will not disturb you.
- Avoid having clients waiting immediately outside the counselling room.

PRIVATE PRACTICE

See also: Administration, Business, Fees, Marketing, Website (personal)

'I have found the difficulties in earning sufficient money from counselling real, enduring, numerous and rarely openly discussed' (Feltham, 1993, p165). Many practitioners explore the possibility of private practice at some point in their career (Feltham, 1993, 1995b, 2002; McMahon *et al.*, 2005; Syme, 1994). We emphasise the problems of private practice here, but many of them are issues for counsellors working in organisations too, and there are also pleasures and rewards, and considerable autonomy.

To start with, private practice means running a small business. Market research – finding out about likely customers, competitors and the probable demand for services – is an important first step. The practice's location is a key factor, as working in a sparsely populated or economically impoverished area is likely to ensure financial insecurity. Business planning, accountancy, marketing, advertising and administration all play a significant part.

There is also a range of professional issues to be considered, such as further training, supervision, communication outside the counselling sessions, privacy, security, confidentiality, punctuality, CPD, note taking, accreditation, after-hours accessibility, the nature and form of contract between the practitioner and the client, and the development of trust and care. Factors, such as the client group seen, whether to engage in open-ended or time-limited counselling, experience and stamina, all affect the number of weekly client contact hours that can safely and ethically be undertaken.

Private practitioners will probably earn less in the first few years and, at the same time, have extra expenses – for their room, perhaps; telephone bills and postage; purchase of equipment; training; professional body and registration fees. There are no paid holidays or sick leave, no employer's superannuation schemes, and the majority of private practitioners work in isolation for most of the working week, with no colleagues to help relieve the pressures of difficult clients or intense counselling sessions.

PROCESS

See also: Contract, negotiating a, Hidden agendas, Immediacy, Parallel process, Self-awareness

The term 'process' is widely used in counselling to refer to *how* something functions, develops or unfolds over time, and can be contrasted with 'content', which refers to *what* is being addressed or *what* the task is. This is often a useful distinction to bear in mind. The content of counselling is generally the most immediate and apparent aspect, but attention to the process and discussion of this with clients is often equally useful in developing clients' awareness and insight and equipping them for the future. This can be useful in a number of ways: drawing attention to their part in the counselling relationship, which may have parallels in other relationships; highlighting how they have made progress and the part they have played in it; helping them to acknowledge the strengths and resources they have drawn on; and helping them to understand the therapeutic techniques and processes they have experienced so that they might apply them to future issues.

It may also be useful to distinguish between process and content when considering the issue of directiveness. While some approaches attempt to avoid giving direction to the client at any level, many approaches would encourage the counsellor to offer direction at a process level, although taking care to avoid it in terms of content. The difference here may be summarised by contrasting 'Here is a way I think we might help you to work out what to do [about an issue]' – for example a particular technique such as brainstorming – with 'Here is what I think you should do [about the issue]'.

Process is often used to refer to what might be going on below the visible surface, as in the following:

- **Personal process** is that which underlies and to some extent determines the functioning of an individual. When a counsellor is unable to empathise, it may be because of particular cues or blocks which are stimulated by the client or the client's issues, and it is sometimes referred to as 'the counsellor's process getting in the way'.

- **Group process** also refers to what is happening under the surface. For example, a decision is required but one member of the group has a need to control; another wants to impress someone else in the group; and a third fears being asked to do more work. All these 'hidden agendas' affect the way a group works. Some groups explore the process, although in meetings it is usually the task which is uppermost. Sometimes, the task cannot proceed because the process gets in the way.

PROFESSIONAL DEVELOPMENT

See: Continuing professional development

PSYCHOBABBLE

See also: Giving information, Theories of counselling

Psychobabble and jargon can be defined either as 'gibberish' or as 'language peculiar and often useful to a particular profession or group'. To an outsider, in this case someone unfamiliar with counselling language, these two things are indistinguishable. Words like 'resistance', 'transference', 'empathy' and 'congruence' can be mystifying and alienating. In a similar vein, you might wish to avoid using clichés or 'counsellor speak' when counselling. Phrases such as 'What I hear you saying is …', or 'It sounds to me like …' can become intensely irritating if used too often. If you tape-record some of your sessions, you can look out for words or phrases that sound clichéd or repetitive.

PSYCHODIAGNOSIS

See also: Assessment, DSM-IV

The best known systems of psychodiagnosis are listed in ICD-10, the World Health Organization's *International Classification of Diseases* (WHO, 1988), and in DSM-IV, the American Psychiatric Association's *Diagnostic and Statistical Manual of Mental Disorders* (APA, 2000). Some counsellors, such as Shlien (1989), regard these systems as a form of evil.

Some of the advantages of psychodiagnosis are as follows:

- It suggests strategies and methods that have been shown to be effective with similar problems.

- It provides a framework for research and for the development of a body of knowledge about various patterns of disorder and their treatment.

- Many practitioners find themselves working in mental health agencies where they are required to make diagnostic classification of client problems. In the USA, this is increasingly being linked to health insurance.

- A classification system enables practitioners and researchers to communicate more easily. It is not necessary to list every one of a client's symptoms in order to discuss the client with a supervisor or colleague. A diagnostic category is sufficient to give a general picture of the kinds of difficulty the client is experiencing, which can be elucidated further by individual detail.

Some criticisms of psychodiagnosis are:

- Diagnosis often places meaningless and poorly defined labels on clients.
- Labels can become self-fulfilling prophecies if the label is perceived as coming from an 'expert' and is interpreted as a statement about the client's general behaviour. Clients can then more easily avoid taking responsibility by 'acting into' the identified symptoms and accepting the patient role.
- Clients diagnosed with particular disorders can be viewed and treated in stereotyped ways by practitioners, friends, relatives and even the clients themselves for a long time after the disorder has disappeared.
- Practitioners can become preoccupied with a client's history and neglect current attitudes and behaviour, losing sight of the client's individual and unique experience.
- As diagnosis has been associated historically with pathology, there is a danger that counsellors will be preoccupied with pathology and underestimate or exclude clients' strengths and resources.
- There is a risk of gender-role socialisation influencing diagnosis. For example, women socialised into being emotionally expressive and putting the needs of others ahead of their own are vulnerable to being diagnosed in particular ways (e.g. histrionic or dependent). Men socialised into being more distant rather than engaging with others may be seen as paranoid or antisocial. In this way, diagnosis may reflect the potential for seeing as pathological those aspects of behaviour that are normative for women and men who have been well socialised.
- Sociocultural influences result in people from particular cultural or ethnic groups being vulnerable to inaccurate diagnosis.
- An emphasis on diagnosis can encourage client dependence on experts.
- Practitioners need to be adequately trained to use the various systems (which still have relatively low reliability and validity).
- The use of psychodiagnosis can appear on the surface as eminently scientific and objective, thus heightening the mystique of professionalism and investing practitioners with authority.

PSYCHOLOGICAL TYPE

See also: Expectations (clients'), Good counsellors, Multiculturalism, Personality, Quiet clients, Rapport, Referral, Self-awareness, Theories of counselling

Psychological type is a theory of personality developed by Myers (Bayne, 2004; Myers with Myers, 1980; Myers *et al.*, 1998) from some of Jung's ideas. She suggested 16 'kinds of people', describing all of them primarily in terms of strengths and potential strengths. The evidence for the theory is good, especially its relationship with the Big Five factor theory of personality now dominating personality research (Bayne, 2005).

The central concepts in MBTI theory are 'preference' and 'type'. Preference can be defined as 'feeling most natural and comfortable with particular ways of behaving and experiencing'. Thus, people generally behave in the ways they prefer but can behave in the opposite way, although usually less frequently and with more effort. At the basic level of type theory, there are four pairs of preferences:

Extraversion (E)	or	Introversion (I)
Sensing (S)	or	Intuition (N)
Thinking (T)	or	Feeling (F)
Judging (J)	or	Perceiving (P).

The meaning of each of the preferences is briefly indicated by the following characteristics, which are behaviours which tend to be associated with the preferences rather than definitions of them:

E	More outgoing and active	More reflective and reserved	I
S	More practical and interested in facts and details	More interested in possibilities and an overview	N
T	More logical and reasoned	More agreeable and appreciative	F
J	More planning and coming to conclusions	More easy-going and flexible	P

A person's 'type' includes one from each of the four pairs of preferences e.g. ENTP or ESTJ. There are 16 such combinations and therefore 16 types.

Type is relevant to counselling in several ways, for example:

- as an approach to self-awareness

- as a way of understanding and accepting four major ways in which clients' personalities vary

- as a type theory, i.e. going beyond the four major personality differences to suggest how each person's personality is organised

- as an approach to personality development and self-esteem: different types have different patterns of development and find self-esteem in different experiences

- as a source of ideas and information on particular topics, e.g. relationships (Tieger and Barron-Tieger, 2000) and careers (Tieger and Barron-Tieger, 2001)

- as an approach to the so far elusive possibility of increasing counselling effectiveness by systematically matching clients, problems, counsellors and techniques.

More specifically, type theory suggests that each person prefers some ways of experiencing and behaving and is more comfortable with these than with others. Table 4 lists the preferences and their implications for clients' behaviour, in counselling and generally. The table does not take type development, or other factors affecting behaviour, into account.

Table 4 Behaviour and experience associated with the preferences (from Bayne, 2004)

People who prefer	Tend to
Extraversion	Be more active Be less comfortable with reflection Be optimistic and energetic
Introversion	Be more at ease with silence Be less comfortable with action Be more private
Sensing	Be concrete and detailed Like a 'practical' approach Not see many options Be uncomfortable with novelty
Intuition	Take a broad view Jump around from topic to topic See unrealistic options See lots of options Overlook facts Like novelty and imaginative approaches
Thinking	Avoid emotions, feelings and values in early conversations Need rationales and logic Be critical and sceptical Want to be admired for their competence Be competitive
Feeling	Focus on values and networks of values Need to care (e.g. about a value, a person or an ideal) Be 'good' clients or patients Want to be appreciated
Judging	Fear losing control Find sudden change stressful Need structure Need to achieve Work hard and tolerate discomfort
Perceiving	Avoid decisions Need flexibility Avoid discomfort

The implications for counselling of the tendencies listed in Table 4 follow fairly directly: for example, if you are an introverted counsellor with an extroverted client, you can consider being more active or discussing this possibility with your client (Bayne, 2004). A general principle here is the standard one of discussing relevant aspects of the relationship, for example using the skill of immediacy to say 'I wonder if you'd rather I spoke more?' A second general principle is to counsel mainly in your own way but to adapt to clients to some extent. Provost takes a different position: that counsellors can learn to 'talk 16 types' (1993, p24). However, this may ask most counsellors to be too versatile, and Provost does also state that 'Although counselors can build rapport by mirroring clients' types, this does not mean that counselors should become the client's type. Counselors must be themselves and work from their own strengths' (p26). Her book illustrates this well, through brief case studies of her counselling clients of each type, but her own type (ENFP) is one of the most versatile.

More generally, psychological type theory suggests that each counsellor, depending on his or her psychological type, is likely to be most comfortable and effective in different schools, styles, stages and skills of counselling, for example:

- Counsellors of one psychological type will tend to be more skilled at observing nonverbal cues than at detecting themes; counsellors of the opposite type will tend towards the reverse pattern.

- Counsellors who find that empathy comes 'naturally' may find challenging more difficult, and vice versa.

- Some types are more comfortable with exploration (tending to neglect action), others with action (tending to neglect exploration).

In counselling generally, there is a marked bias towards preferences for 'feeling' (dealing with people) and 'intuition' (inferring meanings). This does *not* mean that other types should avoid counselling: all psychological types can be good counsellors, but with different patterns of strengths and comfort.

QUESTIONS

See also: Challenging, Empathy, Metaphors in counselling, Miracle question, Paraphrasing, Summaries and 'moving interviews forward'

In searching for an answer or way to help the client, it can be tempting to take a traditional medical role and ask a series of diagnostic questions. This can easily set up a pattern of question and answer, leading to other questions and more answers, with the questioner controlling the direction of the exploration and holding on to the power in the relationship. Indeed, Egan (2007, p124) admits to catching himself asking questions to which he did not want to know the answers!

A series of questions does little to establish a warm and positive climate in which clients are encouraged to take responsibility. It is useful if you can be confident that you are able – by using paraphrases and other reflective responses – to sustain a dialogue with a client without relying on questions so that when you do ask a question it is a pertinent and helpful one. Skilful questioning enables clarification, encourages deeper exploration or reflection, or can be a form of challenge. Therefore, reflect on whether the question you are about to ask will inhibit or further the flow of the session and in what way the answer will help you to help the client or whether it will merely satisfy your curiosity. Very brief questions – 'And you?', 'And?', 'But?' (each of which is also a challenge) – can occasionally be useful, but generally we suggest asking few questions.

One system for categorising questions is as follows:

- **Open questions** (e.g. 'Tell me about ...?') allow freedom of choice of response and are useful for most openings or exploration within the client's frame of reference.

- **Closed questions** (e.g. 'Would you like a drink?') usually have a correct and/or short response. They are useful for obtaining single facts, but limit or control the response.

- **Probe questions** (e.g. 'What happened next?') are intended to follow up or expand on initial response. They are the 'what, when, where, why and how' questions, useful in checking information or gathering more detailed and concrete information. 'Why' should be used with caution if at all, as it can often sound confrontational or can seem 'too big' a question. Generally, questions like 'What is it about ...?' or 'How does ...?' can be constructed, and these are easier to answer and more helpful to the client than 'Why?'

- **Hypothetical questions** (e.g. 'What do you think might happen if he walked into the room now?') invite clients to imagine their reactions to hypothetical situations and can be useful in encouraging them to consider new ideas or to anticipate or rehearse their reactions.

- **Leading questions** (e.g. 'Surely you don't believe that?') usually invite the expected or desired answer or are suggestions disguised as questions ('Have you thought about ...?') and are seldom, if ever, useful in counselling.

- **Multiple questions** (e.g. 'Have you lived there long? Do you like it?') involve two or more questions at once and tend to be confusing or answered only in part.

QUESTIONS (PERSONAL) ASKED BY CLIENTS

See also: Assertiveness, Boundaries, Self-disclosure, Trust

Clients sometimes ask personal questions like 'Are *you* married?'; 'Do you like football?'; 'Have you been depressed?' How you answer depends to some extent on your model of counselling and the particular circumstances, including how much you are taken by surprise! A general factor to take into account is the client's emotional state: whether she or he is feeling vulnerable and insecure, or curious and challenging. One option for dealing with such questions is to give a brief, direct answer and immediately return the focus to the client: for example, 'Yes, I am. Does it make a difference to you?' or 'No, I haven't. Would you feel more understood or optimistic if I had?'

Another possibility, although one that runs the risk of you sounding like a stereotypical psychoanalyst, is to say something like 'I find that an interesting question for you to ask. Can you say what lies behind it?' or – more bluntly – 'What's the statement behind that question?' If you have a sense of what lies behind the question, you can reflect that to the client. Clients may not want a literal answer but are saying something about themselves or their attitude towards you. The underlying question – as with criticisms of you being too young, lacking relevant experience, etc. to be a counsellor – may be 'What are you like?' or 'Can I trust you?', so you might say, for example, 'No, I'm not HIV positive but I've spent some time learning about it, and I want to understand what it's like for you.'

QUIET CLIENTS

See also: Beginnings, Contract, negotiating a, Contraindications for brief counselling, Difficult clients, Exercises, Immediacy, Process, Psychological type, Rapport, Reluctant clients, Silence, Trust

There are many reasons for clients being quiet: they may be reluctant, resistant or stuck; they might not know what is expected of them; the client may be a quiet person or may be reflecting. The most important point seems to be whether the silence is beneficial to the client. Clients might need time to adapt to you, to trust you, to think, or to summon up the courage to take responsibility for themselves. It is for you to establish whether the client has a problem with silence and, if so, why. It is also for you to establish that clients know what is expected in the session and if they really want to be there at all. At least initially, some clients find face-to-face contact threatening. Pencil-and-paper and other exercises can be a gentle way of respecting and coping with this reaction.

RACE

See: Multiculturalism

RAPPORT

See also: Beginnings, Congruence, Contract, negotiating a, Core conditions, Empathy, Multiculturalism, Psychological type, Questions (personal) asked by clients, Readiness to change, Referral, Self-disclosure, Trust

Rapport is implied by such metaphors as 'in tune', 'being on the same wavelength' and 'a meeting of minds'. It is an intuitively compelling but vague idea.

Establishing rapport with a new client is an important part of the initial stages of counselling. One technique is to copy, to some extent, the way each client speaks, uses visual images, and so on. This is too mechanical and contrived for some tastes and could be experienced by clients as a form of mimicry. It could also conflict with being congruent and natural. However, rapport is easier to establish if your way of speaking and the language you use are not completely at odds with those of your client, and some accommodation to another person is itself a natural part of communication.

In the initial stages of counselling, you will be concentrating on listening to and understanding your client; this includes being aware of your client's way of using expression and language. It is possible to maintain your own natural and spontaneous 'way of being' while remaining sensitive to your client's manner and mood. The important thing is to take your time and 'tune in' to your client gradually without trying to force rapport before either of you is ready: rapport develops with trust.

RAPPROCHEMENT

See: Common factors, Integration and eclecticism

READINESS TO CHANGE

See also: Assessment, Contraindications for brief counselling, Expectations (clients'), Furniture, Motivational interviewing, Multiculturalism, Trust

Some people take to counselling much more easily than others. Counselling cannot begin until people recognise their need to change and until they are at least some way towards committing themselves to change.

Prochaska *et al.* (1992) suggested the following four-stage model for assessing how ready a person is to change:

1. **Precontemplation:** in this stage people see little or no point in counselling, at least for themselves. They are 'reluctant clients', who have usually been persuaded by friends or relations to try counselling. They are clearly sceptical and doubt the value of counselling, even though they might admit that they would like situations or people around them to be different. Reluctant clients tend to drop out quickly. The counsellor can check whether clients see themselves as in this stage and the implications.

2. **Contemplation:** people recognise that they have a problem and are thinking seriously about what they might do about it. They are not fully committed to the idea of counselling but tend to be open to exploration and willing to talk about themselves and their problem. Some versions of the model include a preparation stage here, the meaning of which is as it sounds. See the entries on Beginnings and Expectations (clients').

3. **Action:** at this stage, people have tried different ways of coping with their problems. They have some understanding of themselves and the nature of the problem and often have clear ideas about what they want to do. People in this stage are genuinely prepared to commit themselves to counselling but may be impatient to move forward rather than to explore and clarify.

4. **Maintenance:** in this stage people tend to have already made significant changes in their lives. They may have had previously positive experiences of counselling and be fully committed to its value. They seek counselling at this stage to reinforce earlier gains and to develop new strategies and coping skills to prevent the recurrence of problems and to find more positive ways of living.

Feltham and Dryden (2006) argued that counsellors need to be able to recognise a client's stage of readiness to change. They warn that difficulties will be caused by attempting to apply a single therapeutic approach to all clients, irrespective of the stage they are in. Several factors appear to contribute to higher levels of client readiness: these include positive and realistic expectations of counselling and/or the counsellor; intellectual curiosity; willingness to self-disclose; feeling liked by the counsellor; flexible attitudes and defence systems; openness to new perspectives; high level of commitment to counselling; comfortable physical surroundings; and a sense of the counsellor as aware of and respecting differences.

RECORD KEEPING

See also: Administration, Confidentiality, Ethical Framework, Evaluation, Evidence-based practice, Legal system, Note taking, Suicide

Records of counselling have several purposes and potential purposes (Bond, 2000; Bond and Sandhu, 2007). Recent developments, including increased professionalisation, legislation, and the possibility of litigation, have clarified the desirability of keeping records. Some counsellors remain resistant to the idea, but the BACP's Ethical Framework states:

> Practitioners are encouraged to keep appropriate records of their work with clients unless there are adequate reasons for not keeping any records. All records should be accurate, respectful of clients and colleagues and protected from unauthorised disclosure. Practitioners should take into account their responsibilities and their clients' rights under data protection legislation and any other legal requirements. (BACP, 2007)

Records can be valuable in a number of ways, such as:

- to monitor progress
- to record content as an aide-mémoire for the next session and to help identify key issues and themes and to facilitate referral

- to facilitate reflection on your interventions, your feelings, thoughts, sense of self in the relationship with your client and what is going on in the relationship
- to develop an assessment of what is going on for the client
- to develop a therapeutic plan: articulating sense of direction and purpose, goals, strategies, obstacles and possible ways forward
- to identify issues for supervision
- to provide evidence of professional and ethical responsibility
- to be used as evidence in court, bearing in mind that, in the UK, barristers take an adversarial approach.

The Data Protection Act 1998 has stimulated discussion about the openness of records and gaining client's permission to keep them. One reaction is to keep minimal factual records without opinions and including assessment and risk-management information. Clients should be informed about the purpose of the notes, and that they are stored safely and for how long.

What might matter more to you than the purposes listed above is your model of counselling. How much do you need to remember, and how much would your clients like you to remember? Bond and Sandhu (2007) discuss issues such as who has access to records, their use in court, their content and format, where and how they are kept, and how long to keep them. Records of the client's identity (name, address, telephone number, etc.) should be kept *separately* from any case notes, and arrangements should be made for safe disposal of client records, especially in the event of your incapacity or death.

Records should be clear and it is useful to distinguish between the relatively objective content (what was discussed, observed, techniques used, goals and plans agreed, etc.) and more subjective interpretations and impressions, which, if recorded at all, should be owned as such. The BACP's website provides helpful and detailed information sheets on record keeping and access to records.

REFERRAL

See also: Boundaries, Contraindications for brief counselling, Endings, First impressions, Referral letters, Specialisms in counselling, Values

You will not be the best available counsellor for every client or every type of problem, and this could become apparent at any stage of counselling. However, you and your clients can experience a whole range of emotions about referral. While it can bring a sense of relief and hope, referral can also be disruptive and disappointing. Clients can feel hurt, rejected and reluctant to start again with someone else or feel that counselling is not for them anyway. Those who have been passed from one mental health agency to another may come to believe that their problem is too big for any counsellor and that they are beyond help. Other clients in similar situations feel powerless and become very angry.

Referrals in the early stage of the relationship are likely to be less emotionally fraught for both client and counsellor, and the following are some of the circumstances in which it is ethically responsible and appropriate for you to make a referral:

- The client wishes to be referred.

- The client needs longer-term work, an open-ended contract or more frequent sessions than you have available or, if you work for an agency, are possible within the constraints of the agency's policy.

- You feel overwhelmed by, do not understand, or have insufficient training or experience to deal with, the presenting problem.

- The presenting problem is one for which other more appropriate or specialist agencies exist. At a later or action-planning stage of counselling it becomes apparent that the client needs more specialist advice, information, longer-term counselling, or practical help.

- The client persistently fails to respond to your counselling and may be helped more effectively by someone else.

- The client needs medical attention. For example, refer to a GP for unusual headaches, shortness of breath, fatigue and chest pain. For persistent angina (tight, gripping pain in chest, back or arms), send for an ambulance.

- The client shows signs of severe mental illness and is not able to continue without intensive care and support.

- There is, in your view, a real risk of harm to the client or to others.

- Either you or the client is leaving the area to live somewhere else.

- You experience a very strong negative reaction to a client or there is a clash of personalities.

- You discover that you and your client share a close relationship.

Whenever the possibility of referral arises, a decision should be made with your client, although the initial suggestion may come from you. The process can be brief or take weeks or longer, and you may wish to serve as a 'bridge' and provide short-term supportive counselling. Facilitating any referral involves a number of tasks to ensure as far as possible that the client feels generally positive about it. These include:

- checking that the agency or individual will be able to accept the referral

- helping the client to explore, and perhaps resolve, any emotional blocks towards the agency or referral

- working towards bringing the client's perceptions of the problem close enough to that of the referral agency for the referral to 'take'

- explaining the nature of the help that might be offered and perhaps encouraging the client to consider accepting the help

- if necessary, helping the client to make his or her own approach or application

- reviewing what has been achieved with the client and exploring what still needs to be achieved and how the referral agency could contribute to this
- anticipating and exploring ways of coping with possible differences and potential difficulties in starting work with someone else
- letting the client know that referral does not end your care and concern.

In order to increase the number of options and establish an efficient referral system, you should develop your own personal contacts and resources file, listing people in a variety of occupations: lawyers, osteopaths, psychiatrists, but particularly counsellors and psychotherapists with different strengths and specialisms from your own. Lazarus gives some subtle examples of the matching involved, such as referral to somebody who 'has a way with certain words'. He also suggests a form of words for referring a client when you are 'stuck': 'I think we need a second opinion here; I am missing something; I have a high regard for my colleague so and so, and would recommend that you see him or her' (Dryden, 1991, p32).

In addition to listing the nature of the help offered by an agency or individual, it is useful for your resources file to contain full information on each agency, for example:

- name of the contact person, telephone number and address
- whether the agency or individual offers a 24-hour service, drop-in or appointment system
- scale of fees charged, if any, or if financial assistance is available
- probable waiting time
- how the referral can be made and by whom
- whether the agency or individual offers a telephone service
- whether the agency or individual sends information or publications
- theoretical orientation of counsellors
- training and supervision of counsellors
- code of ethics to which counsellors subscribe
- whether the agency offers individual and/or group counselling.

REFERRAL LETTERS

See also: Administration, Psychobabble, Referral

A referral letter is a means by which one professional person communicates with another about a client. Referral letters to the counsellor may contain detailed information or might simply consist of a single-line statement. Although a referral letter could contain important and relevant information, it is also possible that the referrer has a very different picture of the client than the one the counsellor subsequently forms.

A counsellor could be called upon to write a referral letter on behalf of a client. If this is the case, the client needs to be informed that the letter is being written and, wherever possible, his or her permission should be obtained for contact to be made. The form the referral letter will take should be discussed with the client, but generally it includes the client's full name, address and date of birth, as this leaves less room for error in securing, for example, patient notes, and all relevant information (e.g. client's problems) as discussed with the client.

Fact and opinion should be clearly separated, and, as in most writing, short words and paragraphs are best (Bond and Sandhu, 2005).

REFLECTION OF FEELINGS

See also: Core conditions, Emotions, Empathy, Feeling, Paraphrasing

Most counsellors would associate 'reflection of feelings' with Carl Rogers and client-centred counselling, but it is now widely used and part of the range of methods or techniques within almost all approaches to counselling. Reflection of feelings is a way of communicating empathic understanding, but Rogers (e.g. 1987) became increasingly concerned that it was being misrepresented as a simple and rather mechanical technique. For him, empathy was not a matter of 'reflection' in the way a mirror reflects, which he thought was a rather passive process. Rather, he was trying to establish the extent to which his understanding of his clients was accurate, and his responses contained the unspoken question, 'Is this the way the world feels to you at the moment?' Rogers' preferred terms, later in his life, were 'testing understanding' or 'checking perceptions', where he tried to emphasise the active process involved in both gaining deeper empathic understanding and communicating it.

REGULARITY OF SESSIONS

See also: Boundaries, Contract, negotiating a, Frequency of sessions, Length of sessions, Power, Psychological type

Some clients appreciate being offered the same day of the week and the same time of day for their counselling sessions. This has at least three possible advantages. First, you may be seen as consistent and reliable, which will help you establish trust with your client, especially at the beginning of counselling. Secondly, your client may be able to arrange for time away from work or home more easily, especially if childcare arrangements are necessary. Thirdly, it might help to maintain the working alliance as purposeful and concentrated. On the other hand, some clients (e.g. shift workers, pilots, performing artists) and counsellors need flexibility, and short 'bursts' of counselling with gaps may help some clients change more effectively.

RELATIONSHIP BETWEEN COUNSELLOR AND CLIENT

See also: Common factors, Core conditions, Counselling, Empathy, Metaphors for counselling, Psychological type, Rapport, Trust

Research shows that the relationship between counsellor and client is a major factor in successful counselling (Beutler *et al.*, 2004; Norcross, 2002; Stiles, 2006). However, it is not the only important factor and it is not yet clear what *elements* of the relationship are the most influential. The core qualities are well supported, and other likely elements include optimism from the counsellor and the active involvement of the client (Hubble *et al.*, 1999). Moreover, the importance of each element and of the relationship itself probably varies from client to client. A useful way of thinking about and studying the counselling relationship is the 'working alliance' (Bordin, 1979; Stiles, 2006). This assumes and emphasises the collaborative, open nature of an effective counselling relationship and is based on three components:

- agreement on goals
- agreement on strategies
- the emotional bond between counsellor and client.

RELAXATION

See also: Exercise (physical), Exercises, Homework, Imagery, Mindfulness, Stress

Physical relaxation is an obvious way of coping with stress, both immediately and preventively. Two 10-minute sessions of progressive relaxation a day seem to have a beneficial and cumulative effect (Seligman, 1995). However, sometimes attempting to relax is itself stressful. Lazarus and Mayne (1990) discuss such factors as fear of losing control, competitiveness and lack of patience. A flexible approach helps. Some people prefer a well-lit room, others a dark one; some respond best to several two- or three-minute sessions; and so on. Payne (2000) discusses several methods of physical and psychological relaxation in detail, including pitfalls, as well as theory and some of the research on their effects.

Both relaxation and meditation aim to put the body at ease and to clear the mind. They also tend to have similar health benefits, such as decreased blood pressure, reduced stress, increased immune efficiency, reduction of anxiety symptoms and often reduction of depression. Meditation strengthens and focuses the mind, a dynamic component of awakening – becoming more aware of moment-to-moment experiences. Relaxation often works with 'moving to a place of peace' (visualisation) whereas meditation is more concerned with regular practice and focusing the mind in the here and now ('falling awake').

RELIGION

See: Multiculturalism

RELUCTANT CLIENTS

See also: Avoidance, Denial, Difficult clients, Empathy, Expectations (clients'), Giving information, Quiet clients, Readiness to change, Referral

Clients can see counselling as a luxury or a necessity but want, at least in part, to be there. They may also see it as an admission of failure or an indication that they are losing their sanity, and they could therefore be wary of attending. Moreover, some clients are coerced into coming by others (e.g. by family or an institution). Children nearly always attend at the insistence of others. The reasons for a client's reluctance need to be clarified – they may be anything from lack of information to a deep-seated fear – and clients must be reassured that their needs come first. Queries must be answered and confidentiality assured. Some clients like to know about codes of ethics. Good use of listening skills, empathy and information giving are all central to responding well to reluctant clients. However, reluctant clients (as distinct from clients who are resistant to change) often drop out of counselling.

RESEARCH

See also: Evidence-based practice, Freewriting

The term 'research' is best interpreted as 'finding out' rather than anything mysterious. A much wider range of research methods are now accepted by the major journals and textbooks (e.g. see Boynton, 2005; McLeod, 2003b; Robson, 2002) from, for example, 'the joys of reading someone else's mail' (interpreting say the letters between Freud and Jung: Benjamin, 2007) to large-scale meta-analyses. Qualitative and quantitative methods are increasingly seen as complementary rather than rivals; what matters is their appropriateness for the research question and how well they are used.

Leong and Austin (2006) provide a clear, calm guide to carrying out research, with many practical tips and a respect for all phases of research, including finding ideas, dealing with journal editors and reviewers, and writing. For the formal researcher into aspects of counselling, the fifth edition of Bergin and Garfield's handbook (Lambert, 2004) is essential, even though it often exemplifies why practitioners tend to ignore research. Good attempts have also been made to reduce the terrors of statistics, for example by Diamantopoulos and Schlegelmilch (1997).

Writing up research – theory or empirical – is another daunting step for many researchers. One obstacle is the myth that writers find writing easy; however, most rewrite many times, and many regard writing as, at least in part, a punishing process. Nevertheless, writing also helps to clarify thoughts and may help others, and there are techniques to try when inspiration fails, such as freewriting; reading your material aloud (or – this is particularly brave – asking someone else to); writing a detailed outline; writing as if to a friend. Boice (1994, 1997), Elbow (1997) and Bayne (2004) offer views, research findings and advice on writing.

Boice's recommendations include those listed below:

- Write little and often. He specifically recommends 'brief, daily sessions' of 10 minutes to an hour.
- Take at least as long to make notes, play with them and organise them, as to write, rewrite and edit.
- Check for tension while you write (say every few minutes) and relax if necessary.
- Rewrite several times.

Boice's general approach is to make writing more enjoyable, and as a result more productive. His research shows clearly that these strategies work well. However, Boice did not consider individual differences (e.g. psychological type) and each strategy is likely to suit some people more than others.

RESISTANCE

See: Avoidance

RESPECT

See also: Acceptance, Counselling, Core conditions, Warmth

Like the related concepts of acceptance and warmth, respect is considered by most approaches to counselling to be a highly desirable characteristic of the counsellor. Its essential quality is that it is as nonjudgemental and unevaluative as possible. Respect is not the same as 'liking' or 'feeling affection', and it is not an instruction to counsellors about how they should feel for their clients; rather, it is a lack of judgement of a client's present way of being and an acceptance that positive change is possible, even for clients whose behaviour may at present be very destructive towards self or others (Mearns and Thorne, 2007; Merry, 1995; Rogers, 1961).

RESTIMULATION

See: Counter-transference, First impressions

REWARDS OF COUNSELLING

See also: Continuing professional development, Psychological type, Self-awareness, Stress

Counselling can be a very rewarding occupation. Helping someone to overcome very difficult and challenging circumstances can bring great personal fulfilment. Focusing on the life and experience of another person in ways that enable the healing of past emotional hurt and encourage a more creative outlook for the future is, in itself, a rewarding and worthwhile experience.

Other rewards are more indirect. Counsellor training involves the development of understanding and sensitivity towards others, and these qualities can be reflected in a counsellor's personal life and relationships. On the other hand, the intensity and intimacy of some counselling can make other relationships seem mundane. Having an awareness of the way in which destructive behaviour is often a result of damaging life experience can help us to become more tolerant and understanding of others. Knowing that it is possible to transform such behaviour, together with underlying attitudes and values, into something more constructive and creative can help us to remain optimistic for ourselves and others.

RISK MANAGEMENT

See also: Confidentiality, Mental health and mental illness, Record keeping, Scaling, Suicide, Violence and its prevention

With some clients, it is important to recognise that there are risks involved, as a result of the issues they are dealing with, or in relation to engaging in the counselling process. Clients may for example have suicidal ideas, engage in self-harming behaviour, or be psychologically fragile. They may present a risk to others such as family members or even the counsellor if they have difficulties with aggression and violence. They may also be at risk from others, for example abusive partners or relatives, and this risk may be exacerbated if these others are aware that they are seeing a counsellor, or if their behaviour changes as a result. There may also be some risk as a result of the process of counselling: sometimes clients feel worse in the initial stages before they start to feel better.

Risk management in counselling is about assessing the risks realistically, openly and honestly, and developing strategies to manage them: to minimise the risk and have strategies in place to ensure safety should the need arise. It is important to be aware that risk assessment is not a once-only procedure; it should be a dynamic ongoing process which takes account of *fixed factors* (such as age, gender, etc. known to influence risk) and *variable factors* (the client's changing circumstances, life events, mood, and behaviour). It is generally helpful to engage clients actively in the process of monitoring and managing risk: ask regularly how they perceive the risk; consider using rating scales if appropriate, and ask them how best they can ensure their (or others') safety and wellbeing.

Risks that might need to be assessed include:

- risky behaviours:
  - suicide
  - self harm
  - eating disorders
  - addictive behaviours
  - sexual risk taking
  - taking physical risks

- mental health problems, if they include an element of risk
- physical health
- threats to client from significant others
- environmental risks (e.g. living conditions, etc.)
- risks to others:
  - from client (e.g. aggression, violence, abuse)
  - from others known to client (e.g. abuse, intimidation).

Therapeutic work affects risk and is the most effective risk management. For example, clients engaged in counselling are less at risk from suicide, although the risk rises during breaks. Somewhat paradoxically, if risk management is successful, the accuracy of assessment will not be known, and it is important not to allow this to lead to complacency. In other words, if you are effective in managing risk, be wary that it does not lead you to begin to underestimate it in the future.

Counsellors are well advised to familiarise themselves with the risk factors for common presenting problems (such as suicidal ideas) but not to overvalue them at the expense of an empathic understanding of individual clients. It is also useful to develop a repertoire of short-term strategies for managing risk, which can include:

- contracting – either making an explicit agreement that the client will not do a particular thing or that she or he will do something (e.g. phone Samaritans) as a first step in avoiding the risk
- problem management approaches (clear identification of likely triggers, goal, and action plan)
- cognitive-behavioural techniques for challenging self-defeating thoughts, compulsions, etc.
- relaxation techniques or distraction/diversion activities
- developing a range of coping strategies with the client, including people or organisations that can help, alternative behaviours, time out, safe places, etc.

Some risks, for example violence, abuse and particular risks to health, may be severe enough to warrant the involvement of other agencies such as police, GP, social worker, etc. Where possible this should be done with the client's consent, but in cases where there is sufficient risk to the client or others, the BACP's Ethical Framework (BACP, 2007) does allow the counsellor to break confidentiality. Working with a high level of risk with clients can be stressful and demanding and is an issue that needs careful monitoring in supervision, not only from the point of view of maintaining effective risk management but also to monitor the wellbeing and coping resources of the counsellor.

ROLE CONFLICT

See also: Boundaries, Brief counselling, Confidentiality, Counselling, Effectiveness of counselling, Power, Self-awareness, Stress

For some people, counselling is part of a wider professional role. For example, some teachers and nurses offer counselling as one of several ways in which they respond to the needs of others. It is not easy to maintain boundaries between different helping roles with the same person, but many helping professionals are able to achieve this. They seem able to build on their existing relationships, established through their other roles, and offer valuable counselling.

Provided that the distinction between counselling and any other form of helping is explicit, there does not seem to be any ethical objection to someone offering counselling to the same person with whom he or she has, or has had, another role relationship. However, role conflict (as the term suggests) does tend to create some difficulties, five of which are discussed briefly below:

- **Internal conflict:** it can be very difficult and professionally demanding for the same person to be the expert in one role – with in-depth knowledge of a particular field, efficient and skilled in performing tasks *for* others – and then to switch roles and provide a helping relationship in which the responsibility is on the client to work through and come to terms with painful and emotional aspects of his or her own life.

- **Expectations:** clients are also asked to adapt. In the role of the patient, for example, they can justifiably expect a nurse to know some answers and to be able to make some things better but, in the role of the client, they find they can no longer expect things to be made to happen for them in the same way. You may then be faced with the client's hostility or disappointment and, in turn, might doubt your own ability as a counsellor. Clearly, this is a difficulty that any counsellor might face at some time with any client, not just those who are having to switch roles with the same person, but role conflict can intensify the problem, and it can be very hard and often discouraging to deliberately resist a client's expectation of us to be someone who has the answer.

- **Power:** perhaps anyone who sets themselves up to help others in any professional helping role, not just as a counsellor, will automatically become 'superior'. Neutrality in any helping role, including counselling, is probably a myth. The very fact that counsellors place themselves in the position of offering help puts them in a potentially powerful position over the one who temporarily accepts that help. This can feel good and be very seductive. It is important that counsellors recognise this aspect of the counsellor–client relationship so that it can be appropriately controlled and used (Egan, 2007) or put aside as far as possible (Rogers, 1987).

- **Individual needs:** relatively little is known about why people become counsellors. The decision may reflect a special need to help others and to be needed. This source of satisfaction from counselling is quite ethical, unless clients are exploited. A safeguard against this is for counsellors to ensure that their personal lives meet most of their needs sufficiently. Counsellors must monitor what is going on for them and be aware of the ways in which they might misuse their relationships with clients.

- **Pressure of work:** professional helpers tend to be very busy. Within the current ethos of quality control and accountability, there is pressure to get things done as quickly and efficiently as possible so that more can be done for more people. Employers expect results. The difficulty for counselling is that it often takes time – sometimes weeks or months – to establish an effective working relationship with clients and allow them to explore and work through their problems and find the best way of coping effectively. It is very tempting to tell clients what to do or what to think and feel in order (on the surface) to manage or resolve their problems quickly. Counselling does not work like this, but it can be difficult (especially for someone who offers counselling as one of several ways of helping) to put these pressures aside.

ROOM

See: Furniture, Nonverbal communication, Privacy

SCALING

See also: Action planning, Evaluation, Force-field analysis, Goals, Homework

Scaling is a technique used in solution-focused brief therapy (de Shazer *et al.*, 2007) that can be adapted by integrative counsellors and psychotherapists for a number of applications. The technique invites the client to consider the present situation or problem in relation to a scale, usually from 0 to 10, where 0 represents the worst that things have ever been or could be, and 10 represents the best.

1. The client rates the current situation, for example choosing 4.
2. The counsellor would then ask what factors make the current rating 4 rather than 3. This encourages the client to consider ways in which the present situation is a bit better than it might be, hopefully identifying things which she or he is doing, or strengths and resources that she or he is using which are contributing to that.
3. The client is then asked to describe how things would be different if the rating were to reach 5. (It may be useful to look at numbers higher up the scale as well: e.g. 'What would 6 be like?', '7?', etc.)
4. The client can then be encouraged to explore strategies which would help her or him to achieve the next point on the scale. This is likely to include making more use of the positive actions and strengths

identified in step 2. If the step up to the next full point on the scale seems daunting for the client, it can help to suggest aiming for a half-point improvement. ('What could you do to get to 4½?')

5. The scale can then be used in subsequent sessions to evaluate progress and develop further action plans.

Such scales can be used to refer to very specific factors about a client's experience, such as the level of anxiety versus confidence experienced, or a more general evaluation of how she or he stands in relation to a particular problem or, indeed, life in general. Some clients find it helpful to use rating scales as part of journal entries or for self-monitoring in difficult situations; and the process outlined above offers a way of building on this positively rather than simply noting the score.

SELF-AWARENESS

See also: Assertiveness, Big I, Blind spots, Body scan, Drama triangle, Emotions, Feeling, Immediacy, Metaphors in counselling, Mindfulness, Psychological type, Thoughts, Values

All the 'core qualities' and many of the skills of counselling require at least a reasonable degree of self-awareness, in the sense of awareness of your own thoughts, emotions, sensations, intuitions, intentions, fantasies and images. If we become clearer about ourselves in this 'inside' sense, we can:

*   be clearer with other people
*   detect signs of stress earlier
*   have more information on which to base decisions
*   be more ourselves
*   maintain a balance between over-involvement (with consequent stress) and too great a detachment.

Three senses of the term 'self-awareness' are distinguished in Figure 4: first, part of inner self-awareness, as defined above; secondly, self-knowledge, which refers to relatively stable aspects of inner self-awareness, such as talents, values, interests and personality traits; thirdly, outer self-awareness, which refers to awareness of your own behaviour and of how it tends to be interpreted by others.

Counsellor education and training focuses on all three senses of self-awareness, because they all have an impact on counselling. Inner self-awareness provides personal experience, especially emotions, intuitions and insights. Self-knowledge affects your judgements of others and their judgements of you. Outer self-awareness may need to be referred to, for example 'I frowned then because …' or 'I was being flippant. There is a serious point there too …'

The idea that we can become more aware of our emotions through counselling, or other ways of focusing attention inwards, applies to the other elements too and to patterns of emotional responses to people and events,

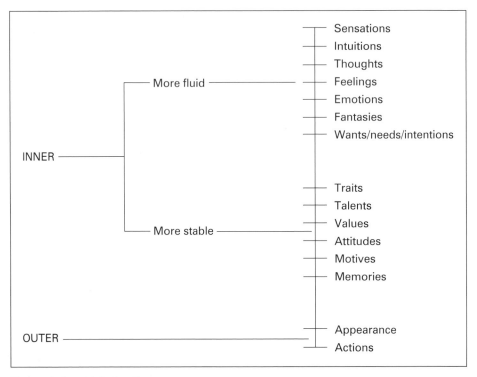

Figure 4 A model of self-awareness

for example the drama triangle. There are of course numerous approaches to increasing self-awareness (e.g. Bond, 1986; Merry, 1995).

SELF-DISCLOSURE

See also: Assertiveness, Boundaries, Challenging, Congruence, Furniture, Hot flushes, Immediacy, Multiculturalism, Nonverbal communication, Questions (personal) asked by clients, Self-awareness, Trust

By clients

Many clients do not tell their counsellors everything, or even everything relevant to their problems (Farber, 2003, 2006; Manthei, 2007). Most of the reasons given are obvious, for example shame, lack of trust, fear. Manthei (2007) suggests reassuring clients that this is OK, and that 'it is probably better for them to exercise caution in this area rather than feel "pushed" into doing something they don't want to do' (p18).

By counsellors

Three senses of self-disclosure by counsellors can be distinguished: historical revelation (e.g. 'I've been jealous too'); expression of here-and-now reactions (e.g. 'I'm feeling stuck'); and nonverbal (e.g. furniture, facial expression). The first should be rare in counselling, although occasionally it is very helpful; the second is a counselling skill; the third is inevitable.

Egan (2007) calls self-disclosure in the historical-revelation sense 'direct self-disclosure' and comments that so far the research on it 'has led to mixed and even contradictory conclusions' (p166). The gains are potentially worthwhile, especially for the relationship, and clients tend to rate counsellor self-disclosure as helpful for increasing trust, or putting their own situation in perspective. Thus, as Hanson (2005, p103) commented: 'simply to avoid self-disclosure in order to avoid the possibility of exploitation risks doing a disservice to clients'. The risks, however, are substantial. In particular, the client may be baffled and perhaps try to help you. It follows that your purpose in self-disclosure should be clear to both you and your client, and that you should be direct, brief and relevant.

SEXUAL ATTRACTION

See also: Abuse, Assertiveness, Boundaries, Ethical Framework, Immediacy, Self-awareness, Transference

Of clients for counsellors

Clients often enter counselling at a time when they feel most vulnerable (e.g. after the breakdown of an important relationship) and in particular need of understanding and warmth. It is not surprising, therefore, that clients sometimes become sexually attracted to their counsellors, especially when they feel accepted and valued.

Occasionally, clients make sexual suggestions or advances to their counsellors. Some forms of counselling, particularly psychodynamic counselling, view this as a form of 'transference' (having feelings for the counsellor which originate in, and belong to, past relationships). Whatever the theoretical explanation, it is most important to hear and acknowledge such feelings, but never directly to act on them. It is best to respond with a gentle but firm 'No', and to do this in such a way that your client will not feel rejected as a person.

A brief explanation in terms of ethics and boundaries is also likely to be appropriate; then, of course, it is a matter of listening to your client's reaction and (again, if appropriate and consistent with your approach to counselling) disclosing some of your reactions. To give a rather clinical perspective, you are demonstrating the difference between expressing feelings on the one hand and acting on those feelings on the other.

Of counsellors for clients

The counselling relationship can be very special and close. Counsellors may feel great warmth and love for their clients, and sometimes feelings of sexual attraction. This is not a matter of shame or even regret. However, it is important both to acknowledge these feelings and not to act on them directly.

Acknowledging them may mean talking about them with someone you trust, perhaps a supervisor or in a supervision group, although this may feel risky. Some approaches to counselling suggest sharing your feelings with your client; this may, in some circumstances, be sound advice, but we suggest caution and (perhaps in supervision) a role play first.

Becoming sexually involved with a client is always unethical, although defining 'sexual' can be a problem (Russell, 1993). It is most important to protect the integrity of the counselling relationship, to be sensitive to and caring of the needs and feelings of your client, to protect and value the professional nature of the counselling activity, and to be true to your own professional, ethical and moral standards. The priority of your concerns should be the client, professional issues and the counsellor, in that order.

The ethics of sexual involvement with an ex-client are more arguable. Russell (1993) suggested, on the basis of models of loss and grief, a six-month period before ex-clients (not counsellors) make contact socially. Factors like the length and nature of the counselling relationship seem relevant, while imposing an absolute ban does not do justice to the possibility of love between counsellor and ex-client, or respect client autonomy. On the other hand, some counsellors and organisations believe that some or all counselling relationships are never ended, and therefore that a sexual relationship between counsellor and client will always be an abuse of power and Bond (2000, p145) suggested that:

> most prudent counsellors would prefer to avoid sex with former clients unless the counselling relationship had been extremely brief, lacking in emotional intensity and therefore not involving the dynamics of transference and power which might persist or recur in a subsequent non-counselling relationship.

SEXUAL ORIENTATION

See: Multiculturalism

SHOULDS

See: Thoughts

SILENCE

See also: Empathy, Immediacy, Paraphrasing, Questions

Silences – pauses, intervals, moments of tension – can be very caring and effective, depending on the kind of silence. Some silences are 'working' ones: your client is trying to clarify or disentangle something. Some are natural breaks: there is nothing more to say about something, at least for the moment. These silences can be very peaceful. Other silences are lost, rejecting or hostile: your client has had enough or is stuck. The best option here is probably to try to be (gently) empathic, for example by saying 'You seem very fed up with this?' or 'You're finding it difficult to talk about this?' If you cannot tell from the context or the client's expression what is going on, you could say something like 'We've been quiet for some time. I'm not sure what's happening.' Ladany *et al.* (2004) concluded, in part, that 'No specific recommendations can be made in terms of when to use silence', and that 'There are no standard patterns for length of silence' (p88).

SOCIAL CLASS

See: Multiculturalism

SPECIALISMS IN COUNSELLING

See also: Common factors, Counselling, Multiculturalism, Referral

Two obviously opposed views on specialisms in counselling are, first, that at least some of them are justified, and, secondly, that they are marketing ploys and specious. At first glance, it seems an obviously good idea to develop skills and expertise in working with particular groups of people or with particular 'problems'. Particular people, or particular kinds of problems, the argument goes, need experts with specialist knowledge or experience. In most, perhaps all, of the client groups discussed in this book – people with dyslexia, PTSD, etc. – some of the people concerned would probably benefit from specialist counselling.

While this argument has some merit, it is in danger of creating a profession that has abandoned the idea that counselling consists of a general set of values, attitudes and relationship skills that can benefit all people, no matter what the 'presenting problem'. Instead, counselling becomes a 'technology' based on the accurate identification of subgroups and possible problems, each with its own experts.

Moreover, there is often as much variety within such subgroups as there is between them. Being a member of a particular group does not necessarily mean that an individual is typical of that group. Identifying subgroups can lead to stereotyping and treating people as if they are representative of their group, rather than as unique individuals who have some things in common with others, but also many differences. Furthermore, if it is true that the source of healing resides in clients themselves, together with their experience of being understood in a therapeutic relationship, then specialist knowledge of specific problems or groups is obviously less important.

STRESS

See also: Assertiveness, Boundaries, Burnout, Exercise (physical), Mindfulness, Post-traumatic stress disorder, Private practice, Referral, Relaxation, Rewards of counselling, Self-awareness, Supervision, Support groups, Thoughts, Values, Writing (expressive)

Stress is difficult to define well (Jones and Bright, 2001). However, a useful working definition is 'the experience of unpleasant over or under stimulation, as defined by the individual in question, that actually or potentially leads to ill health' (Bond, 1986, p2). This definition emphasises individual experience, hints at feeling threatened and strained to the extent of being overwhelmed, and includes too much stimulation as well as too little, as in 'bored out of my mind'.

Four types of stress can be suggested. First, too little stimulation can result in the stress of boredom or 'rustout'. Secondly, there is having too high expectations of oneself, doing or giving too much, without enough input of relaxation, self-care, play or fun, so that your life becomes out of balance in terms of work 'overload', which if it goes on for too long can cause burnout. Thirdly, there is the stress of change or of seemingly impossible goals, usually imposed from outside us but occasionally self-imposed, with which people perceive they cannot cope successfully; this can produce a sense of being out of control and create 'pressure stress'. Finally, there is the physical, emotional and mental stress which can result from a particular trauma: physical or emotional 'traumatic stress'.

One of the sources of confusion about stress is that the word 'stress' is often used to refer to the situation which causes unwanted bodily reactions. It is clearer if the situation as perceived by the stressed person is called the 'stressor' and the word 'stress' is used for the effects on the person.

Several kinds of stressor have been suggested as relevant to counsellors. In a research review, Brady *et al.* (1995) distinguished seven 'burdens', which are:

- patient (client) behaviours such as suicide, dependence, not turning up
- working conditions – for example, too many clients, inadequate resources
- emotional depletion
- physical isolation
- therapeutic relationships
- personal disruption – the counsellor's own problems affecting the quality of his or her counselling
- 'psychic isolation' – lack of intimacy and emotional support.

On therapeutic relationships, Brady *et al.* (1995, pp15–16) wrote (perhaps rather dramatically): 'We alternate between sleepless nights fraught with recollections of hostility and anxiety incurred from characterologically impaired patients, and fleeting moments of realisation that we have genuinely assisted a fellow human being.' They end their review on a *fairly* positive note: 'Most of us feel enriched, nourished and privileged in conducting counselling, but these benefits come at a significant cost' (p23).

Feelings of inadequacy or lack of skill, knowledge or experience in dealing with some very challenging or complex issues can also be very stressful. Good supervisory and other support is essential at these times. Counsellors need to develop the self-awareness and professional judgement that are required to refer clients whom they find too difficult to other counsellors or forms of help, without accompanying feelings of personal failure or inadequacy.

Working in private practice brings its own stresses. Finding enough clients willing or able to pay an appropriate fee can be a problem, especially when starting out and more so in some geographical areas than others. The need to keep proper accounts for tax purposes and to pay for consulting rooms and insurance, for example, can cause anxiety and a feeling of insecurity. Clients who are in employment may need appointments in the evenings or at weekends, and this can disrupt family life and erode opportunities for recreation and relaxation. Difficult counselling sessions can leave counsellors unable or unwilling to attend to the needs of their children, and there are many other problematic aspects of working from home (see entry on Private practice).

Effects of stress

When a person is overstressed, their thinking and emotions are likely to be affected, as is their body. Thoughts often become more negative. Some people become anxious, others angry and yet others depressed, but in all these moods there are usually associated negative thoughts about self, others, or a particular situation. At the same time, the autonomic nervous system stimulates the body to produce signs of stress. Powerful hormones (e.g. cortisol and adrenaline) are released. The heart rate becomes faster, the breathing more shallow, the digestive system slows down and muscles tense. All these changes can make the stressed person tired, irritable or ill.

Coping with stress

Often it is hard to realise that you are too stressed. It is only when they become ill that most people realise that something is wrong, and even then they may regard the illness as something outside their control. The first step in overcoming stress is often to understand its nature. After this, it is a matter of seeing which of the three components of stress you can most readily or usefully alter: the stressor, your mind or your body.

The stressor can be altered, modified or eliminated, but sometimes just help in understanding it may be beneficial. Counselling (or writing or meditation) may help to sort out negative thoughts, attitudes and perceptions and so generally improve your mental state. For your body, exercise, relaxation and breathing exercises can all be beneficial. It is advantageous if you use coping strategies for both your body and your mind: if they are relaxed and in harmony, you are better able to cope with the stressors of life. See Bond (1986), Rosenthal (1993), Palmer and Dryden (1995) and Jones and Bright (2001) for discussion of strategies.

Effective coping with stress therefore involves:

- noticing your own *early* signs of too much stress
- finding strategies that suit you
- using a variety of strategies.

As in counselling, small steps and gradual change are more likely to succeed for most people. Reading about the 'successes' and 'failures' of other counsellors can be helpful (e.g. Mearns 1990a, b; Yalom, 1989). It may also help to believe – really believe – that, in counselling and the health professions generally, there is always more to do, and that it is up to each of us to set our own priorities and boundaries. Proper rest and recovery time is part of being an effective counsellor.

The International Stress Management Association's website and the StressBusting website have useful information.

SUICIDE

See also: Confidentiality, Crisis counselling, Depression, Mental health and mental illness, Record keeping, Risk management

Suicide and the threat of suicide are frightening and taboo subjects for many people. People who threaten to commit suicide are typically in a state of overwhelming anguish, highly emotional and ambivalent, and absorbed by their problems. They frequently experience rejection or loss and hostility towards self and others. They tend to think in unusually constricted ways that lead them to see suicide as the only logical answer to their problems. Bond (2000) discussed in depth the 'acute ethical dilemma' facing a counsellor whose client is 'seriously intent on suicide': 'The choice is between respecting the client's autonomy or intervening with the intent of preserving the client's life. Counsellors are divided about how best to resolve this ethical dilemma' (p97).

A client mentioning suicide must be taken seriously and the possibility talked about with the client straight away. Some clients, however, only hint at suicide, so it is necessary to listen carefully for clues and confront the client gently: 'It sounds like you feel life isn't worth living for you and you want to end it.' If they question whether there is anything to live for, acknowledge the truth of this for them, and ask if they will give you a chance to listen to them, talk about their feelings and find out if there *is* anything for them to live for.

The BACP (2004) and Duffy and Ryan (2004) offer some useful ideas and research findings about suicide to bear in mind when assessing risk and challenging your clients:

- Factors associated with suicide include being a male, age (15–25 and over 75), social isolation, being single, job loss, certain jobs (e.g. doctor, dentist, farmer), mental illness, abuse, specific plan made, previous attempts at suicide, family history of suicide or suicide attempts.

- It is not true that people who talk about suicide never commit it. People who commit suicide often give clues or definite warnings about their intention.

- People who attempt suicide are not necessarily fully intent on dying. Most are undecided about living or dying and sometimes 'gamble with death', leaving it to others or 'fate' to save them. They may not be aware of their motives.

- Apparent improvement does not mean that the risk of suicide is over. Many suicides occur some months after apparent recovery from a suicidal crisis and when the person has the energy to act.

- People are not 'suicidal people' as such; they are people who want (or think they want) to kill themselves but are suicidal only for a limited time.

Joiner's theory states that people who commit suicide:

- believe that they are a burden to others and that they no longer make a useful contribution
- feel disconnected and isolated
- have got used to fear, pain, and suffering.

These risk factors suggest that treatment and prevention should focus on helping clients to engage socially and contribute to others and society. Joiner (2006) recommends focusing on the client's sense of being a burden and feeling alone: clients can list their disruptive feelings and emotions, ranking them in order of most upsetting and looking at strategies to try for each (this could increase control and hope) and challenging negative thoughts.

Most approaches to preventing suicide suggest various tasks and stages, and assume that the counsellor will be relatively active and directive; the following is an example:

1. Establish a positive relationship.
2. Clarify the problem.
3. Assess the risk and reassess it from time to time:
   - Precipitating factors: identify possible stressful events and assess whether the level of stress is chronic or acute, recent, episodic or longer term.
   - Symptoms: assess the severity of symptoms and whether there has been any sharp, noticeable and sudden onset, e.g. severe depression, withdrawal, delusions, hallucinations, etc.
   - Suicide plan: assess the degree of detail and clarity of any plan. Does the client know when, where and how he or she intends to commit suicide? In particular, how specific is the intended timing and how lethal and realistic is the proposed method?

- Is there a history of suicide or depression?
- Client's resources: assess the nature and level of social support and the client's ability to make use of it. Explore the client's view of what other people think of him or her. A lack of sympathy or understanding can increase the risk of suicide.

4. Form a plan of action. Try to help the client identify possible alternatives to suicide. Counsellors are typically more directive than usual, offering some guidance and suggestions. Although many clients will view themselves as helpless, most will have some strengths and resources. Initial plans need to be short term, identifying any potential 'low' spots in the day and ways of coping differently with them. Some counsellors negotiate a 'no-suicide pact' in which clients promise not to attempt suicide before the next counselling session, or before contacting the counsellor.

Your choice of strategy depends partly on the degree of suicide risk. If there is a high risk that a client will actually commit suicide, it might be necessary to refer him or her for treatment or hospitalisation, or to inform their GP, friends or relatives. Such action could mean breaking confidentiality. In this instance, counsellors normally try to encourage their clients to take the particular course of action for themselves; failing that, they ask the client's permission or agreement, and in the last resort simply tell the client what they are going to do before they do it. It can be helpful for counsellors to tell their clients that they do not want to carry the responsibility of the knowledge alone.

Most counsellors dealing with seriously suicidal clients should contact their supervisor as soon as possible. It is also essential to keep detailed case notes of the assessment, and of decisions or action taken, with supporting evidence, together with times and dates, i.e. to act in a considered and professional way. In particular, record specifically how your client expressed suicidal feelings or intentions; how you responded; the factors affecting your assessment of risk; and any actions you took, including consultations (BACP, 2004).

The following are useful contacts: Samaritans – phone 08457 909090 (24 hours) and website; Calm – phone 0800 585858 (5pm–3am); Survivors of Bereavement to Suicide – phone 0870 167 1677; the American Association of Suicidology's website and the website of Students Against Depression, which includes a self-help resource on coping with suicidal thinking.

SUMMARIES AND 'MOVING INTERVIEWS FORWARD'

See also: Challenging, Counselling, Paraphrasing, Questions

A summary of what your client has said should help them to clarify what they mean, feel and think, and to make more sense of it. In addition, it may increase your client's sense of control and hope, or reduce feelings of being overwhelmed. Summaries need to be tentative (they could be wrong in content or emphasis) and have a flavour of 'This is where we are so far, in outline, so where next?' 'Where next? may be further exploration, a focus on one problem or aspect of a problem or the end of counselling. Gilmore (1973) discussed ways of offering clients a way forward: for example, you might add the question 'Is there one of these you'd like to talk about first?' to your summary (the client may choose differently from you!). Or you might use a hunch: 'Perhaps your main worry is ...' or 'What seems to be most important is ...' Alternatively, you might suggest focusing first on something which seems relatively straightforward (Gilmore, 1973).

A further variation is to add a hypothetical question to your summary. Gilmore (1973) called this 'requesting a contrast'. For example, you might say in the preliminary summary 'You're unhappy about your work, especially whether you can cope with your boss's bullying. You'd love to be fitter and sleep better. And you're worried about being late for work, both because it lets your colleagues down and because being on time matters to you.' (Pause for your client to respond if she or he wishes.) A 'contrast' for this client would be to add: 'Suppose you were sleeping well. Do you think any of your other problems might look different?'

Sometimes, requesting a contrast works very well: it helps a client clarify a present feeling or focus on a key point. The risks, however, are also potent: it can look like (or become) premature problem solving (the instant solution) or lead to a general, speculative discussion. Again, how you say something and your attitude and general approach are central, and there is a strong artistic element: timing, how you speak, and the quality of the relationship between you and your client all play a part.

A final variation is to ask your client to summarise.

SUPERVISION

See also: Ethical Framework, Freewriting, Multiculturalism, Peer supervision, Process, Tape-recording, Therapeutic plan, Transference

In the UK, all counsellors are required to discuss their work regularly with a third party, the supervisor (c.f. Feltham, 1996). Supervision is primarily for addressing the needs of clients, but it is also to support the counsellor. In addition, the relationships between counsellor and client, and counsellor and supervisor, and the supervisor's 'process' all need to be kept in mind. A useful resource to work with, as it shows much of what actually happened in the session, not just what is reported, is a tape of a counselling session.

Supervision is preferably carried out by someone who does not have another role (e.g. line manager) in relation to the counsellor, and who therefore can concentrate solely on the counselling.

Hawkins and Shohet (2006) distinguish between seven modes of supervision that may be used together or at different times, although they say that supervisors might avoid one or more of these 'out of habit or lack of familiarity and practice' (p84). The modes are as follows:

- Reflect on what the client said and did, avoiding premature theorising.

- Explore the strategies and interventions used by the counsellor, and possible alternatives.
- Explore the counselling process and relationship.
- Focus on the supervisee.
- Focus on the supervisory relationship (c.f. 'parallel process').
- Focus on the supervisor's or supervision group's 'process'.
- Focus on the wider context (e.g. multicultural factors, codes of ethics, politics).

In choosing or working with a supervisor, it is worth negotiating a working agreement. Issues to negotiate can include:

- time, place, frequency and length of session
- length of contract and regular review sessions
- fee and method of payment (when and how)
- notice required for cancellation of sessions and missed session payment
- method of presentation and recording of clients (e.g. tape-recordings)
- what you want from supervision
- any training-course requirements.

In presenting a client for supervision, it is often useful to decide whether to focus on the entire counselling process or only on parts of it, on the client and his or her problems, or on your own sense of effectiveness and wellbeing. If, for example, you find a particular client difficult or challenging, you might want to present and discuss the difficulties you experience as issues in themselves, rather than specifically talk about a certain client.

One way of presenting a client for supervisions is to use a simple series of 'prompts'. As in the following examples, these offer ways of focusing on your feelings and thoughts about your relationships with your clients:

- What do I wish to accomplish through presenting this case?
- What specific difficulties do I experience with this client?
- Does this client remind me of aspects of myself and what do I think and feel about those aspects?
- What does this client hope to accomplish in counselling?
- What am I doing well with this client?
- What could I do better with this client?
- What am I learning about myself as a person and as a counsellor from this client?

Another, more structured and detailed, possibility is to select from the frameworks below:

1. **Identification**
   (a) First name only, gender, age/life stage
   (b) Your first impressions, client's physical appearance

2. **Antecedents**
   (a) How the client came to see you – e.g. self-referred
   (b) Context – e.g. agency, private practice, hospital clinic
   (c) What you knew about the client before you first met. How you used this information. Any existing relationship with the client and possible implications

3. **Presenting problem and contract**
   (a) Summary of presenting problem
   (b) Your initial assessment: duration of problem, precipitating factors (i.e. why the client came at this point), current issues
   (c) Contract – frequency, length and number of sessions

4. **Questions for supervision**
   (a) Key issues

5. **Content**
   (a) Description of the client in Gilmore's (1973) framework:
   (i)   work – significant activities, interests
   (ii)   relationships – significant people
   (iii) identity – feelings and attitudes towards self
   (iv)   further possible elements are the implications of cultural, economic, social, political and other systems, and the client's early experiences, strengths and resources, beliefs, values, hopes, fears and fantasies
   (b) Problem definition
   (i)   Construct a picture of the client's view of the present problem
   (ii)   What would the client like to happen? How would the client like things to be?
   (c) Assessment – how you account for and explain the presenting problem:
   (i)   Are there any patterns/themes connections?
   (ii)   Which theoretical concepts or models apply? Hunches? New perspectives?
   (d) Counselling or therapeutic plan
   (i)   Direction or focus for future work?
   (ii)   Criteria for change?
   (iii) Review and/or formulate plan(s)

6. Process

    (a) Strategies and interventions

        (i)   What strategies and interventions have you used?

        (ii) What was your intention?

        (iii) What was their impact on the client?

        (iv) What alternative strategies are there?

    (b) Relationship

        (i)   What was happening between you and the client? Reframe the relationship; try a metaphor

        (ii) What was happening within the client (transference)?

        (iii) What was happening within you (counter-transference)?

        (iv) What changes have there been in the relationship?

        (v) Evaluate the 'working alliance'

7. Parallel process

    (a) What is happening between you and the supervisor?

    (b) Any parallels with you and the client?

8. Critical incident analysis

    (a) Description

        (i)   What did the client say and do at the particular point?

        (ii) What did you say and do?

        (iii) How did the client respond?

        (iv) What was happening within you?

    (b) Analysis

        (i)   What was happening within the client?

        (ii) What was going on between you and the client?

        (iii) Intention and impact of interventions/responses

        (iv) What hunches/hypotheses did you have at the time? And now?

        (v) Review

9. Listening to aspects of covert communication

    (a) What was happening within you?

        (i)   How well did you listen to your own emotional response to a client?

        (ii) You may be aware of your feelings first and thoughts later, or the reverse

        (iii) What did the client do and say to make you feel the way you did?

        (iv) What does the client want from you and what sort of feeling is she or he trying to arouse in you to get it?

(b) What was happening within the client? Observe and reflect back when appropriate:

    (i)   changes in voice quality, which might indicate an inner focus on something that is being seen or felt differently

    (ii)   nonverbal communication: e.g. silence, gazing into space, posture

    (iii) idiosyncratic words or phrases

    (iv) aspects of content you do not understand; perhaps the client does not either

    (v)   statements about other people or situations which may, at some level, actually be about the client.

SUPPORT GROUPS

See also: Assertiveness, Boundaries, Challenging, Contract, negotiating a, Immediacy, Stress, Trust

The main purposes of a support group are to offer support to each member of the group, by, for example, listening carefully to them, and to enable you to receive support yourself. Good social and psychological support has been shown to reduce stress and lessen the effects and risk of some stressors (e.g. Jones and Bright, 2001; Nichols and Jenkinson, 2006). On the other hand, other methods are also effective and some claims seem not to be justified (e.g. Coyne *et al.*, 2007). Support groups are not encounter groups, or for therapy, or for attempting to solve other people's problems. They are for each person to talk as openly as they comfortably can about important concerns and worries.

Guidelines

- Confidentiality is vital. We suggest agreeing not to discuss what happens in your group outside the group with anyone, not even with another group member or the person concerned.

- Bond (1986) distinguished between several kinds of support. The most relevant for peer support groups are listening (pp158–170), sharing factual information, sharing personal information, and advice and encouragement (pp147–151).

- The section on pitfalls in giving and receiving support (Bond, 1986, pp173–176) may also be useful. Pitfalls include refusing support when you need it, feeling obliged to take unnecessary support, and choosing the wrong kind of support.

- At the end of each meeting, review what is going on in the group, your reactions and if you would like to change anything.

Practical issues

- How many people? (3–6)
- How often will you meet? (No accepted right amount. Weekly?)
- For how long? (Try an hour? And an initial contract of, say, six meetings?)
- How will you structure each session and allocate time?
- If it is a peer support group, do you want one of the group to be the leader? Or take turns? Or …?
- Where will you meet?
- When will you meet? (If you meet irregularly, who will arrange meetings?)

TAPE-RECORDING

See also: Assertiveness, Confidentiality, Contract, negotiating a, Ethical Framework

A recording of a counselling session can be extremely valuable for supervision or as a means of self-monitoring. The most obvious ethical principle involved is to consult the clients beforehand and for their permission to be freely given. This means telling them what the recording is for, who will listen to it and what will happen to the tape once it has been used, and listening hard to the client's reaction. If the client gives permission initially, check again at the end of the session.

Many clients have no objection to being recorded or are enthusiastic about it, but some are very uneasy, and their wishes should of course be respected. Sometimes, clients appreciate knowing that they can switch off the tape at any point, and this possibility should be part of your agreement before recording begins. Another option for dealing with uneasy clients is to offer them the tape or a copy of it. If you do this, you might also want to suggest that the clients wait a few days before listening to it, and discuss where and how they will listen to the tape and the possible effects it could have. You may also want to discuss confidentiality (whether anyone else will hear the tape).

TEA AND COFFEE

See: Drinks/refreshments

TEAMS (MULTIDISCIPLINARY)

See also: Assertiveness, Boundaries, Confidentiality, Record keeping

Counsellors may work as part of, or in liaison with, a multidisciplinary team. Such teams are usually a group of workers involved in the care of an individual.

For example, clients with a history of psychiatric disorder may have a psychiatrist, a social worker and a psychologist involved in their care. A hospice is another example of a multidisciplinary team in action. Similarly, residential drug projects may have more than one worker involved in the care of a resident, and many counsellors now find themselves part of a multidisciplinary team when they work in general practices.

There are a number of issues to consider when working as part of a multidisciplinary team. First, the boundaries related to individual roles need to be defined, understood and agreed so that each person involved in the team understands the needs of the other team members and the work each will be undertaking with the client. Secondly, you need to decide what information is to be made available to the team and what should remain confidential between the client and counsellor. This also means being clear with the client about the parameters of confidentiality, which in turn has an impact on the type of notes taken and their storage, including access.

Open, frequent communication is central and Kwiatkowski and Hogan (1998) suggest several ways of achieving this and therefore improving a team's effectiveness. They include activities for exploring and clarifying how you construe your membership of groups, and ways of analysing groups and making sense of them. Their optimistic approach is justified: people have always worked in teams, often very effectively. Other factors which contribute to effectiveness are clarity about the task that team members are there for and their different roles, listening to each other, and challenging and respecting each other (Fay *et al.*, 2006; West, 2004).

TELEPHONE COUNSELLING

See also: Brief counselling, Coaching, Nonverbal communication, Online counselling

The most obvious difference between telephone counselling and face-to-face counselling is the absence of visual information (and the related assumptions and prejudices). However, voice tone, pitch and accent will all contribute to the impressions the client and counsellor form of each other. Some telephone counsellors negotiate with clients to exchange photographs, but others prefer to work without any visual clues. Rosenfeld (2006) suggests that the anonymity of some telephone counselling is liberating and increases intensity. It may therefore demand more effort and concentration and be more tiring. It is also easier for clients to end a session simply by putting the phone down, and clients may have different expectations of telephone counselling than they do of face-to-face counselling.

Telephone counselling is especially useful for crisis work and for clients who are ill or have limited mobility, and it obviously saves the time and cost of travelling. As with most brief or time-limited counselling, it is often necessary to work in a focused way on specific issues, drawing on explanatory concepts and techniques from a variety of theoretical orientations. Telephone counselling also has a place as an adjunct or follow-on process for clients who have previously been seen face to face, for example to overcome geographical or scheduling difficulties associated with moves, periods of study away, changes in work patterns, etc. Rosenfeld (2006) lists the elements of a contract and discusses relevant ethical issues, such as using a premium rate number and difficulties in keeping the fact of being counselled private.

THEORIES OF COUNSELLING

See also: Integration and eclecticism, Metaphors in counselling, Personality

Although there are over 400 individual therapeutic approaches, most fall within one of the four major theoretical schools: psychodynamic, humanistic, cognitive-behavioural and transpersonal. Some key concepts for each of these schools are:

- humanistic – fulfilment, growth, self as organism
- psychodynamic – predetermination, the dynamic unconscious, defences
- cognitive-behavioural – interaction of physiology, cognition, behaviour and emotion
- transpersonal – angst, authenticity, spirituality.

Formulating a harmonious and coherent grand theory from two or more theories which make radically different assumptions about human nature and about how, and to what extent, people can change may be impossible. For example, the concept of a 'dynamic unconscious' is central to psychoanalytic theories of counselling but is absent from many other theories where the evidence for a dynamic unconscious is open to alternative and simpler interpretations. Thus, slips of the tongue may reflect conscious feelings or feelings which are just below the surface, rather than hypothetical 'deeply submerged' ones, or they may simply be speech errors.

Nelson-Jones (1985, p131) suggested four elements of a theory of counselling:

- an indication of basic assumptions
- an explanation of how functional and dysfunctional feelings, thoughts and behaviour are acquired
- an explanation of how they are perpetuated or sustained
- practical suggestions for changing and modifying dysfunctional feelings, thought and behaviour that are internally consistent with the preceding elements.

These elements are the same as those in theories of personality. Those approaches to counselling that place little if any importance on the origin of psychological problems would be found lacking as a theory if these elements were accepted. However, there are problems with this idea: Nelson-Jones is not explicit about the kind of basic assumptions, and the practical component is vague, providing no guidelines on the type or nature of practical suggestions for change and no criteria for internal consistency.

Mahrer (1989) offered a different view. He argued that a theory of psychotherapy (or counselling) is *not* the same as a theory of personality. Its components are different, as are the issues and questions with which it deals, even though he recognises that it may imply or give birth to a theory of psychotherapy. He identified seven components of a theory of psychotherapy:

- useful material to be elicited from the client
- how to listen and what to listen for
- explanatory concepts to describe the client's presenting problem and targets for change
- therapeutic goals and direction of change
- general and more specific principles of change
- strategies, techniques and procedures
- description of what strategies to use under what circumstances or conditions.

Similarly, Beitman (1990) argued that counselling is a practical endeavour, intended to help people change, and therefore its theories must be connected to practical goals. He was critical of all the efforts to develop theories of personality and the emphasis placed on explanatory frameworks of the origin of psychological difficulty. He argued that theories of counselling must pay greater attention to the process of change and the factors maintaining psychological difficulty.

There is at present much interest in the integration of theories of counselling. However, without a clear analysis of what constitutes a theory it is difficult to know what it is that is being integrated. While there remains no consensus on a template for the analysis of a theory, four constituent elements of a comprehensive model of counselling emerge from the literature (Horton, 1998):

- **Personal belief system:** this is the philosophical element that describes the basic assumptions underpinning the other elements. It is typically concerned with world view – an individual's unique way of making meaning or construing reality – and with the counselling relationship and process.

- **Formal theory:** this is concerned with human nature and development. It may provide explanations of how both normal (or functional) and abnormal (or dysfunctional) thoughts, feelings and behaviours are acquired and how they are perpetuated. Alternatively, it may describe the position taken on the need for such explanatory frameworks. Explanations of the origin of psychological problems are not always seen as useful or relevant. Formal theory may emphasise the importance of social or cultural factors and identify targets or levels of change.

- **Clinical theory:** this is the functional theory that explains what counsellors do and why they do it. It would typically include some account of the general principles and mechanisms of change; the counselling process and how it develops; the nature and function of the therapeutic relationship; and clinical procedures such as assessment, therapeutic goals or tasks, contracting, etc.

- **Therapeutic operations:** this describes core skills and strategies. Bond (1995, personal communication from Tim Bond) illustrates the relationship of these elements in Bond's pond, a pictorial metaphor. The four elements are levels of water. At the bottom of the pond is the personal belief system in dark, murky and often stagnant water: yet Bond says that 'it contains rich and fertile soil, living creatures, flora and fauna and the unregenerate sludge and detritus of our own culture'. The formal and clinical theories are the next levels of water, with therapeutic operations as the clearly visible water on the surface of the pond. This is what counsellors actually do with clients to implement the other theoretical elements.

THERAPEUTIC PLANNING

See also: Assessment, Common factors, Counselling, Evaluation, Goals, Relationship between counsellor and client

The term 'therapeutic plan' refers to deciding (or in our view agreeing with your client) goals and strategies for your client's counselling. This can range from a general sense of direction to being very concrete. It may be developed from an assessment and should be open to change.

Research into the working alliance (see Relationship between counsellor and client) suggests that the level of agreement between therapist and client about the goals of therapy and the tasks to be undertaken in order to achieve those goals are key factors in achieving successful outcomes. Therapeutic planning in collaboration with the client is therefore an important consideration if you are to maximise the chances of success.

We suggest the following three-stage model for therapeutic planning, where Stage 1 represents the initial phase of the counselling process; Stage 2 is the 'working' phase; and Stage 3 the ending phase. (See Counselling.)

Therapeutic planning should be seen as a dynamic and evolving process, not something which is agreed initially and fixed. It is good practice to record in your notes goals for therapy and agreed approach and tasks, and to review these regularly both in supervision and with your client. In some cases, it may also be useful for the client to keep a note of plans agreed, and it is particularly important that the client participates fully in ongoing evaluation of the work you are doing. (Questions like 'What is helping?', 'What are you finding most useful?', 'What is less helpful?', 'Your goals were ... how do those feel now?' are helpful in initiating that process.)

Table 5 A model of therapeutic planning

Stage 1	Stage 2	Stage 3
Assess and negotiate	Monitor and revise	Evaluate
• Identify focus and therapy aims • Negotiate contract • Negotiate tasks of therapy – what we will be doing in sessions	• Monitor progress and goals • Monitor and review approach, techniques used, etc. • Evaluate and renegotiate	• Contract-ending procedures • Review learning and achievements, what can be taken away for future • Forward planning

THOUGHTS

See also: Assertiveness, Behaviour, Beliefs (irrational), Challenging, Depression, Emotions, Self-awareness, Values

Some counsellors and theories of counselling emphasise the role of thoughts – especially irrational self-defeating thoughts and underlying irrational beliefs – in troublesome emotions and behaviour (e.g. Ellis and Dryden, 1998; Moorey, 2007). A central idea in this approach is that when we repeatedly tell ourselves something like 'I must not make mistakes' we are likely to become upset and demoralised.

To avoid this damaging pattern, the following steps can be taken:

1. Identify the negative automatic thought – 'pinning it down' can be a helpful way of putting this.
2. Challenge it.
3. Replace it with a more realistic thought.
4. Act on the new thought.

For example, suppose you catch yourself or a client believing 'I should be able to do everything well', and see this as explaining or at least contributing to feeling incompetent, upset and anxious. You can help to dispute this thought by creatively using one of three types of disputation strategy:

- **Empirical:** 'Where is the evidence that you must do everything well?'
- **Logical:** 'Just because you do something badly, how does it logically follow that you are a bad person?'
- **Pragmatic:** 'How does believing that you must do everything well help you feel better?'

Having disputed the negative thoughts, the next step is to replace the self-defeating thought with a more realistic one: for example, 'I would prefer to do everything well but I do not have to'; 'I would prefer to do everything well; however, it is not the end of the world if I don't'. The last step is to reinforce and consolidate the new thinking through action. The client might have been avoiding studying for fear of not doing well and as a result of this analysis now signs up for a course.

This approach to changing thoughts is consistent with the assertiveness approach to rights. The list of rights in the entry on assertiveness contains negative thinking by implication, for example 'People ought to respect me' or 'I mustn't make mistakes and it is catastrophic if I do.' However, it is important to find each person's own variations.

Counsellors may have their own specialised irrational beliefs, such as 'I must be effective with all clients and client problems'; 'Rogers or Ellis would help this client'; 'Because I'm a counsellor, I shouldn't get stressed, tired, depressed, or anxious'. A general principle is to treat 'musts' and 'shoulds' not as absolutes but as *preferences*. For example, 'I should be effective with all clients' now becomes 'I would prefer to be effective with all clients; however, there is no law of the universe that says I must.' Unmet desires are seen as regrettable rather than as deeply upsetting.

There are many types of cognitive intervention: examples are identifying thinking errors such as 'all or nothing thinking'; using constructive self-talk; the deserted island technique; cost–benefit analysis; problem-solving training and thought stopping (Palmer and Dryden, 1995).

Thought stopping

Many people find themselves with unwelcome and unwanted thoughts. Thought stopping is perhaps one of the most widely used of the cognitive interventions. The following are two of the techniques:

- The client is asked to think of an unwelcome thought and then to visualise a 'STOP' sign. Once this has happened, the client tries to replace the unwanted thought with a more realistic or pleasant thought or image.
- The client is asked to wear an elastic band around his or her wrist and to flick the band when an unwanted thought happens. The sensation induced can distract the client from the thought.

Some people are repelled by this kind of technique, seeing it as 'brainwashing' and superficial; others see the techniques as using imaginative power for self-control and as worth trying for their economy, keeping other approaches in reserve.

TIME BOUNDARIES

See also: Boundaries, Endings, Length of sessions, Sexual attraction, Stress

There is considerable agreement among counsellors that it is part of your professional responsibility to be ready to start a session on time, but less agreement about when to end. Some counsellors believe that they should be careful to end within 30 to 60 seconds of the appointed time, and that this should be done without an apology, simply stating to the client that the time is up (Langs, 1982). Others have a more flexible approach, ending each session when it feels appropriate to do so within the time constraints and circumstances of both counsellor and client. They argue that a rigid adherence to boundaries is based on little more than convention. Most counsellors, however, feel that it is important to try to bring a session to a natural close near to the time originally agreed with the client.

There are strong arguments in favour of paying attention to ending on time. Maintaining time boundaries by starting and ending each session promptly can symbolise containment, 'holding' and reliability and provide a client with a sense of security and safety. Only if you keep reasonable time boundaries can your clients learn to use the time that is available. It is quite common for clients to start talking about a significant issue, or to make an apparently throw-away comment, towards the end of a session. This may be a test of their own courage or of your reaction in the relative safety of the limited time available, knowing at some level of awareness that it is possible to avoid taking the issue too deeply, at least in that session. Alternatively, it may be an attempt to manipulate you to spend more time with them.

A small, quiet clock visible to both you and your client allows you to say when there are only 5 or 10 minutes left and in this way begin to work towards ending and avoid an abrupt halt. Especially with brief counselling, it can be useful to conclude a session with some form of review. You can summarise what has been achieved and what needs to be discussed further or invite your client to do so.

At the end of some sessions a client may still be very distressed. Some counsellors remain silent, giving the client a few moments to recover. They believe that clients have the responsibility for dealing with their own distress and that they must learn to deal with it in their own way. Other counsellors prefer to offer an attention-switching or celebratory exercise (Evison and Horobin, 2006) to help their clients gain composure. An ideal situation would be to allow clients to sit quietly in another room until they feel ready to leave. In many settings, however, this is not possible.

TIME MANAGEMENT

See: Assertiveness, Boundaries, Psychological type, Stress, Values

TOUCH

See also: Assertiveness, Boundaries, Crying, Mistakes, Nonverbal communication, Sexual attraction

Some counsellors believe that it is never or rarely helpful to touch their clients. Others argue that touch can be very natural and positive and that it should depend on your client's needs and your careful judgement rather than on a fear of censure or a taken-for-granted taboo (Swade *et al.*, 2006).

'Careful judgement' involves several factors, as discussed by Hunter and Struve (1998) and others: for example, client's consent, control and choice over all aspects of touch; that the counsellor is comfortable with touch; timing; multicultural elements. The main problem is that touch, like most nonverbal communication, is highly ambiguous. It can be interpreted as caring, patronising, threatening, sympathetic, dominant, sexual, intimate, or an expression of fear.

It can also vary dramatically in its effects. For example, a hug is sometimes a very unhelpful thing to do, because it can block awareness of feelings. It can be more useful to talk about a desire to touch than to initiate it. However, touch is also a very basic way of making contact (perhaps especially when it is not done as a technique).

In some cultures, including some European ones, kissing as a greeting or as a farewell is a ritual that need not have any special (i.e. sexual) significance, but, even so, this form of physical contact usually happens only when people have known each other for some time. Also, different cultural groups have very different attitudes to kissing. Some find it very offensive; for others it is a normal ritual. Amongst some Europeans, kissing only *appears* to happen; there is no actual physical contact. Also, even if your culture expects or accepts 'ritual kissing', your client might not.

The real danger here is that a kiss can be misinterpreted, or invested with more significance than it really has. Even when you feel that you know your client very well, and have enjoyed a long relationship, it is best to be careful about how much physical contact, even of a ritualised kind, you allow. If problems do arise they can, of course, be talked through, and if you or your client has made a mistake this can be accepted and explored just like any other incident in counselling.

TRANSFERENCE

See also: Common factors, Counselling, Counter-transference, Empathy, First impressions, Immediacy, Relationship between counsellor and client, Supervision

'Transference' is a term used to describe the displacing of an emotion or attitude from one relationship to another. In essence, it involves having feelings towards, or behaving towards, someone on the basis of feelings or attitudes that exist or existed towards someone else. At some level the current relationship generates reminders or triggers, which reactivate the feelings or attitudes from the earlier relationship. These triggers may be to do with physical appearance or other aspects of the dynamics of the relationship, such as authority, care and understanding, or trust and intimacy, and are often outside conscious awareness.

In psychoanalysis, transference is more specifically used to refer to clients' feelings and attitudes towards the therapist, which may be transferred from their feelings and attitudes towards significant others in their lives (often parents, lovers, or authority figures). Indicators that transference is a factor include unexpected reactions, such as too intense, inconsistent or ambivalent. The counsellor is idealised, imitated or hated (Stewart, 2005). O'Brien and Houston (2007, p149) remark, gently, that 'how the client approaches the therapist and experiences the relationship may not entirely reflect the reality of what the therapist is like, either as a person or in the relationship with the client.'

Freud developed the idea of using transference to discover more about the deeper emotional state and early conflicts of clients. In this approach, the therapist offers little of themselves in order to present a 'blank screen' to the client where the transference can develop and be explored. An alternative approach is to try to prevent its development and, if it does develop, to challenge it, separating yourself from the person your client would like to believe you are. Empathy and congruence reduce transference, and humanistic theory (and much counselling research) would suggest that there are more benefits to be gained from a genuine person-to-person relationship in the majority of cases.

TRANSITIONS

See: Loss

TRUST

See also: Boundaries, Contract, negotiating a, Contraindications for brief counselling, Empathy, Immediacy, Multiculturalism, Questions (personal) asked by clients, Respect, Transference

Although some clients are very trusting right from the start, development of trust is usually a gradual process. Clients will have had mixed experiences of previous relationships. Some will have been let down very badly, and for these people trusting you will naturally take some time. Once counselling is under way, clients may test you by revealing things about themselves, or by asking you questions.

Fong and Cox (1983, p164) proposed six ways in which clients test for trust and suggested that behind each statement or question the client has a hidden and sometimes unconscious motive or a 'real' question (indicated here in brackets after each test):

- requesting information about the counsellor's personal experience, circumstances or knowledge, e.g. 'Are you married?' ('Can you understand me if you have not had a similar experience?')
- revealing, often unexpectedly and out of context, a potentially embarrassing secret, e.g. 'My brother masturbates with me' ('Can I be vulnerable with you?')
- asking the counsellor a favour, e.g. 'Can I borrow that book?' ('Do you think I am honest and reliable?')
- saying something bad or negative about him- or herself, e.g. 'I always make a mess of things' ('Can you accept the real me?')
- inconveniencing the counsellor in some way, e.g. 'Could I use your phone before we start?' ('Do you have consistent limits?')
- questioning the counsellor's motives, e.g. 'I bet it is hard to listen to other people's problems all day' ('Do you really care for me?').

It is important to take these tests seriously and to show that you can be trusted by being nonjudgemental. You might not want to answer, or you might think it inappropriate to answer some direct questions put to you by clients, but these situations can also be seen as opportunities for you to respond to the real issue or underlying motive. If a counsellor misreads the situation and sees the client's questions as defensive, resistant or even hostile and responds accordingly or only at a surface level, the process of developing trust may be delayed or fail.

TWO-CHAIR TECHNIQUE

See also: Exercises

The Gestalt two-chair technique, which can seem a very strange thing to offer to clients, can be introduced in this way:

> There seem to be two parts of you arguing here, and going round and round, so that you feel exhausted and helpless. I'd like to suggest a kind of experiment to try and clarify the two sides. It means you sitting in this chair when you're arguing one way and in this chair for the other side. Would that be OK?

Clarke and Greenberg (1986) compared the effectiveness of two kinds of intervention aimed at helping clients with decisions: one (problem solving) intended to help clients change their way of thinking, the other (the Gestalt two-chair method) focused more on emotions. Four counsellors trained in the two-chair method and four trained in problem solving each saw four clients, all of whom were volunteers facing a 'difficult, personal decision'. There was also a 'waiting list' group (a group that received no counselling). The research design had many good methodological points: for example, the eight counsellors were equally experienced in and positive about their own approach, and the sessions themselves were taped so that they could be rated for actual use of the two approaches. You may at this point like to predict the results.

Both methods reduced indecision more effectively than being on the waiting list, and the two-chair method was more effective than problem solving. The authors discussed the strengths and limitations of their study, but perhaps the main point is that although they were doing what most counsellors do anyway – comparing different methods to help them decide which is 'best' – they were doing it in a more systematic and explicit way. The study was also relevant to theoretical issues about the relative importance of thoughts and emotions. Elliott *et al.* (2004, p523) briefly review other research on 'two-chair dialogue'. This is at an early stage but seems promising.

UNCONDITIONAL POSITIVE REGARD

See: Respect

UNITED KINGDOM COUNCIL FOR PSYCHOTHERAPY (UKCP)

2nd Floor
Edward House
2 Wakely Street
London EC1V 7LT

The UKCP has a website.

VALUES

See also: Acceptance, Assertiveness, Contract, negotiating a, Exercises, Multiculturalism, Personality, Self-awareness, Stress, Trust

Values are enduring beliefs about what matters and does not matter. They can therefore be important in making decisions and reducing stress and, like emotions, are energising. People vary considerably in how clear or confused they are about their values and in the extent to which they act on them. Counsellors can help clients clarify their values by listening, being empathic and challenging, and by using exercises. Authentic or core values are chosen after reflection and experience, and from a range of alternatives.

It is usually assumed that each person has only a few core values, on the basis that it is not possible to do everything well and that our time and energy are limited. 'Laddering', a special form of brief interview, is one technique (Bannister and Mair, 1968). A series of statements is each followed by the question 'What is it about X that is important to you?' until no more answers appear. Patrick (2003, p30) gave the following example: 'I must have the beds made by 10' led to 'if not, someone might find out how untidy I am', which led to 'I prefer people not to know how I really am; if they knew they wouldn't like me', which led to 'I wouldn't have any friends', which led to 'I'd have no social life'.

A variation of the laddering technique is to ask for the names of, for example, three animals or foods and then ask these questions:

- Can you tell me one way in which two of them are the same and the other is different?
- Which would you prefer?
- Why?
- Why is that important?

And so on, until a core value appears to have been reached or the person has had enough. Some people may respond more to 'What is appealing about that?' For other subtleties of laddering, see Fransella and Dalton (2000).

Clearly, laddering requires considerable self-awareness (and possibly patience) but Patrick's experience was that through using it she found 'several values, stumbling around ownerless' and some stimulating clashes between espoused values (e.g. equality) and values she actually used (e.g. being in control). She found the process particularly useful in choosing a model of counselling and in identifying sources of discomfort (Patrick, 2003).

Another potentially demanding approach is to ask clients to write their epitaph or obituary, or to imagine they have one year of their life left and what they would do.

Some key questions about core values are:

- What are your core values?
- Do any of them conflict with each other?
- Where do they come from?
- Do you act on them?
- Do you want to act *more* on any of them?
- If you do, what will you do less of?
- How do they affect other people?

Clients are likely to become aware of their counsellor's values on a number of issues, however neutral she or he tries to be, and you might need to be explicit about one or more of your values either before or during counselling. For example, a counsellor and client may have different values about sexuality, abortion or assertiveness. Such differences can be discussed sensitively, preferably with awareness of multicultural factors. As Walker (1993) points out, counselling contracts do not usually have exclusion clauses allowing counsellors to withdraw if they do not like their client's views, so it is more professional to view differences in values as an opportunity to explore and clarify our own values (while of course focusing primarily on the client and, we would add, not ruling out the option of referral). The desired balance here is between having clear, firmly based values (but not letting them get in the way of counselling) and being open to reviewing and changing them.

VICARIOUS TRAUMATISATION

See also: Burnout, Stress

Vicarious traumatisation (VT) refers to 'harmful changes that occur in professionals' views of themselves, others and the world as a result of exposure to graphic and/or traumatic material' (Baird and Kracen, 2006, p182). It is associated with disruption to beliefs or schemas in the areas of safety, trust, esteem, intimacy and control, and it is a normal response to such exposure.

The differences, if any, between VT, compassion fatigue, burnout, counter-transference and secondary traumatic stress are unclear, but the research so far suggests (among other things) that having a personal history of trauma is linked to the development of VT and that supervision is a protective factor.

VICTIM

See: Drama triangle

VIOLENCE AND ITS PREVENTION

See also: Anger, Assertiveness, Empathy, Furniture, Paraphrasing, Touch

Although the risk of violence during counselling is small, prevention is worthwhile (Breakwell, 1997; Jones, 2004). Most of the contributors to Jones (2004) worked or work at HMP Grendon, which specialises in new ways of working with offenders convicted of violent crimes.

Below are some preventive steps to consider:

- Whenever possible, avoid working in a building alone with a client, especially in the evenings, or in buildings away from a main public thoroughfare. If you are working alone, maintain a strict appointment service and do not operate a drop-in clinic. If possible, tell the caretaker that you will be working alone and when you expect to finish, but certainly inform a colleague or friend.

- If you make a home visit, inform a colleague or friend where you are going and the time you expect to return.

- Have a phone readily available and consider having an alarm or 'panic' button installed in your counselling room. Know someone will answer it, with an agreed plan of action! Carry a personal security device in situations in which you feel vulnerable.

- If you suspect danger, it may be advisable to cancel the appointment or, if actually working with a client, to bring the session to a close. The BACP's ethical framework (BACP, 2007) requires counsellors to take responsibility for working within their competence.

- Take particular care with arrangements to work with any clients who have a history of acting out any form of violence or aggression.

- Discover and examine your beliefs about violence; for example, do you believe that it is unprofessional to 'run away'?

- Some counsellors consider it advisable and good practice to avoid any form of physical contact with clients apart from a handshake.

- Arrange the chairs for counsellor and client equidistant from the door, so that you both have equal access. If the counsellor's chair is nearer the door, your client could feel trapped or closed in. Ideally, the room will have a glass panel in the door, a calm 'feel' and no ornaments that could be used as weapons.

- Calmness *and* empathy – sometimes calmness alone infuriates someone further. Acknowledge the other person's feelings and your own.

At an organisational level, there should be a system for recording and following up violent incidents, and support for those attacked, such as counselling, paid leave or help with legal action.

VISUALISATION

See: Imagery

WARMTH

See also: Acceptance, Emotions, Love (styles of loving), Multiculturalism, Paraphrasing, Psychological type, Readiness to change, Respect, Sexual attraction

Being warm and affectionate is the opposite of being distant or aloof; it implies a liking for people and a caring approach, especially to people who are distressed or confused. Warmth, however, is not necessarily something you will always feel or feel equally for every client, and some clients are likely to experience you as warmer than others. Warmth, like trust, is often a developing process rather than something established immediately, as the expression 'to warm to somebody' implies. It helps if you have an open and inviting attitude towards your clients when you first meet them, allowing yourself time to get to know them and for them to get to know you.

Excessive warmth can be as much of a problem as no warmth at all. Some clients may feel overpowered or uncomfortable if you are overly warm towards them. It can be very difficult for clients to express angry feelings towards you, for example if you allow your natural warmth to spill over into being overprotective or overfriendly. Similarly, clients can feel reticent about expressing what they think of as their negative aspects if they feel that they risk withdrawal of your affection. This might have very strong echoes of the past for many clients. Some clients prefer a formal, businesslike approach.

WEBSITE (PERSONAL)

See also: Advertising, BACP, Client information handout, Marketing

Your own website advertising your own counselling can increase your number of clients and possibly the variety. The BACP runs a website hosting service for members or will design a website for you or host your existing site. (A host has its computer on all the time.)

The BACP needs text in electronic form: for example, an introduction and overview; a profile of you as counsellor; a statement about your approach to counselling, confidentiality and ethics; your hours etc. and how to contact you. Colours, photos, drawings and perhaps a logo can all add appeal to your design. There is a detailed guide on the BACP's website or phone the BACP's IT department.

Huxstep (2003) asked some stimulating questions about personal websites, such as how they fare in attracting clients compared with a postcard in the library foyer. He found a friend's advice that 'some simple sites are among the best' a relief, but he was surprised that Google, Yahoo and other search engines do not list your site at once and that you have to meet their criteria to be listed. Two other problems were finding a website name that had not already been taken, and an office or factory address to use when registering (for security). However, he ends on a positive note: 'My site is now being "hit" about 10 times a day; most are spam generating robots but some are not. I am earning money from clients who have found me on the web' (Huxstep, 2003, p49).

WORKING ALLIANCE

See: Relationship between counsellor and client

WRITING (EXPRESSIVE)

See also: Confidentiality, Counselling, Drawings, Exercises, Force-field analysis, Freewriting, Homework, Narrative, Scaling

Studies by Pennebaker and others (e.g. Frattaroli, 2006; Lyubomirsky *et al.*, 2006; Pennebaker *et al.*, 1990) provide strong evidence for the value to the writer of writing about troubling experiences. In one study, first-year students wrote continuously for 15 to 20 minutes on three consecutive days on their 'deepest feelings and thoughts' about coming to college. A control group wrote about what they had done that morning; they were asked to be 'objective', i.e. not to mention emotions, feelings, or opinions. In line with previous findings showing improved functioning of the immune system, the first group visited the health centre less often in the following months than the control group. Interview data supported an insight rather than a catharsis interpretation. Alternatively, both processes might be at work but in different ways.

In another study, participants were asked to write about their deepest feelings and thoughts each day for two weeks. On two of the days, they were given some words to include, such as 'negative' emotions, insight words like 'realise' and causation words like 'because'. They reported that on these days the writing was the least personal and most difficult to do but also the most meaningful. In a third study, without provided words, it was found that the participants who benefited most were those who used low rates of cognitive words on their first day of writing compared with their last (Pennebaker, 1993); thus they explored emotions first, then insights and ideas.

The research therefore strongly supports the ideas that, first, not talking (or writing) about upsetting experiences is stressful because there is a basic need to talk about them which is actively inhibited, and, secondly, translating them into language helps the person clarify and think them through. Writing is of course much cheaper than counselling, more private and more under the person's control; and it has a long history (Freud and Horney both wrote about self-analysis). However, this is not to say that written (or oral) self-analysis makes counselling redundant.

A general model of counselling is clear in Pennebaker's and others' discussions: first, express and feel the problem fully; secondly, analyse and think it through. Like counselling, writing a journal aims to reduce confusion, clarify emotions, feelings, wishes, values and thoughts, and therefore to free us to act more in the present.

Some clients find writing about some things easier than talking about them, just as others prefer to draw or use other means of expression. Wright (2005, p118), reflecting on one client's experience of writing therapy during brief workplace counselling, found several other benefits: 'immediacy, availability, client control, privacy, permanency and extension of therapeutic control' but suggested using it cautiously because of its potential to cause distress and because others may read it without permission. She also points to some risks for the counsellor, for example being drawn into reading and commenting outside the allotted time. A way round this is to say 'I'd rather you tell me what you've found that's important'.

An example of expressive writing using three stages and consistent with the integrative model of counselling outlined in the entry on Counselling is shown below.

1. Write freely

> Longer run than usual on Monday. In the night pain in my knee woke me up, and yesterday it was stiff and I hobbled. Felt despairing and angry: I'll have to stop running. Also annoyed that I'd just bought new running shoes, and disturbed by the strength of my reaction. I was flat and ill most of the day at work, and abrupt with some of my colleagues. During the day my knee eased. This morning it's near normal. Feel much more buoyant and constructive. [End of Step 1, at least on this occasion]

2. Analyse

> I'm left wondering about my reaction to injury (and illness).
>
> 1. I believe it's awful and catastrophic not to be able to run.
> 2. It's a recurring pattern. It may be related to lots of illness as a child, especially being scared I'd stop breathing.
> 3. Everyone is ill or injured sometimes (especially good athletes!). It's normal.

3. Act

> Look up knee injuries. Preventive measures?
>
> Ask Dave's advice.
>
> Make a special effort re 'flatness' next time: perhaps explain to other people, 'go into' my feelings, treat it like loss. [End of Step 3]

Comment on the example

The steps overlap but give some shape and sense of direction. Step 2 is relatively neglected: some good thoughts, but it could be more argued. The actions are feasible, but could be expressed more specifically.

In outline, the three steps are:

1. Write freely (explore)

   Write as freely as you can about a reaction or experience that matters to you.

2. Analyse (analyse more objectively)

   Analyse your reactions and perhaps challenge them, e.g.:

   - Be more specific about what actually happened.
   - What other ways (however unlikely) are there of looking at what happened?
   - What is the evidence for any assertions, beliefs?
   - Is there a familiar feeling or pattern there?
   - What assumptions are you making?
   - Do your reactions tell you anything else about yourself, e.g. suggest important values?
   - How realistic are you being?

3. Act (possible actions)

   Generate possible actions, choose from them, make the chosen one(s) specific, do it or them, evaluate. 'Specific' means saying when, how, etc.

Rainer (1978, p18) saw writing expressively as 'a practical psychological tool that enables you to express feelings without inhibition, recognize and alter self-defeating habits of mind, and come to know and accept that self which is you'. It can help you discover genuine interests, nourish you, clarify goals, free intuition, and record insights.

There are many approaches to expressive writing, including freewriting and 'games you can play with your inner consciousness to get to know it better' (Rainer, 1978, p26). Some examples from Rainer (1978), Adams (1990), Waines (2004) and Bolton *et al.* (2004, 2006) are:

- lists, e.g. of desires, things you feel uneasy about, things you're happy about, beliefs you have discarded, loves
- 'portraits', e.g. describe a friend
- describe a day
- at the end of a day, write one adjective to describe it and another to describe how you would like the next day to be
- freewriting, i.e. writing quickly and without stopping or editing
- sitting quietly for a few moments before writing (to allow the most important incidents and feelings to begin to surface)

- writing with your other hand (the speculative idea is to improve contact with emotions)
- writing about yourself in the third person
- writing dialogues, e.g. with someone else, with an object, between part of you and another part of you.

ZEST

See: Assertiveness, Burnout, Mistakes, Psychological type, Rewards of counselling, Self-awareness, Stress

REFERENCES

Adams, K. (1990) Journal to the Self: 22 Paths to Personal Growth. New York: Warner Books.

Ainscough, C. and Toon, K. (2000) *Breaking Free: Help for Survivors of Child Sexual Abuse*. London: Sheldon Press.

Alston, M. (2003) Asperger syndrome in the counselling room. *Counselling and Psychotherapy Journal*, June, 10–12.

American Psychiatric Association (2000) *Diagnostic and Statistical Manual of Mental Disorders*. Washington, DC: American Psychiatric Association, 4th edn.

Anderson, I. (1997) Psychiatry: evidence-based but still value-laden. *British Journal of Psychiatry*, **171**, 226.

Angus, L.E. (1996) An intensive analysis of metaphor themes in psychotherapy. In J. S. Mio and A. N. Katz (eds) *Metaphor: Implications and Applications*. Mahwah, N. J.: Lawrence Erlbaum.

Angus, L.E. and McLeod, J. (2004) (eds) *Handbook of Narrative and Psychotherapy: Practice, Theory and Research*. London: Sage.

Anthony, K. (2006) Electronically delivered therapies. In C. Feltham and I. Horton (eds) *The Sage Handbook of Counsellors and Psychotherapy*. London: Sage, 3rd edn.

Baird, K. and Kracen, A.C. (2006) Vicarious traumatization and secondary traumatic stress: a research synthesis. *Counselling Psychology Quarterly*, **19**, 181–188.

Bannister, D. and Mair, J. (1968) *The Evaluation of Personal Constructs*. London: Academic Press.

Barkham, M. (2007) Methods, outcomes and process in the psychological therapies across four research generations. In W. Dryden (ed.) *Individual Therapy*. Milton Keynes: Open University Press, 5th edn.

Barrett-Lennard, C.T. (1993) The phases and focus of empathy. *British Journal of Medical Psychology*, **66**, 3–14.

Bass, E. and Davis, L. (2002) *The Courage to Heal: A Guide for Women Survivors of Child Sexual Abuse*. Vermilion: London.

Bayne, R. (2004) *Psychological Types at Work. An MBTI Perspective*. London: Thomson.

Bayne, R. (2005) *Ideas and Evidence. Critical Reflections on MBTI Theory and Practice*. Gainesville FL: Center for Applications of Psychological Type.

Beck, A.T., Emory, G. and Greenberg, R. (2005) *Anxiety Disorders and Phobias: A Cognitive Perspective*. New York: Basic Books.

Beitman, B. (1990) Why I am an integrationist. In W. Dryden and J.C. Norcross (eds) *Eclecticism and Integration in Counselling and Psychotherapy*. Loughton, Essex: Gale Centre Publications.

Bell, L. (2003) *Managing Intense Emotions and Overcoming Self-Destructive Habits: A Self-Help Manual*. Hove: Brunner-Routledge.

Benjamin, L.D. (2007) Confessions of an archival addict. *The Psychologist*, **20**, 352–355.

Berne, E. (1964) *Games People Play*. New York: Grove Press.

Berne, E. (1973) *Sex in Human Loving*. Harmondsworth: Penguin.

Beutler, L.E., Malik, M., Alimohamed, S., Harwood, M.T., Talebi, H., Noble, S. and Wongo, E. (2004) Therapist variables. In M.J. Lambert (ed.), *Bergin and Garfield's Handbook of Psychotherapy and Behavior Change*. Chicago: Wiley, 5th edn.

Bimrose, J. (1996) Multiculturalism. In R. Bayne, I. Horton and J. Bimrose (eds) *New Directions in Counselling*. London: Routledge.

Bohart, A.C., Elliott, R., Greenberg, L.S. and Watson, J.C. (2002) Empathy redux: The efficacy of therapist empathy. In J. Norcross (ed.), *Psychotherapy Relationships that Work*. New York: Oxford University Press.

Boice, R. (1994) *How Writers Journey to Comfort and Fluency. A Psychological Adventure*. London: Prager.

Boice, R. (1997) Strategies for enhancing scholarly activity. In J.M. Moxley and T. Taylor (eds) *Writing and Publishing for Academic Authors*. London: Bowman and Littlefield.

Bolton, G., Field, F. and Thompson, K. (eds) (2006) *Writing Works. A Resource Handbook for Therapeutic Writing Workshops and Activities*. London: Jessica Kingsley.

Bolton, G., Hawlett, S., Lago, C. and Wright, J.K. (2004) (eds) *Writing Cures: An Introductory Handbook of Writing in Counselling and Therapy*. London: Brunner-Routledge.

Bonanno, G. (2004) Loss, trauma, and human resilience: Have we underestimated the human capacity to thrive after extremely aversive events? *American Psychologist*, **59**, 20–28.

Bond, M. (1986) *Stress and Self-awareness. A Guide for Nurses*. London: Heinemann.

Bond, T. (2000) *Standards and Ethics for Counselling in Action*. London: Sage, 2nd edn.

Bond, T. (2006) Responding to complaints. In C. Feltham and I. Horton (eds) *The Sage Handbook of Counselling and Psychotherapy*. London: Sage, 2nd edn.

Bond, T. and Sandhu, A. (2005) *Therapists in Court. Providing Evidence and Supporting Witnesses*. London: Sage.

Bond, T. and Sandhu, A. (2007) *Record-Keeping and Confidentiality: Recording Confidences*. London: Sage.

Bordin, C. (1979) The generalizability of the psychoanalytic concept of the working alliance. *Psychotherapy*, **16**, 252–260.

Boynton, P.M. (2005) *The Research Companion. A Practical Guide for the Social and Health Sciences*. Hove: Psychotherapy Press.

Brady, J.L., Healy, F.C., Norcross, J.C. and Guy, J.D. (1995) Stress in counsellors: an integrative research review. In W. Dryden (ed.) *The Stresses of Counselling in Action*. London: Sage.

Brantley, J.B., (2003) *Calming your Anxious Mind*. Oakland, CA: New Harbinger Publications.

Breakwell, G. (1997) *Facing Physical Violence*. Leicester: British Psychological Society.

Brems, C. (2001) *Basic Skills in Psychotherapy and Counselling*. London: Brooks/Cole.

Brenner, D. (1982) *The Effective Psychotherapist*. Oxford: Pergamon.

British Association for Counselling (1993) The BAC Basic Principles of Counselling. *Counselling*, August, 155–6.

British Association for Counselling (1998) *Code of Ethics and Practice for Counsellors*. Rugby: BACP.

British Association for Counselling and Psychotherapy (2002) *Ethical Framework for Good Practice in Counselling and Psychotherapy*. Rugby: BACP, revised edn.

British Association for Counselling and Psychotherapy (2004) *Working with the Suicidal Client*. Information Sheet P7. Rugby: BACP.

British Association for Counselling and Psychotherapy (2007) *Ethical Framework for Good Practice in Counselling and Psychotherapy*. See www.bacp.co.uk/ethical framework

British Psychological Society (2006) *Understanding Personality Disorder*. Can be downloaded in full at www.bps.org.uk/6lnq

Brown G.W. and Harris T.O. (1978) *The Social Origins of Depression*. London: Tavistock.

Bugental, J.F.T. and Bugental, E.K. (1980) The far side of despair. *Journal of Humanistic Psychology*, **20**, 49–68.

Calnan, J. (1991) Handling complaints. In R. Corney (ed.) *Developing Communication and Counselling Skills in Medicine*. London: Routledge.

Charles, R. (2004) *Intuition in Psychotherapy and Counselling*. London: Whurr.

Chester, A. and Glass, A.C. (2006) Online counselling: a descriptive analysis of therapy services on the Internet. *British Journal of Guidance and Counselling*, **34**, 145–160.

Cheston, R. and Bender, M. (2003) *Understanding Dementia*. London: Jessica Kingsley.

Clarke, K.M. and Greenberg, L.S. (1986) Differential effects of the Gestalt two-chair intervention and problem-solving in resolving decisional conflict. *Journal of Counseling Psychology*, **33**, 11–15.

Claxton, G. (1997) *Hare Brain, Tortoise Mind: Why Intelligence Increases When You Think Less*. London: Fourth Estate.

Claxton, G. (1998) Investigating human intuition: knowing without knowing why. *The Psychologist*, **11**, 217–20.

Cockerill, I.M. and Riddington, M.E. (1996) Exercise dependence and associated disorders: a review. *Counselling Psychology Quarterly*, **9**, 119–129.

Collard, P. (2006) Multimodal stress therapy: an integrative approach. In E. O'Leary and M. Murphy (eds) *New Approaches to Integration in Psychotherapy*. Abingdon: Taylor and Francis.

Collett, P. (2004) *The Book of Tells*. London: Bantam.

Cooper, J. (2007) Sleeping Beauty gets assertive. *Therapy Today*, May, 39–41.

Corey, G. (2006) *Theory and Practice of Group Counselling*. London: Thomson Learning, 6th edn.

Costa, P.T. and McCrae, R.R. (1986) Personality stability and its implications for clinical psychology. *Clinical Psychology Review*, **6**, 407–23.

Coyle, E.F. (2005) Very intense exercise training is extremely potent and time efficient: a reminder. *Journal of Applied Physiology*, **98**, 1983–1984.

Coyne, J.C., Stefanek, M. and Palmer, S.C. (2007) Psychotherapy and survival in cancer: the conflict between hope and evidence. *Psychological Bulletin*, **133**, 367–394.

Daines, B., Gask, L. and Howe, A. (2007) *Medical and Psychiatric Issues for Counsellors*. London: Sage, 2nd edn.

Dalton, P. (1992) Chapter 2. In W Dryden (ed.) *Hard-earned Lessons from Counselling in Action*. London: Sage.

d'Ardenne, P. (1993) Transcultural counselling and psychotherapy in the 1990s. *British Journal of Guidance and Counselling*, **21**(1), 1–7.

Davenport, R.B. and Pipes, D.S. (1990) *Introduction to Psychotherapy: Common Clinical Wisdom*. London: Prentice-Hall.

Department of Health (2001) *Treatment Choice in Psychological Therapies and Counselling – Evidence Based Clinical Practice Guideline*. London: Department of Health Publications.

de Shazer, S., Dolan, Y. and Korman, H. (2007) *More than Miracles. The State of the Art of Solution-focused Therapy*. New York: Haworth Press.

Diamantopoulos, A. and Schlegelmilch, B.B. (1997) *Taking the Fear out of Data Analysis*. London: The Dryden Press.

Dickson, A. (1987) *A Woman in Your Own Right*. London: Quartet, revised edn.

Donahoe, G. and Ricketts, T. (2006) Anxiety and panic. In C. Feltham and I. Horton (eds) *The Sage Handbook of Counselling and Psychotherapy*. London: Sage, 2nd edn.

Draucker, C.B. and Martsoff, D. (2006) *Counselling Survivors of Childhood Sexual Abuse*. London: Sage, 3rd ed.

Dryden, W. (1991) *A Dialogue with Arnold Lazarus. 'It Depends'*. Milton Keynes: Open University Press.

Dryden, W. (ed.) (2007) *Dryden's Handbook of Individual Therapy*. London: Sage, 5th edn.

Duan, C. and Hill, C.E. (1996) The current state of empathy research. *Journal of Counseling Psychology*, **43**(3), 261–74.

Duffy, D. and Ryan, T. (eds) (2004) *New Approaches to Preventing Suicide: A Manual for Practitioners*. London: Jessica Kingsley.

Dweck, C. (2006) *Mindset*. New York: Random House.

Egan, G. (1975) *The Skilled Helper*. Monterey, CA: Brooks/Cole.

Egan, G. (2007) *The Skilled Helper*. Monterey, CA: Brooks/Cole, 8th edn.

Elbow, P. (1973) *Writing Without Teachers*. Oxford: Oxford University Press.

Elbow, P. (1997) Freewriting and the problem: Wheat and tares. In J.M. Moxley and T. Taylor (eds) *Writing and Publishing for Academic Authors*. London: Bowman and Littlefield, 2nd edn.

Elliott, R., Greenberg, C.S. and Lieteaer, G. (2004) Research on experiential psychotherapies. In M. J. Lambert (ed.) *Bergin and Garfield's Handbook of Psychotherapy and Behavior Change*. New York: Wiley, 5th edn.

Ellis, A. and Dryden, W (1998) *The Practice of Rational Emotive Behaviour Therapy*. London: Free Association Books.

Ellis, A., Gordon, J. Neenan, M. and Palmer, S. (1997) *Stress Counselling: A Rational-Emotive Approach*. London: Cassell.

Evison, R. and Horobin, R. (2006) Co-counselling. In C. Feltham and I. Horton (eds) *The Sage Handbook of Counselling and Psychotherapy*. London: Sage, 2nd edn.

Farber, B.A. (2003) Patient self-disclosure: A review of the research. *Journal of Clinical Psychology*, **59**, 589–600.

Farber, B.A. (2006) *Self-disclosure in Psychotherapy*. London: Guilford Press.

Fay, D., Borrill, C., Amir, Z., Haward, R. and West, M.A. (2006) Getting the most out of multidisciplinary teams: A multi-sample study of team innovation in health care. *Journal of Occupational and Organizational Psychology*, **79**, 553–567.

Feltham, C. (1993) Making a living as a counsellor. In W. Dryden (ed.) *Questions and Answers on Counselling in Action*. London: Sage.

Feltham, C. (1995a) *What is Counselling?* London: Sage.

Feltham, C. (1995b) The stresses of counselling in private practice In W. Dryden (ed.) *The Stresses of Counselling in Action*. London: Sage.

Feltham, C. (1996) Beyond denial, myth and superstition in the counselling profession. In R. Bayne, I. Horton and J. Bimrose (eds) *New Directions in Counselling*. London: Routledge.

Feltham, C. (1997) *Time Limited Counselling*. London: Sage.

Feltham, C. (2002) Starting in private practice. In J. Clark (ed.) *Freelance Counselling and Psychotherapy. Competition and Collaboration*. Hove: Brunner-Routledge.

Feltham, C. (2003) Letter. *Counselling and Psychotherapy Journal*, December, 18.

Feltham, C. (2006) Goals. In C. Feltham and I. Horton (eds) *The Sage Handbook of Counselling and Psychotherapy*. London: Sage, 2nd edn.

Feltham, C. and Dryden, W. (2006) *Brief Counselling. A Practical Integrative Approach*. Maidenhead: OU Press, 2nd edn.

Feltham, C. and Horton, I. (eds) (2006) *The Sage Handbook of Counselling and Psychotherapy*. London: Sage, 2nd edn.

Fong, M.L. and Cox, B.G. (1983) Trust as an underlying dynamic in the counselling process: How clients test trust. *Personnel and Guidance Journal*, November, 163–167.

Fransella, F. and Dalton, P. (2000) *Personal Construct Counselling in Action*. London: Sage, 2nd edn.

Frattaroli, J. (2006) Experimental disclosure and its moderators: a meta-analysis. *Psychological Bulletin*, **132**, 823–865.

Frost, G. (2006) Hot and bothered. *Therapy Today*, November, 34–36.

Frude, N. (2005) Prescription for a good read. *Counselling and Psychotherapy Journal*. February, 28–31.

Funder, D. (2007) *The Personality Puzzle*. London: W.W. Norton, 4th edn.

Geddes, J.R. and Harrison, P.J. (1997) Closing the gap between research and practice. *British Journal of Psychiatry*, 171, 220–225.

Gendlin, E.T. (1981) *Focusing*. London: Bantam, 2nd edn.

Gilbert, P. (2006) Depression. In C. Feltham and I. Horton (eds) *The Sage Handbook of Counselling and Psychotherapy*. London: Sage, 2nd edn.

Gilmore, S.K. (1973) *The Counselor-in-Training*. London: Prentice-Hall.

Goss, S. and Anthony, K. (2003) *Technology in Counselling and Psychotherapy: a Practitioner's Guide*. Basingstoke: Palgrave/Macmillan.

Grande, L. and Bayne, R. (2006) Adult dyslexia – the challenge to counsellors. *Therapy Today*, April, 31–34.

Green, H. (1964) *I Never Promised You a Rose Garden*. London: Pan.

Greenberg, L.S. and Safran, J.D. (1990) *Emotion in Psychotherapy*. New York: Guilford Press.

Gunarata, B. (2002) *Mindfulness in Plain English*. Boston: Wisdom Press.

Haines, S. (1999) *The Survivor's Guide to Sex: How to Have a Great Sex Life Even If You've Been Sexually Abused*. Pittsburgh, PA: Cleis Press.

Hall, E., Hall, C. Stradling, P. and Young, D. (2006) *Guided Imagery. Creative Interventions in Counselling and Psychotherapy*. London: Sage.

Hanson, J. (2005) Should your lips be zipped? How therapeutic self-disclosure and non-disclosure affects clients. *Counselling and Psychotherapy Research*, **5**, 96–104.

Hawkins P. and Shohet, R. (2006) *Supervision in the Helping Professions*. Milton Keynes: Open University, 3rd edn.

Hawley, D. (2003) A fair day's work for a fair day's pay. *Counselling and Psychotherapy Journal*, December, 15–17.

Hayman, P. and Allen, F. (2006) Working together on depression. *Therapy Today*, April, 45–48.

Hill, A. and Brettle, A. (2005) The effectiveness of counselling with older people: Results of a systematic review. *Counselling and Psychotherapy Research*, **5**, 265–272.

Hill, C.E. (2003) *Helping Skills. Facilitating Exploration, Insight and Action*. Washington, DC: American Psychological Association.

Hodgkinson, P.E. (2006) Post-traumatic stress disorder. In C. Feltham and I. Horton (eds) *The Sage Handbook of Counselling and Psychotherapy*. London: Sage, 2nd edn.

Hollon, S.D., Stewart, M.D. and Strunk, D. (2006) Enduring effects for cognitive behavior therapy in the treatment of depression and anxiety. *Annual Review of Psychology*, **57**, 285–315.

Hook, A. and Andrews, B. (2005) The relationship of non-disclosure in therapy to shame and depression. *British Journal of Clinical Psychology*, **44**, 425–438.

Horton, I. (1998) Principles and practice of a personal integration. In S. Palmer and R. Woolfe (eds) *Eclectic and Integrative Counselling and Psychotherapy*. London: Sage.

Horton, I. (2006) Integration. In C. Feltham and I. Horton (eds) *The Sage Handbook of Counselling and Psychotherapy*. London: Sage, 2nd edn.

Hubble, M., Duncan, B. and Miller, S. (1999) *The Heart and Soul of Change*. Washington, DC: APA Press.

Hunter, M. and Struve, J. (1998) *The Ethical Use of Touch in Psychotherapy*. London: Sage.

Huxstep, G. (2003) Do websites work? *Counselling and Psychotherapy Journal*, December, 46–49.

Inskipp, F. (1996) *Skills Training for Counselling*. London: Cassell.

Jenkins, P. (2007) *Counselling, Psychotherapy and the Law*. London: Sage, 2nd edn.

Jennings, L. and Skovholt, T.M. (1999) The cognitive, emotional and relational characteristics of master therapists. *Journal of Counseling Psychology*, **46**, 3–11.

Jinks, G. (2006) Specific strategies and techniques. In C. Feltham and I. Horton (eds) *The Sage Handbook of Counselling and Psychotherapy*. London: Sage, 2nd edn.

Joiner, T. (2006) *Why People Die by Suicide*. Harvard: Harvard University Press.

Jones, D. (ed.) (2004) *Working with Dangerous People: The Psychotherapy of Violence*. London: Radcliffe Medical Press.

Jones, F. and Bright, J. (2001) *Stress. Myth, Theory and Research*. Harlow: Pearson.

Joseph, S and Worsley, R. (2005) *Person-centred Psychopathology: A Positive Psychology of Mental Health*. Ross-on-Wye: PCCS Books.

Kabat-Zinn, J. (1990) *Full Catastrophe Living*. London: Piatkus Books.

Kahn, M. (1991) *Between Therapist and Client*. New York: W. H. Freeman.

Kahn, M. (1997) *Between Therapist and Client. The New Relationship*. New York: W.H. Freeman, revised edn.

Karpman, S.B. (1968) Fairy tales and script drama analysis. *TA Bulletin*, **VII**(26), 39–43.

Kennedy-Moore, E. and Watson, J.C. (1999) *Expressing Emotion: Myths, Realities and Therapeutic Strategies*. London: Guilford Press.

King, M., Sibbald, B., Ward, E., Bower, P., Lloyd, M., Gabbay, M. and Byford, S. (2000) Randomised controlled trial of non-directive counselling, cognitive behaviour therapy, and usual general practitioner care in the management of depression as well as mixed anxiety and depression in primary care. *British Medical Journal*, **321**, 1383–1388.

Kohut, H. (1987) *The Kohut Seminars on Self Psychology and Psychotherapy with Adolescents and Young Adults*. New York: W.W. Norton.

Kwiatkowski, R. and Hogan, D. (1998) Group membership. In R. Bayne, P. Nicolson and I. Horton (eds) *Counselling and Communication Skills for Medical and Health Practitioners*. Leicester: BPS Books.

Ladany, N., Hill, C.E. Thompson, B.J. and O'Brien, K.M. (2004) Therapeutic perspectives on using silence in therapy: a qualitative study. *Counselling and Psychotherapy Research*, **4**, 80–89.

Lago, C. (2006) *Race, Culture and Counselling*. Maidenhead: OU Press, 2nd edn.

Lambert, M.J. (2004) *Bergin and Garfield's Handbook of Psychotherapy and Behavior Change*. Chichester: Wiley, 5th edn.

Lambert, M.J. and Ogles, B.M. (2004) The efficacy and effectiveness of psychotherapy. In M.J. Lambert (ed.) *Bergin and Garfield's Handbook of Psychotherapy and Behavior Change*. Chichester: Wiley, 5th edn.

Langs, R. (1982) *Workbooks for Psychotherapists, Vol. II Listening and Formulating*. Emerson, NJ: Newconcept Press.

Lazarus, A.A. (1977) Towards an egoless state of being. In Ellis, A. and Grieger, R. (eds) *Handbook of Rational Emotive Therapy*. New York: McGraw-Hill.

Lazarus, A. (1989) *The Practice of Multimodal Therapy*. Baltimore: Johns Hopkins University Press.

Lazarus, A. and Mayne, T.J. (1990) Relaxation: some limitations, side effects and proposed solutions. *Psychotherapy*, **22**, 261–266.

Leahy, R. (2003) *Cognitive Therapy Techniques: A Practitioner's Guide*. New York: Guilford.

Leahy, R. and Holland, S.C. (2000) *Treatment Plans and Interventions for Depression and Anxiety Disorders*. New York: The Guilford Press.

Lee, J. (1988) Love styles. In R.J. Sternberg and M.C. Barnes (eds) *The Psychology of Romantic Love*. London: Yale University Press.

Leong, F.T.L. and Austin, J.T. (2006) (eds) *The Psychology Research Handbook*. London: Sage, 2nd edn.

Ley, P. (1988) *Communicating with Patients*. London: Croom Helm.

Loftus, E.F. (1993) The reality of repressed memories. *American Psychologist*, **48**(5), 518–537.

Lovell, K. (2006) Behavioural psychotherapy. In C. Feltham and I. Horton (eds) *The Sage Handbook of Counselling and Psychotherapy*. London: Sage, 2nd edn.

Lumley, M.A. (2004) Alexithymia, emotional disclosure, and health: a program of research. *Journal of Personality*, **72**, 1271–1300.

Lyubomirsky, S., Sousa, L. and Dickerhoof, R. (2006) The cost and benefits of writing, talking, and thinking about life's triumphs and defeats. *Journal of Personality and Social Psychology*, **90**, 692–708.

Mackay, H.C., Barkham, M., Rees, A. and Stiles, W.B. (2003) Appraisal of published reviews of research on psychotherapy and counselling with adults 1990–1998. *Journal of Consulting and Clinical Psychology*, **71**, 652–656.

Maddi, S.R. (2005) On hardiness and other pathways to resilience. *American Psychologist*, **60**, 261–262.

Mahrer, A.R. (1989) *The Integration of Psychotherapies*. New York: Human Science Press.

Mann, J. (1973) *Time Limited Psychotherapy*. Cambridge, MA: Harvard University Press.

Manthei, R.J. (2007) Clients talk about their experience of the process of counselling. *Counselling Psychology Quarterly*, **20**, 1–26.

Markides, K.S. (2007) (ed.) *Encyclopaedia of Health and Ageing*. London: Sage.

Marzillier, J. (2004) The myth of evidence-based psychotherapy. *The Psychologist*, **17**, 392–395.

Maslach, C. and Goldberg, J. (1998) Prevention of burnout: new perspectives. *Applied and Preventive Psychology*, **7**, 63–74.

McAdams, D. (1995) What do we know when we know a person? *Journal of Personality*, **63**, 365–396.

McLeod, J. (1990) The client's experience of counselling and psycho-therapy: a review of the research literature. In D. Mearns and W. Dryden (eds) *Experiences of Counselling in Action*. London: Sage.

McLeod, J. (1997a) Reading, writing and research. In I. Horton with V. Varma (eds) *The Needs of Counsellors and Psychotherapists*. London: Sage.

McLeod, J. (1997b) *Narrative Psychotherapy*. London: Sage.

McLeod, J. (2001) *Qualitative Research in Counselling and Psychotherapy*. London: Sage.

McLeod, J. (2003a) *An Introduction to Counselling*. Buckingham: OU Press, 3rd edn.

McLeod, J. (2003b) *Doing Counselling Research*. London: Sage, 2nd edn.

McLoughlin, D., Leather, C. and Singer, P. (2002) *The Adult Dyslexic. Interventions and Outcomes*. London: Whurr.

McMahon, G., Palmer, S. and Wilding, C. (2005) *The Essential Skills for Setting Up a Counselling and Psychotherapy Private Practice*. London: Routledge.

McMullen, L.M. and Conway, J.B. (1996) Conceptualizing the figurative expressions of psychotherapy clients. In. J.S. Mio and A.N. Katz (eds) *Metaphor: Implications and Applications*. Mahwam, N. J.: Lawrence, Erlbaum.

Mearns, D. (1990a) The counsellor's experience of failure. In D Mearns and W. Dryden (eds) *Experiences of Counselling in Action*. London: Sage.

Mearns, D. (1990b) The counsellor's experience of success. In D. Mearns and W. Dryden (eds) *Experiences of Counselling in Action*. London: Sage.

Mearns, D. (1993) Against indemnity insurance. In W. Dryden (ed.) *Questions and Answers on Counselling in Action*. London: Sage.

Mearns, D. and Thorne, B. (2007) *Person-Centred Counselling in Action*. London: Sage, 3rd edn.

Mellor-Clark, J. and Barkham, M. (2006) The CORE system: developing and delivering practice-based evidence through quality evaluation. In C. Feltham and I. Horton (eds) *The Sage Handbook of Counselling and Psychotherapy*. London: Sage, 2nd edn.

Merry, T. (1995) *Invitation to Person Centred Psychology*. London: Whurr.

Merry, T. (1999) *Learning and Being in Person-Centred Counselling*. Ross-on-Wye: PCCS Books.

Miller, T.R. (1991) The psychotherapeutic utility of the five-factor mode of personality: a clinician's experience. *Journal of Personality Assessment*, **57**(3), 415–433.

Miller, W.R. (1991) *Motivational Interviewing*. New York: Guilford Press.

Miller, W.R. and Rollnick, S. (2002) *Motivational Interviewing. Preparing People for Change*. New York: Guilford Press, 2nd edn.

Milner, J. and O'Byrne, P. (2003) *Assessment in Counselling Theory, Process and Decision Making*. Basingstoke: Palgrave Macmillan.

Milner, P. and Palmer, S. (1998) *Integrative Stress Counselling. A Humanistic Problem-Focused Approach*. London: Cassell.

Moorey, S. (2007) Cognitive therapy. In W. Dryden (ed.) *Dryden's Handbook of Individual Therapy*. London: Sage, 5th edn.

Moos, R.H. (ed.) (1991) *Coping with Life Crises – An Integrated Approach*. New York: Plenum.

Mothersole, G. (2004) CORE: what is it good for? *Counselling and Psychotherapy Journal*, August, 18– 21.

Mothersole, G. (2006) The use of CORE System data to inform and develop practitioner performance assessment and appraisal: an experiential account. *European Journal of Psychotherapy and Counselling*, **8**, 177–192.

Mountford, C.P. (2005) One size does not fit all. *Counselling and Psychotherapy Journal*, June, 43–45.

Murray, R. (1997) *Ethical Humanities in Health Care: A Practical Approach through Medical Humanities*. Cheltenham: Stanley Thornes.

Murray, R. (1998) Communicating about ethical dilemmas: a medical humanities approach. In R. Bayne, P. Nicolson and I. Horton (eds) *Counselling and Communication Skills for Medical and Health Practitioners*. Leicester: British Psychological Society.

Myers I.B. with P.B. Myers (1980) *Gifts Differing*. Palo Alto CA: Consulting Psychologists Press.

Myers, I.B., McCaulley, M.H., Quenk, N.L. and Hammer, A.L. (1998) *Manual: A Guide to the Development and Use of the Myers-Briggs Type Indicator*. Palo Alto, CA: CPP.

Nay, W.R, (2004) *Taking Charge of Anger*. London: Guilford Press.

Neenan, M. and Dryden, W. (2001) *Life Coaching*. Hove: Brunner-Routledge.

Nelson-Jones, R. (1985) Eclecticism, integration and comprehension in counselling theory. *British Journal of Guidance and Counselling*, **13**, 129–138.

NICE (2004a) *Anxiety: Management of Anxiety (panic disorder, with or without agoraphobia, and generalised anxiety disorder) in Adults in Primary, Secondary and Community Care*. Clinical Guideline No. 22. www.nice.org.uk

NICE (2004b) *Depression: Management of Depression in Primary and Secondary Care*. Clinical Guideline No. 23. www.nice.org.uk

Nichols, K.A. and Jenkinson, J. (2006) *Leading a Support Group*. Milton Keynes: Open University Press.

Nicolson, P., Bayne, R. and Owen, J. (2006) *Applied Psychology for Social Workers*. Basingstoke: Palgrave Macmillan, 3rd edn.

Nicolson, R. (2005) Dyslexia: beyond the myth. *The Psychologist*, **18**, 658–659.

Norcross, J. (ed.) (2002) *Psychotherapy Relationships That Work: Therapist Contributions and Responsiveness to Patients*. New York: Oxford University Press.

Nyman, S.R. (2007) A balancing act? *The Psychologist*, **20**, 420–421.

Oatley, K., Keltner, D. and Jenkins, J.M. (2006) *Understanding Emotions*. Oxford: Blackwell, 2nd edn.

O'Brien, M. and Huston, G. (2007) *Integrative Therapy. A Practitioner's Guide*. London: Sage, 2nd edn.

Okiishi, J., Lambert, M.J., Nielsen, S.I. and Ogles, B.M. (2003) Waiting for supershrink: an empirical analysis of therapist effects. *Clinical Psychology and Psychotherapy*, **10**, 361–373.

O'Leary, E. and Barry, N. (2006) Counselling older adults. In C. Feltham and I. Horton (eds) *The Sage Handbook of Counselling and Psychotherapy*. London: Sage, 2nd edn.

Orenstein, M. (2001) *Smart but Stuck: Emotional Aspects of Learning Disabilities and Imprisoned Intelligence*. New York: Haworth Press.

Packwood, P. (2006) Enabling dyslexics to cope in employment. *Selection and Development Review*, **22**, 17–21.

Palmer, S. and Dryden, W. (1995) *Counselling for Stress Problems*. London: Sage.

Parry, G. (1990) *Coping with Crises*. London: BPS/Routledge.

Patrick, E. (2003) Values? Now where did I put them? *Counselling and Psychotherapy Journal*, August, 30–31.

Payne, R. (2000) *Relaxation Techniques: A Practical Handbook for the Health Care Professional*. London: Churchill Livingstone.

Peake, T.H., Borduin, C.M. and Archer, R.P. (1988) *Brief Psychotherapies – Changing Frames of Mind*. London: Sage.

Pedersen, P. (1987) Ten frequent assumptions of cultural bias in counseling. *Journal of Multicultural Counseling and Development*, **16**, 36–40.

Pennebaker, J.W. (1993) Putting stress into words: health, linguistic and therapeutic implications. *Behaviour Research and Therapy*, **31**(6), 539–548.

Pennebaker, J.W., Colder, M. and Sharp, L.K. (1990) Accelerating the coping process. *Journal of Personality and Social Psychology*, **58**(3), 528–537.

Perren, S. (2003) Being involved in a research study – a counsellor's view. *Counselling and Psychotherapy Research*, **3**, 246–248.

Pines, A.M. and Keinan, G. (2005) Stress and burnout: the significant difference. *Personality and Individual Differences*, **39**, 625–635.

Pipes, R.B., Schwartz, R. and Crouch, P. (1985) Measuring client fears. *Journal of Consulting and Clinical Psychology*, **53**(6), 933–934.

Ponteretto, J. (ed.) (2001) *Handbook of Multicultural Counselling*. London: Sage.

Prochaska, J.O., DiClemente, C.C. and Norcross, J.C. (1992) In search of how people change. *American Psychologist*, **47**, 1102–1114.

Provost, J.A. (1993) *A Casebook: Applications of the Myers–Briggs Type Indicator in Counseling*. Gainesville, FL: Center for Applications of Psychological Type, 2nd edn.

Rainer, T. (1978) *The New Diary*. New York: St Martin's Press.

Rakos, R. (1991) *Assertive Behaviour: Theory, Research and Training*. London: Routledge.

Reddy, M. (1987) *The Manager's Guide to Counselling at Work*. London: BPS/Methuen.

Reid, D., Leylan, J. and Gill, L. (2005) Does client self-booking reduce 'did not attends' (DNAs) in a counselling service? *Counselling and Psychotherapy Research*, **5**, 291–294.

Reynolds, F. (1999) Distress and coping with hot flushes at work: implications for counsellors in occupational settings. *Counselling Psychology Quarterly*, **12**, 353–361.

Ridley, C. (2005) *Overcoming Unintentional Racism in Counselling and Therapy: A Practitioner's Guide to Intentional Intervention*. London: Sage 2nd edn.

Robson, C. (2002) *Real World Research. A Resource for Social Scientists and Practitioner-Researchers*. Oxford: Blackwell, 2nd edn.

Rogers, C.R. (1957) The necessary and sufficient conditions for therapeutic personality change. *Journal of Consulting Psychology*, **21**(2), 95–103.

Rogers, C.R. (1959) A theory of therapy, personality and interpersonal relationships as developed in the client-centred relationship. In S. Koch (ed.) *Psychology: A Study of a Science, Vol. III*. New York: McGraw Hill.

Rogers, C.R. (1961) *On Becoming a Person*. London: Constable.

Rogers, C.R. (1980) *A Way of Being*. Boston, MA: Houghton Mifflin.

Rogers, C.R. (1986) Rogers, Kohut and Erickson: A personal perspective on some similarities and differences. *Person-Centred Review*, **1**, 125–140.

Rogers, C.R. (1987) Comments on the issue of equality in psychotherapy. *Journal of Humanistic Psychology*, **27**(1), 38–40.

Rogers, C.R. and Sandford, R.C. (1980) Client-centred psychotherapy. In H. Kaplan, B. Sadock and A. Freeman (eds) *Comprehensive Textbook of Psychiatry, Vol. 3*. Baltimore: Williams and Wilkins.

Rogers, J. (2004) *Coaching Skills. A Handbook*. Maidenhead: OU Press.

Rogers, J. (2006) *Developing a Coaching Business*. Maidenhead: OU Press.

Rosen, G.M. (1987) Self-help treatment books and the commercialization of psychotherapy. *American Psychologist*, **42**(1), 46–51.

Rosen, G.M., Glasgow, R.E. and Moore, T. (2003) Self-help therapy. In S.O. Lilenfeld, S.J. Lynn and J.M. Lohr (eds) (2003) *Science and Pseudoscience in Clinical Psychology*. London: The Guilford Press.

Rosenfeld, M. (2006) Telephone counselling. In C. Feltham and I. Horton (eds) *The Sage Handbook of Counselling and Psychotherapy*. London: Sage, 2nd edn.

Rosenthal, R. (1990) How are we doing in soft psychology? *American Psychologist*, **45**, 775–777.

Rosenthal, T. (1993) To soothe the savage breast. *Behaviour Research and Therapy*, **31**, 439–462.

Rowland, N. (2001) *Clinical Guidelines for Treatment Choice Decisions in Psychological Therapies and Counselling*. Information Sheet 16. Rugby: BACP.

Russell, J. (1993) *Out of Bounds: Sexual Exploitation in Counselling and Therapy*. London: Sage.

Sanderson, C. (2006) *Counselling Adult Survivors of Child Sexual Abuse*. London: Jessica Kinsley, 3rd edn.

Sackett, D.L.A., Richardson, W.S., Rosenberg, W. and Haynes, R.B. (1997) *Evidence-Based Medicine: How to Practice and Teach EBM*. London: Churchill Livingstone.

Scott, M.J. and Stradling, S.E. (2006) *Counselling for Post Traumatic Stress Disorder*. London: Sage, 3rd edn.

Segal, J. (1995) The stresses of working with clients with disabilities. In W. Dryden (ed.) *The Stresses of Counselling in Action*. London: Sage.

Segal, Z.V., Williams, J.M. and Teasdale, J.D. (2002) *Mindfulness-Based Cognitive Therapy for Depression*. London; New York: Guilford Press.

Seligman, M.E.P. (1995) *What You Can Change ... And What You Can't*. New York: Fawcett Columbine.

Seligman, M.E.P., Rashid, T. and Parks, A.C. (2006) Positive psychotherapy. *American Psychologist*, **61**, 774–788.

Shillito-Clarke, C. (1993) Book review. *Counselling*, August, 219.

Shlien, J.M. (1989) Boy's person-centred perspective on psycho-diagnosis – a response. *Person Centred Review*, **4**(2), 157–162.

Sills, C. (ed.) (2006) *Contracts in Counselling and Psychotherapy*. London: Sage, 2nd edn.

Singer, J.A. (2005) *Personality and Psychotherapy. Treating the Whole Person*. London: The Guilford Press.

Snape, C., Perren, S., Jones, L. and Rowland, N. (2003) Counselling – why not? A qualitative study of people's accounts of not taking up counselling appointments. *Counselling and Psychotherapy Research*, **3**, 239–245.

Stewart W. (2005) *An A–Z of Counselling Theory and Practice*. Cheltenham: Nelson Thornes, 4th edn.

Stiles, W.B. (2006) The client-therapist relationship. In C. Feltham and I. Horton (eds) *The Sage Handbook of Counselling and Psychotherapy*. London: Sage, 2nd edn.

Stiles, W.B., Shapiro, D.A. and Elliott, R. (1986) Are all psychotherapies equivalent? *American Psychologist*, **41**, 165–180.

Stiles, W. B., Barkham, M., Twigg, E., Mellor-Clark, J. and Cooper, M. (2006) Effectiveness of cognitive-behavioural, person-centred and psychodynamic therapies as practised in UK National Health Service settings. *Psychological Medicine*, **36**, 555–566.

Storr, A. (1990) *The Art of Psychotherapy*. London: Heinemann/Secker and Warburg, 2nd edn.

Sugarman, L. (2004) *Counselling and the Life Course*. London: Sage.

Sutherland, N.S. (1998) *Breakdown: A Personal Crisis and a Medical Dilemma*. Oxford: Oxford University Press, new edition.

Swade, T., Bayne, R. and Horton, I. (2006) Touch me never? *Therapy Today*, November, 41–42.

Syme, G. (1994) *Counselling in Independent Practice*. Milton Keynes: Open University Press.

Tavris, C. (1984) On the wisdom of counting to ten. Personal and social dangers of anger expression. In P. Shaver (ed.) *Review of Personality and Social Psychology, Vol.5*. London: Sage.

Tavris, C. (1989) *Anger: The Misunderstood Emotion*. London: Touchstone Books/Simon & Schuster, 2nd edn.

Thayer, R.E. (1996) *The Origin of Everyday Moods: Managing Energy, Tension, and Stress*. New York: Oxford University Press.

Thorne, B. (1992) Psychotherapy and counselling: the quest for differences. *Counselling*, **3**(4), 244–248.

Thorne, B. (1995) Contribution to I. Horton, R. Bayne and J. Bimrose (eds) New directions in counselling: a roundtable. *Counselling*, **6**, 34–40.

Thorne, B. (1999) The move towards brief therapy: its dangers and its challenges. *Counselling*, February, 7–11.

Tieger, P.D. and Barron-Tieger, B. (2000) *Just Your Type: the Relationship You've Always Wanted Using the Secrets of Personality Type*. London: Little, Brown.

Tieger, P.D. and Barron-Tieger, B. (2001) *Do What You Are*. London: Little, Brown. 3rd edn.

Tompkins, P., Sullivan, W. and Lawley, J. (2005) Tangled spaghetti in my head. *Therapy Today*, October, 32–36.

Townsend, R. (1984) *Further Up the Organisation*. London: Hodder & Stoughton.

Tudor, K. (1998) Value for money? issues of fees in counselling and psychotherapy. *British Journal of Guidance and Counselling*, **26**, 477–493.

Tudor, K. and Worrall, M. (2002) The unspoken relationships: financial dynamics in freelance therapy. In J. Clark (ed.) *Freelance Counselling and Psychotherapy. Competition and Collaboration*. Hove: Brunner-Routledge.

van Deurzen Smith, E. (2001) *Existential Counselling and Psychotherapy in Practice*. London: Sage, 2nd edn.

Waines, A. (2004) *The Self-Esteem Journal: Using a Journal to Build Self-Esteem*. London: Sheldon.

Walker, M. (1992a) *Surviving Secrets*. Milton Keynes: Open University Press.

Walker, M. (1992b) Chapter 10. In W. Dryden (ed.) *Hard-earned Lessons from Counselling in Action*. London: Sage.

Walker, M. (1993) When values clash. In W. Dryden (ed.) *Questions and Answers on Counselling in Action*. London: Sage.

Walker, M. (1996) Working with abuse survivors: The recovered memory debate. In R. Bayne, I. Horton and J. Bimrose (eds) *New Directions in Counselling*. London: Routledge.

Walker, M. (2006) Sexual abuse in childhood. In C. Feltham and I. Horton (eds) *The Sage Handbook of Counselling and Psychotherapy*. London: Sage, 2nd edn.

Weaks, W., McLeod, J. and Wilkinson, H. (2006) Dementia. *Therapy Today*, April, 12–15.

Wessely, S. (2001) Randomised controlled trials: the gold standard. In C. Mace, S. Moorey and B. Roberts (eds) *Evidence in the Psychological Therapies*. Hove: Brunner-Routledge.

West, M.A. (2004) *Effective Teamwork: Practical Lessons from Organizational Research*. Oxford: Blackwell.

White, M. and Epson, D. (1990) *Narrative Means to Therapeutic Ends*. New York: Norton.

Williams, E. and Scott, M. (2006) Auger control. In C. Feltham and I. Horton (eds) *The Sage Handbook of Counselling and Psychotherapy*. London: Sage, 2nd edn.

Wills, F. and Sanders, D. (1997) *Cognitive Therapy for Depression*. London: Sage.

Worden, J.W. (2004) *Grief Counselling and Grief Therapy: A Handbook for the Mental Health Practitioner*. London Brunner: Routledge, 3rd edn.

World Health Organization (1988) *International Classification of Diseases*. Geneva: WHO, 10th revision.

Wortman, C.B. and Silver, R.C. (1989) The myths of coping with loss. *Journal of Consulting and Clinical Psychology*, **57**(3), 349–57.

Wortman, C.B. and Silver, R.C. (2001) The myths of coping with loss revisited. In M.S. Stroebe, R.O. Hansson, W. Stroebe and H. Schut (eds) *Handbook of Bereavement Research: Consequences, Coping, and Care*. Washington, D.C: American Psychological Association.

Wright, D.B., Ost, J. and French, C.C. (2006) Recovered and false memories. *The Psychologist*, **19**, 352–355.

Wright, J.K. (2005) Writing therapy in brief workplace counselling. *Counselling and Psychotherapy Research*, **5**, 111–119.

Yalom, I.D (1989) *Love's Executioner and Other Tales of Psychotherapy*. Harmondsworth: Penguin.

Yalom, I.D. (2001) *The Gift of Therapy. Reflections on Being a Therapist*. London: Piatkus.

Yalom, I.D. and Leszcz, M. (2005) *The Theory and Practice of Group Therapy*. New York: Basic Books, 5th ed.